Medieval History-Based Writing Lessons

Implementing the Structure and Style® Writing Method

Teacher's Manual

Lori Verstegen

Illustrated by Travis Wells

Fifth Edition © January 2019
Institute for Excellence in Writing, L.L.C.

Also by Lori Verstegen

Advanced U.S. History-Based Writing Lessons
All Things Fun and Fascinating Writing Lessons
Ancient History-Based Writing Lessons
Bible Heroes Writing Lessons
Canadian History-Based Writing Lessons
Dress-Ups, Decorations, and Delightful Diversions
Medieval History-Based Writing Lessons (Student Book)
U.S. History-Based Writing Lessons
World History-Based Writing Lessons

The purchase of this book allows its owner access to PDF downloads that accompany *Medieval History-Based Writing Lessons*. See blue page for details and download instructions. Our duplicating/copying policy for these resources is specified on the copyright page for each of these downloads.

Copyright Policy
Medieval History-Based Writing Lessons: Implementing the Structure and Style® Writing Method
Fifth Edition, January 2019

ISBN 978-1-62341-312-5

Additional copies of this Teacher's Manual may be purchased from IEW.com/MHW-T.

Institute for Excellence in Writing (IEW®)
8799 N. 387 Road
Locust Grove, OK 74352
800.856.5815
info@IEW.com
IEW.com

Printed in the United States of America

These lessons are not intended as a history curriculum replacement, but rather their purpose is to broaden subject knowledge while students learn to write.

Accessing Your Downloads

Teacher's Manual

The purchase of this book allows its owner access to PDF downloads of the following:

- the optional *Medieval History-Based Writing Lessons Reproducible Checklists* (31 pages)
- the *Student Resource Packet* (174 pages*)
- the optional *Medieval History-Based Writing Lessons Simplified Source Texts*
- the optional *Medieval History-Based Writing Lessons Advanced Additions*
- the *Medieval History-Based Writing Lessons Exemplars*

To download these e-resources, please follow the directions below:

1. Go to our website: IEW.com.
2. Log in to your online customer account. If you do not have an account, you will need to create one.
3. After you are logged in, type this link into your address bar: IEW.com/MHW-TE.
4. Click the checkboxes next to the names of the files you wish to place in your account.
5. Click the "Add to my files" button.
6. To access your files now and in the future, click on "Your Account" and click on the "Files" tab (one of the gray tabs).
7. Click on each file name to download the files onto your computer.

Please note: You may download and print these e-books as needed for use within *your immediate family or classroom*. However, this information is proprietary, and we are trusting you to be on your honor not to share it with anyone. Please see the copyright page for further details. Thank you.

*If you would prefer to purchase the *Student Resource Packet* as a preprinted packet, it is available at this web page: IEW.com/SRP-S.

If you have any difficulty receiving these downloads after going through the steps above, please call 800.856.5815.

Institute for Excellence in Writing
8799 N. 387 Road
Locust Grove, OK 74352

Contents

Inventive Writing (IEW Unit 7)

Formal Essay Models (IEW Unit 8)

Formal Critique and Response to Literature (IEW Unit 9)

Just for Fun

Appendices

Welcome to *Medieval History-Based Writing Lessons.* This Teacher's Manual shows reduced copies of the Student Book pages. Instructions to teachers, answers to questions, sample key word outlines, brainstorming ideas, review games, and helps for motivating students are inserted. This format allows a teacher to teach directly from the Teacher's Manual without the need of a copy of the Student Book. Simply read through the Teacher's Manual and follow the inserted instructions and helps.

Lesson instructions are directed to the student, but teachers should read them over with their students and help as necessary, especially with outlining and structure and style practice. It is assumed that teachers have attended IEW's *Teaching Writing: Structure and Style* seminar either live or via DVD and own the *Seminar Workbook*. Before each new unit, teachers should review the appropriate information in that workbook and DVD.

Introduction

The lessons in this book teach Structure and Style in writing. As they move through medieval history themes, they incrementally introduce and review most of the models of structure and elements of style found in the Institute for Excellence in Writing's *Teaching Writing: Structure and Style*.

Have students look at and tab each appendix in their books.

Student Book Contents

- **Scope and Sequence Chart** (pages 8–9)
- **The Lesson Pages**
  This is the majority of the text. It contains the instructions, source texts, worksheets, and checklists you will need for each lesson.
- **Appendix I: Modified MLA Format**
- **Appendix II: Magnum Opus Notebook and Keepsake**
  This appendix explains the Magnum Opus Notebook and includes a checklist.
- **Appendix III: Critique Thesaurus**
  The Critique Thesaurus provides a list of literary terms and their synonyms that are often used when critiquing various forms of literature. This page will help you include specific words to make your critique and literature analysis essay sound sophisticated.
- **Appendix IV: Adding Literature**
  This appendix suggests various novels set in the Middle Ages to be read or listened to alongside the writing lessons. It also includes templates of literature-response pages if teachers would like to assign such pages for students who will be adding the literature. These great stories will enhance the students' understanding of medieval times, provide background for the compositions they will write for some of the lessons, and model skillful use of various elements of structure and style.
- **Appendix V: Vocabulary Chart and Quizzes** (Cards in Student Book only)
  The vocabulary words are an important part of these lessons. You will be instructed to cut out one set of cards for some of the lessons. You should try to include some of these words in each composition you write. You will also be quizzed over the words periodically. The goal is that these great words will become part of your natural writing vocabulary.

This Teacher's Manual includes an additional appendix: Appendix VI—Motivating Students: Tickets and Games. Some of the games require a little preparation, so be sure to read the Teacher's Manual a few days before class. Please also note that some of the games require the use of dice.

Checklists

Each lesson includes a checklist that details all the requirements of the assignment for you and your teacher. You (students) should check off each element when you are sure it is included in your paper. With each assignment, turn in the checklist to be used by the teacher for grading.

The last item of the checklist is for the vocabulary words that you are encouraged to try to use in each composition that you write. Doing so will help you master these quality words. Your teacher will decide how to reward you for using vocabulary words. If point values are assigned, the new total points possible will be written on the custom total line.

Reproducible checklists are available. View the blue page for download information.

Teacher's Manual

The Teacher's Manual includes all of the Student Book contents (except the vocabulary cards) with added instructions for teachers, including sample key word outlines and style practice ideas, answers to questions, review games, answers to vocabulary quizzes, and ideas for motivating students. Teachers may teach directly from this manual without the need of their own copy of the Student Book.

The *Student Resource Packet*

The *Student Resource Packet* (SRP) is a downloadable PDF used throughout these lessons. Please follow the instructions on the blue page for downloading this very helpful resource. If you prefer not to print so many pages, you may purchase a hard copy from IEW.

The Magnum Opus Notebook and Keepsake

If you want to save your work in a special way, make any changes to your final draft suggested by your teacher and remove the stylistic technique markings. Feel free to create illustrations for your work and then place this new draft in a binder in clear sheet protectors with the original IEW stylistic labeled draft hidden behind it.

At the end of the year, you will have a collection of a variety of types of compositions that move through major themes in medieval history. See Appendix II for more details about the Magnum Opus Notebook.

Customizing the Checklist

The total point value of each assignment is indicated at the bottom of each checklist. This total reflects only the basic items and does not include the vocabulary. If this is used, add the appropriate amount of points and write the new total on the custom total line.

Important: Teachers and parents should remember IEW's EZ+1 Rule. The checklist should include only those elements of style that have become easy plus one new element. If students are not yet ready for a basic element on the checklist, simply have them cross it out. Subtract its point value from the total possible and write the new total on the custom total line at the bottom. If you would like to add elements to the checklist, assign each a point value and add these points to the total possible, placing the new total on the custom total line.

Grading with the Checklist

To use the checklists for grading, do not try to add all the points earned. Instead, if an element is present, put a check in the blank across from it. If an element is missing, write the negative point value on its line or box. Total the negative points and subtract them from the total possible (or your custom total).
Note: Students should have checked the boxes in front of each element they completed.

In addition to the SRP, encourage students to bring a thesaurus to class. Most students enjoy using an electronic thesaurus, but for those who prefer books, IEW offers a unique one entitled *A Word Write Now*.

This schedule is provided to emphasize to parents and students, particularly in a class setting, that teachers and students should not expect to complete an entire lesson in one day. Spreading work throughout the week will produce much better writing with much less stress. Parents teaching their own children at home should follow a similar schedule.

Suggested Weekly Schedule

In general, lessons are designed to be taught weekly and to be completed as follows.

Days 1 and 2 require teacher instruction. If your class meets only once per week, Days 1 and 2 should be combined and taught on the day of class.

Day 1

1. Review concepts from previous lessons using review activities in the Teacher's Manual.
2. Together, teacher and students learn or review the structure for the new composition.
3. Follow the lesson instructions to read the source text, make a key word outline, and tell back the meaning of each line of notes.
4. Learn the vocabulary words for the current lesson.

Day 2

1. Review the key word outline from Day 1. If a note is unclear, check the source text and add what you need in order to understand it.
2. If a new element of style is introduced, read about it and complete the practice exercise for it. Use the Structure and Style Practice pages to discuss ideas for including these elements.
3. After you are sure you understand your notes, begin to write a paragraph using only the outline and the structure and style practice ideas to guide you. Try not to look back at the source text while you are writing. Write in your own words. Follow the checklist and indicate the required elements as instructed.

Days 3 and 4 may be completed by students more independently, but parents or teachers should be available to help as necessary and to edit.

Day 3

1. Finish writing your composition. Check each item on the checklist when you are sure you have completed it. Let an editor proofread.
2. Review all vocabulary words learned thus far.

Day 4

1. Write or type a final draft by making any corrections your editor asked you to make. Check off each item on the checklist when you have included and labeled it.
2. Let an editor proofread again. He or she should check that all elements of structure and style are included and labeled as instructed on the checklist. Paperclip the checklist to your final draft to be turned in.
3. If work from a previous lesson has been returned with corrections to be made, revise this work with the help of a parent. Remove the stylistic technique markings, and if you would like to, add a picture. The final draft will be placed in the Magnum Opus Notebook (see page 6) with the original IEW stylistic labeled draft behind it in the same sheet protector. *There is a Magnum Opus checklist on page 264.*

Hold up the picture side of a page of vocabulary cards from a Student Book. Read one definition at a time. Can the students guess from the pictures which word matches the definition?

Scope and Sequence

Lesson	Subject and Structure	Style (First Introduced)	Vocabulary	Literature Suggestions
Unit 1 1	The Middle Ages	introduction to Structure and Style	fetid, massive, dilapidated, intrepid	
Unit 2 2	Anglo-Saxons	-ly adverb	capably, tenaciously, brazenly, benevolently	*The Story of King Arthur and His Knights* retold by Tania Zamorsky or *King Arthur: Tales from the Round Table* by Andrew Lang
3	Monasteries		reverently, astutely, earnestly, pursue	
4	Justinian the Great title rule	*who/which* clause	resolutely, uniformly, nobly, opulently	
Unit 3 5	Beowulf		fatally, hastily, spew, brandish	
6	The Archbishop of Canterbury	strong verb banned words: *go/went, say/said*	extol, flee, rebuke, intrigue	*One Thousand and One Arabian Nights* by Geraldine McCaughrean
7	Mohammed	*because* clause	proclaim, retreat, embellish, deduce	
8	The Sword in the Stone		disclose, contritely, scowl, dislodge	
Unit 4 9	Charlemagne topic and clincher sentences		reform, restrain, apprehend, renowned	*The King's Shadow* by Elizabeth Alder or *Wulf the Saxon* by G.A. Henty
10	Vikings	quality adjective banned words: *good/bad, big/little*	wanton, merciless, imminent, unrivaled	
11	Alfred the Great	*www.asia* clause	prominent, myriad, virtuous, bestow	
12	The Battle of Hastings	#2 prepositional opener	endure, smug, proficient, treacherous	
Unit 5 13	The Samurai and the Dragon		relish, scramble, bewildered, anguish	*Robin Hood* by J. Walker McSpadden or other children's version
14	Llama Saves the Day		din, cower, brim, frantically	
15	The Magic Lamp		gravely, fatigued, insolent, scorn	

Lesson	Subject and Structure	Style (First Introduced)	Vocabulary	Literature Suggestions
Unit 6 16	Medieval Cathedrals fused outlines	#3 -ly adverb opener	grandiose, serene, toil, contrive	Elementary: *The Door in the Wall* by Marguerite de Angeli Junior and Senior High: *Winning His Spurs: A Tale of the Crusades* by G.A. Henty
17	Knights, Part 1	#6 vss	primarily, elite, allegiance, impeccable	
18	Knights, Part 2 bibliography		agile, devoted, feeble, clad	
19	King Richard			
Unit 7 20	Favorite Amusements, Part 1 body paragraphs	#5 clausal opener *www.asia.b* clause		
21	Favorite Amusements, Part 2 introduction and conclusion			Elementary: *Adam of the Road* by Elizabeth Janet Gray Junior and Senior High: *The Kite Rider* by Geraldine McCaughrean
22	Chivalry, Part 1 body paragraphs		credible, foremost, stymie, indolent	
23	Chivalry, Part 2 introduction and conclusion			
24	Descriptive Time Travel Diary	#1 subject opener #4 -ing opener		*Marco Polo* by Demi
Unit 8 25	Knights, Part 3 introduction and conclusion			*Crispin: The Cross of Lead* by Avi
26	The Renaissance, Part 1			
27	The Renaissance, Part 2			
Unit 9 28	"Genghis Khan and His Hawk," Part 1		analyze, aghast, tragic, rash	
29	"Genghis Khan and His Hawk," Part 2			
30	Character Analysis "Seven in One Blow"			
Bonus	Vocabulary Story		review all	

Adapting the Schedule and Lessons

Adapting the Schedule

Groups who follow a schedule with fewer than thirty weeks will have to omit some lessons. Because there are several lessons for each of the nine IEW units, this is not a problem. Teach lessons that introduce new concepts and omit some of those that do not.

Simplified Source Texts

If students are younger or have special needs, teachers may choose to download the optional *Medieval History-Based Writing Lessons Simplified Source Texts* e-book (see blue page). This e-book provides a simplified version of the same source texts used in the basic lessons in the Student Book. When using these simplified source texts, IEW students should follow the directions for each lesson in the Student Book but replace the Student Book source text with the simplified version. Teachers should remember IEW's EZ + 1 rule. Every item on a student's checklist should be easy, plus one new item to challenge him or her.

Advanced Additions

Experienced IEW students who would benefit from additional challenges may be encouraged to download and use the optional *Medieval History-Based Writing Lessons Advanced Additions* e-book (see blue page). This e-book adds more advanced elements of Structure or Style to the basic lessons and checklists in the Student Book. Experienced IEW students should follow the directions for each lesson in the Student Book first, then add the suggested challenges *only if they are ready for them*. Teachers should remember IEW's EZ + 1 rule. Every item on a student's checklist should be easy, plus one new item to challenge him or her.

Lesson 1: The Middle Ages

Structure: IEW Unit 1: Note Making and Outlines

Style: Introduction to Style

Writing Topic: The Middle Ages

In a class that meets weekly, follow Day 1 and 2 instructions together with students. Then read Days 3 and 4 so students understand how to complete the lesson during the remainder of the week.

Teaching Writing: Structure and Style

Watch the sections for Unit 1 (Note Making and Outlines). At IEW.com/twss-help reference the TWSS Viewing Guides.

Lesson 1: The Middle Ages

UNIT 1: NOTE MAKING AND OUTLINES

Lesson 1: The Middle Ages

vocab quickly

Goals

- to be introduced to the Unit 1 Note Making and Outlines structural model
- to create a key word outline (KWO)
- to retell the content of a source text using just your outline
- to correctly use new vocabulary words: *fetid*, *massive*, *dilapidated*, *intrepid*

Assignment Schedule

Note: Classes that meet only one day per week should complete Days 1 and 2 on class day.

Day 1

1. Read the Introduction to Structure and Style on pages 12–13.
2. Read "The Middle Ages" on page 14. Then read it again. As you do, choose no more than three key words from each sentence that will best help you remember the meaning of the sentence. Write the words on the blank outline on page 15.

   Note: You may use symbols, numbers, and abbreviations freely. They do not count as words. However, be sure you can remember what they mean.
3. Cover the source text and tell the meaning of each line of notes *in your own words*.
4. Learn the vocabulary words for Lesson 1: *fetid*, *massive*, *dilapidated*, *intrepid*. Store cards in a pencil pouch where you can easily retrieve them when writing or studying for a quiz.

Write class ideas on the whiteboard. Students may copy these or use their own ideas. See the sample key word outline (KWO) on page 15.

Use a student's book. Hold up the page of cards for Lesson 1. Read each definition and ask the students to guess which word it matches by looking at the pictures.

Day 2

1. Reread the paragraph on page 14; then, turn the page so you cannot see it. Using only your key word notes on page 15, try to tell back the information in complete sentences *in your own words*. You should not memorize the source text word for word. Rather, you should let the key words remind you of the key ideas; then, state the ideas in your own words. If a note is unclear, check the source text and fix your note.

Day 3

1. Try to add a vocabulary word to the outline of the Middle Ages paragraph.

Day 4

1. Prepare to give an oral report from your key word outline. Practice telling back the information one line at a time. Look at a line; then, look up and talk about it. Then look down at the next line, look up, and talk about it. Continue through the outline this way. Practice until the paragraph is smooth.

   It is important to realize that you are not trying to memorize the exact words of the source text. You are trying to remember the ideas and communicate those ideas in your own words.

Unit 1: Note Making and Outlines

2. Review the vocabulary words.
3. If you will be reading the suggested literature, obtain a children's version of the tales of King Arthur for Lessons 2–5. Two are suggested in Appendix IV.

In this book you will learn many ways to make your writing more exciting and more enjoyable to read. You will learn to write with *structure* and with *style*.

Introduction to Structure and Style

Structure

What is *structure*? The dictionary defines structure as "the arrangement of and relations between the parts or elements of something complex."

What has structure? Think of a castle. What had to happen before the castle was built? Someone had to draw out the plans for the builders to follow. The builders had to follow the plans so that each part was in its proper place. The royal family certainly would not have wanted the moat placed around their thrones or a torture chamber in their bedroom. Each part had to be placed in its own special spot, and each step had to be completed in its proper order, giving the castle its proper structure.

Writing a paper, in some ways, is similar to building a castle. A paper contains many facts and ideas. If we were just to begin writing without planning, our facts and ideas would probably not be arranged in the most logical way. Our composition would not be structured well and would not communicate our thoughts effectively. So, in this course you will "draw plans" for everything before you write. Your "plans" will be outlines, and they will follow a particular model of structure for each type of composition.

Style

What comes to your mind when you hear the word *style*? Many people think of clothes. Clothes come in a variety of styles. A maiden would dress differently to go to a royal ball than she would to tend her garden. That is because formal events require a formal style of clothing, whereas casual settings do not.

There are also different styles of language. Below are two sentences that communicate the same information in different styles. Which do you like better? Why?

> *He fell!*
>
> *The young knight plummeted headlong from his horse, dashing his hopes of winning the fair princess.*

Lesson 1: The Middle Ages

You probably like the second sentence better because it is more descriptive. Indeed, if it were part of a written story, the second would most likely be better. However, what if you were at the joust with your friend and the knight was your brother? Which of the above sentences would you be more likely to exclaim? *He fell*! would be more appropriate in this case. The second would sound silly. Why the difference?

When you are speaking to people, they are there with you, experiencing the same scene and event as you are. You do not need to fill in the details. When you write, however, you must realize that the readers are not with you and cannot see, hear, or feel what is in your mind. You must fill in the details and paint vivid pictures with your words. You must help them see, hear, feel, and experience the scene you are writing about as the second sentence does. IEW elements of style will help you do this.

Key Word Outlines

Before you begin to write, you will practice the first step of learning *structure* in writing: key word outlining.

Structure is how you organize the things you write. Key word outlining will help you gather information and help you organize that information in your compositions.

When you outline, you will want to use or create some symbols or abbreviations to help you outline quickly. There are some commonly accepted symbols and abbreviations listed for you in the *Student Resource Packet*. You may use these or make up some of your own. Below are a few symbols that we could use today. What do you think each means?

Practice key word outlining by following the assignment instructions under Day 1 of the Assignment Schedule.

↓ = down, downfall > = greater, huge, a lot

 = go, went; led to  = king w/ = with

Unit 1: Note Making and Outlines

Source Text

The Middle Ages

The Middle Ages began with the crumbling of the great Western Roman Empire in the fifth century. At that time several tribes of barbarians* from the North invaded Europe. Much of Roman culture and knowledge was lost. Over time, though, the Roman Catholic Church increased in power. Huge majestic cathedrals were built, and monasteries were established. Kings and nobles also rose to power in different territories. They constructed massive castles and hired knights to protect their land. However, most people were poor peasants who worked from sunup to sundown farming for the few wealthy noblemen. The Middle Ages lasted for one thousand years and ended with a time called the Renaissance.

****Note***: Romans called anyone who was not Roman a barbarian. The people north of the Roman Empire were also known as Germanic tribes. Many lived in what is now Germany and Scandinavia. They were very different from the Romans. They had light hair and eyes, and they worshiped different gods. They were warriors who valued bravery above all else.

Sample

Lesson 1: The Middle Ages

Key Word Outline

I. *M-A, began, w/. ↓, W. Rom, Emp. 5th cent.*

1. *barbarians, N., → Europe*
2. *Rom., culture, lost*
3. *power, Rom. Catholic, ⛪ ↑*
4. *cathedrals, monasteries, built*
5. *♔s, nobles, ↑ power, territories*
6. *castles, hired, knights*
7. *most, ppl, poor, peasants*
8. *M-A, 1000 yrs, ended, w/Renaissance*

Unit 1: Note Making and Outlines

Lesson 2: Anglo-Saxons

Structure: IEW Unit 2: Writing from Notes

Style: -ly adverb

Writing Topic: Anglo-Saxons

Optional Student Reading Assignment: During Lessons 2–5, students may read an appropriate version of the tales of King Arthur. Please see Appendix IV.

Teaching Writing: Structure and Style

Watch the sections for Unit 2 (Writing from Notes). At IEW.com/twss-help reference the TWSS Viewing Guides.

UNIT 2: WRITING FROM NOTES

Lesson 2: Anglo-Saxons

Goals

- to be introduced to the Unit 2 Writing from Notes structural model
- to create a key word outline about Anglo-Saxons
- to retell the content of a source text using just your outline
- to write a paragraph about Anglo-Saxons from the key word outline
- to correctly add a dress-up: -ly adverb
- to correctly use new vocabulary words: *capably, tenaciously, brazenly, benevolently*

Assignment Schedule

Note: Classes that meet only one day per week should complete Days 1 and 2 on class day.

Day 1

1. Read the Review, Writing from Key Word Outlines, and New Symbols for Key Word Outlining sections on pages 18–19.
2. Read "Anglo-Saxons" on page 20. With the help of your teacher, write a key word outline by writing no more than three key words from each sentence. You may also use as many symbols and abbreviations as you need. Use the blank outline on page 21.
3. Retell the content of the source by covering the source text and telling the meaning of each line of notes.
4. Learn the new vocabulary words for Lesson 2: *capably, tenaciously, brazenly, benevolently*.

Day 2

1. Retell the content of the source by reviewing your outline from Day 1. Be sure you understand everything on it. If a note is unclear, check the source text and add what you need to in order to understand it.
2. Read and complete page 22, "In Your Own Words."
3. Learn a new dress-up, the -ly adverb, on page 23 and practice style ideas for including an -ly adverb and vocabulary words on page 24.
4. Using your key word outline as a guide, begin to write a paragraph *in your own words*. As you write, try to include some of the ideas for -ly adverbs and vocabulary words from your style practice. Write the first few sentences together as the teacher models the process.
5. Go over the checklist on page 25. You will need to underline one -ly adverb. You may use more than one, but only underline one. Also label the vocabulary words you use. Put a ✔ in the box for each requirement on the checklist you have completed.
6. See Appendix I. It explains how to format your papers from this point forward.

Here is a sample start:

(voc) With the collapse of the Roman Empire, intrepid Anglo-Saxons poured into Britain. They consisted of Angles, Saxons, and Jutes, who boldly crossed the North Sea and took over the land. …

Note: As you model writing from the KWO, stress the importance of writing in your own words. Be sure students understand that they should not try to remember and write the exact words of the source text. They should use their notes to understand the key ideas and write those ideas in their own words. One note may become two or more sentences or two notes may become one sentence.

Day 3

1. Finish writing your paragraph using your key word outline, your style practice ideas, and the checklist to guide you. Let an editor proofread.
2. Review all vocabulary words learned thus far.

Day 4

1. Write or type a final draft, making any corrections your editor asked you to make. Check off each item on the checklist when you are sure it is completed.
2. Let an editor proofread again. He or she should check that all elements of structure and style are included and labeled as instructed on the checklist. Paperclip the checklist to your final draft to be turned in.

Literature Suggestion

With Lessons 2–5, read a children's version of the tales of King Arthur. Two are suggested in Appendix IV.

Review

When making a key word outline, how many words may you write for each sentence of a source text? What else may you use to help you remember ideas?

Play No-Noose Hangman. See the Teacher's Manual.

Share your oral report from Lesson 1.

Review

You may use up to 3 words per line.

You may use symbols, abbreviations, and numbers freely.

No-Noose Hangman

Instructions for No-Noose Hangman are in Appendix VI.

For the first puzzle, use FEARLESS. Once solved, ask, "Which vocabulary word means fearless?" (*intrepid*)

For the next puzzle, use the phrase KEY WORD OUTLINE. Once solved, ask the student who solved it, "How many words from each sentence may you write in a key word outline? (3) What else may you use freely?" (*symbols, abbreviations, numbers*)

Lesson 2: Anglo-Saxons

Writing from Key Word Outlines

In Lesson 1 you learned a little about structure by making a key word outline. In this lesson you will learn to use a key word outline as a guide to write a paragraph. You will also practice using one of the IEW dress-ups.

New Symbols for Key Word Outlining

Here are some symbols that may be helpful for this week's outline. What do you think each stands for?

ea [wave symbol] ppl

ea = each [wave symbol] = sea ppl = people

Unit 2: Writing from Notes

Source Text

Anglo-Saxons

When the Roman Empire fell, Anglo-Saxons invaded Britain. They came from Europe across the North Sea. The Anglo-Saxons divided Britain into seven sections, each with its own king. The southern part of the land was called *Angle-land*, which eventually evolved into *England*. At first, the Anglo-Saxons were pagans who worshiped many gods. That is why in the English language, four of the days of the week are named after some of their gods.* However, in 598 a monk named Augustine traveled there, and many converted to Christianity. The Anglo-Saxons ruled England until 1066.

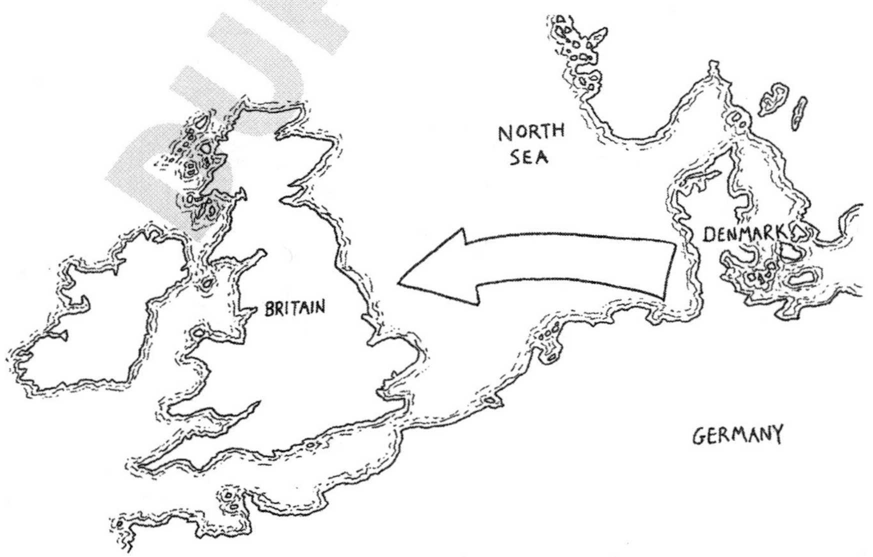

****Note***: Tuesday was named after Tiu, Wednesday came from Woden's Day (Woden was king of the Norse gods.), Thursday was named after Thor, and Friday was from Freya.

Sample

Lesson 2: Anglo-Saxons

Key Word Outline

I. *Rom. Emp, ↓, Anglo-Saxons, → Britain*

1. *from, Europe, → N.* (waves)
2. *÷, 7, sections, ea, own,* (crown)
3. *S., Angle-land → England*
4. *1st, pagans, many, gods*
5. *4 days, from, gods*
6. *598, monk, Augustine, converted*
7. *A-S, ruled, England, → 1066*

Unit 2: Writing from Notes

Key Word Outlines

In Your Own Words

When you write from key word notes, it is important that you use your own words, not the exact words of the source text. To help you say the ideas from your outline in your own words, complete the practice exercise below.

Practice

This is the first sentence of the source text:

When the Roman Empire fell, Anglo-Saxons invaded Britain.

Your notes might look something like this:

I. *Rom. Emp., ↓ Anglo-Saxons, →, Britain*

In the first line, avoid using the exact words *fell* and *invaded*. How could you communicate the idea of the first line without using those exact words? Use a thesaurus for help. (***Example***: With the collapse of the Roman Empire, Anglo-Saxons were able to take over Britain.)

Note your idea for Roman numeral I:

Since the once-mighty Roman Empire had been dilapidated, Anglo-Saxons were able to successfully raid Britain.

New Style

-ly Adverb Dress-Up

There are many IEW elements of style. The first elements we will learn are called *dress-ups* because they will help you "dress-up" your writing. The IEW dress-ups are descriptive words, phrases, or clauses. Today we will have fun practicing one of these: the *-ly adverb.*

An -ly adverb is simply an adverb that ends in -ly. Adverbs are words that modify verbs, adjectives, or other adverbs. Most often they tell *how or when* something is done. Can you think of any such words? There is a long list of -ly adverbs in the *Student Resource Packet* (SRP). You may turn there for help when you write.

Practice

Choose different -ly adverbs to plug into the sentences below and notice how the meaning of the scene is changed. You may use the -ly adverbs in the box below, some from the SRP, or -ly adverbs you think of on your own.

1. The king walked ___*happily/angrily*___ to his throne room.
2. There, a young knight was ___*nervously/boldly*___ waiting for him.
3. "What do you want?" the king asked ___*kindly/hatefully*___.
4. "Her," the knight replied ___*humbly/savagely*___.
5. "Me?" the princess ___*sweetly/woefully*___ gasped.

angrily	excitedly	humbly	longingly	smugly
anxiously	fearfully	hysterically	nervously	stubbornly
boldly	happily	innocently	rudely	suspiciously
eagerly	hatefully	intrepidly	savagely	sweetly
evilly	hopefully	joyfully	sheepishly	woefully

Vocabulary words are in bold.

Style Practice

-ly Adverb Dress-Up

Write ideas for adding -ly adverbs. Then, choose your favorite idea to write in the blank of the sentence. You may use the SRP or a thesaurus for help. Also, some of your vocabulary words for Lesson 2 may be used. See the chart on pages 274–275.

1. Anglo-Saxons *boldly* raided Britain.

   -ly adverb ideas *boldly, **intrepidly**, successfully, brutally, savagely, greedily, **tenaciously**, ferociously*

   Which vocabulary words from Lesson 2 might work in the above sentence? *brazenly*

2. A monk named Augustine *adeptly* shared Christianity with the Anglo-Saxons.

   -ly adverb ideas *boldly, diligently, lovingly, adeptly, successfully, kindly, wisely*

   Which vocabulary words from Lesson 2 might work in the above sentence? *benevolently, capably*

3. Anglo-Saxons ruled England *mightily* until 1066.

   -ly adverb ideas *arrogantly, mightily, proudly, powerfully, ably, strictly*

   Which vocabulary words from Lesson 2 might work in the above sentence? *tenaciously, capably*

Vocabulary Practice

In each blank, write a vocabulary word from Lesson 1 that would make sense.

1. Anglo-Saxons were *intrepid* warriors.

2. Because the Roman Empire had been *dilapidated*, Anglo-Saxons seized the opportunity to invade Britain.

Lesson 2: Anglo-Saxons

Unit 2 Composition Checklist

Lesson 2: Anglo-Saxons

Writing from Notes

Institute for Excellence in Writing
Listen. Speak. Read. Write. Think!

Name: ______________________________

STRUCTURE

☐ MLA format (see Appendix I)	______	6 pts
☐ title centered on top line	______	5 pts
☐ checklist on top, final draft, rough draft, key word outline	______	5 pts

STYLE (one of each in each paragraph)

¶1 Dress-Up (underline)	(5 pts each)	
☐ -ly adverb	______	5 pts

MECHANICS

☐ capitalization	______	1 pt
☐ end marks and punctuation	______	1 pt
☐ complete sentences (Does it make sense?)	______	1 pt
☐ spelling and usage	______	1 pt

VOCABULARY

☐ vocabulary words - label *(voc)* in left margin or after sentence

Total:	______	25 pts
Custom Total:	______	pts

Unit 2: Writing from Notes

Lesson 3: Monasteries

Structure: IEW Unit 2: Writing from Notes

Style: no new stylistic techniques

Writing Topic: Monasteries

Optional Student Reading Assignment: During Lessons 2–5, students may read an appropriate version of the tales of King Arthur. Please see Appendix IV.

UNIT 2: WRITING FROM NOTES

Lesson 3: Monasteries

Goals

- to practice the Unit 1 and 2 structural models
- to create a key word outline about monasteries
- to retell the content of a source text using just your outline
- to write a paragraph about monasteries
- to practice the -ly adverb dress-up
- to correctly use new vocabulary words: *pursue*, *reverently*, *earnestly*, *astutely*

Assignment Schedule

Note: Classes that meet weekly should complete Days 1 and 2 in class.

Day 1

1. Read the Review section on page 28.
2. Read "Monasteries" on page 30. With the help of your teacher, write a key word outline on page 31.
3. Retell the content of the source by covering the source text and telling the meaning of each line of notes.
4. Learn the new vocabulary words for Lesson 3: *pursue*, *reverently*, *earnestly*, *astutely*.

Day 2

1. Retell the content of the source by reviewing your outline from Day 1. Be sure you understand everything on it. If a note is unclear, check the source text and add what you need to in order to understand it.
2. Practice style ideas for an -ly adverb and vocabulary words on page 32.
3. Begin to write your own paragraph, using only the outline and the style practice ideas to guide you. Do not look back at the source text. *Write in your own words*. Follow the checklist.

Day 3

1. Finish writing your paragraph. Include and underline the element of style on the checklist, page 33. Check off each item when you are sure you have completed it. Let an editor proofread.
2. Review all vocabulary words learned thus far.

Tip

Collect all quizzes from Appendix V of the Student Books. That way, if a student comes to class without his book on quiz day, you will have his quiz.

Day 4

1. Write or type a final draft, making any corrections your editor asked you to make.
2. Let an editor proofread again. He or she should check that all elements of structure and style are included and labeled as instructed on the checklist. Paperclip the checklist to your final draft to be turned in.

Study for Vocabulary Quiz 1. It will cover words from Lessons 1–3.

Review

Play a vocabulary game to prepare for the quiz next week. See Appendix VI of the Teacher's Manual.

Unit 2: Writing from Notes

Source Text

Monasteries

During the Middle Ages, some Christians believed that in order to be more holy, they needed to separate from society. Many escaped into the wilderness to live as hermits in caves. Eventually, though, people who believed this gathered into groups and built homes called monasteries or abbeys. The men were called monks, and the head monk was called the abbot, meaning father. Because most monks could read and write, they made copies of the scriptures and other books. They also wrote records of important events that occurred during their time. Monasteries became places of learning. They also became inns for travelers, who were given food and lodging whether or not they could pay. Monasteries were places of peace and hope during the difficult days of the Middle Ages.

Sample

Lesson 3: Monasteries

Key Word Outline

I. *M-A, ✝, > holy, separate*

1. *➔ wilderness, caves, hermits*
2. *groups, ⌂s, monasteries = abbeys*
3. *♂, monks, ↑ = abbot, (father)*
4. *copied, scriptures, books*
5. *recorded, important, events*
6. *monasteries, places, learning*
7. *+ inns, free, poor*
8. *places, peace, difficult, M-A*

Symbols you might find useful:

⌂ = home/house

♂ = man/men/male

Vocabulary words are in bold.

Ask students to share aloud sentences that use vocabulary words. Offer a ticket for each word that could be used in the writing assignment. (See Appendix VI for an explanation of tickets.)

Style Practice

-ly Adverb Dress-Up

Write ideas for adding -ly adverbs. Then, choose your favorite idea to write in the blank of the sentence. You may use the SRP, a thesaurus, and your vocabulary words for help. See the chart on pages 274–275.

1. The head monk was ***reverently*** called abbot, meaning father.

   affectionately, respectfully, ***reverently****, warmly*

2. Monks ***earnestly*** copied the scriptures.

   diligently, carefully, reverently, meticulously, astutely, ***earnestly***

3. Monasteries ***benevolently*** welcomed and lodged travelers.

   benevolently*, affectionately, kindly, compassionately, commonly, generously*

Vocabulary Practice

In each blank, write a vocabulary word from Lessons 1–3 that would make sense. You may use any form of a vocabulary word. For example, you may remove an -ly or add an -ed or -ing. See the chart on pages 274–275.

1. Men who became monks *earnestly* desired to *pursue* a life of holiness.

2. Most monks were *astute* men who could read and write.

Lesson 3: Monasteries

Unit 2 Composition Checklist

Lesson 3: Monasteries

Writing from Notes

Name: ______________________________

Institute for Excellence in Writing

STRUCTURE

☐ MLA format (see Appendix I)	______	6	pts
☐ title centered on top line	______	5	pts
☐ checklist on top, final draft, rough draft, key word outline	______	5	pts

STYLE (one of each in each paragraph)

¶1 Dress-Up (underline) (5 pts each)

☐ -ly adverb	______	5	pts

MECHANICS

☐ capitalization	______	1	pt
☐ end marks and punctuation	______	1	pt
☐ complete sentences (Does it make sense?)	______	1	pt
☐ spelling and usage	______	1	pt

VOCABULARY

☐ vocabulary words - label *(voc)* in left margin or after sentence

Total:	______	25	pts
Custom Total:	______		pts

Unit 2: Writing from Notes

Lesson 4: Justinian the Great

Structure: IEW Unit 2: Writing from Notes
title rule

Style: *who/which* clause

Writing Topic: Justinian the Great

Optional Student Reading Assignment: During Lessons 2–5, students may read an appropriate version of the tales of King Arthur. Please see Appendix IV.

UNIT 2: WRITING FROM NOTES

Lesson 4: Justinian the Great

Goals

- to practice the Unit 2 structural model
- to create a 2-paragraph key word outline
- to write a 2-paragraph report about Justinian the Great
- to correctly add a new dress-up: *who/which* clause
- to correctly create a title
- to take Vocabulary Quiz 1
- to correctly use new vocabulary words: *uniformly*, *resolutely*, *nobly*, *opulently*

Assignment Schedule

Note: Classes that meet weekly should complete Days 1 and 2 in class.

Day 1

1. Begin class with Vocabulary Quiz 1.
2. Read "Justinian the Great" on page 38. With the help of your teacher, write a key word outline on page 39. Notice that this source text has two paragraphs. Each Roman numeral of the blank key word outline represents one paragraph. (***Note***: If you are comfortable with key word outlining on your own, your teacher may have you do some or all of the outline at home.)
3. Tell back the meaning of each line of notes.
4. Learn the new vocabulary words for Lesson 4: *uniformly*, *resolutely*, *nobly*, *opulently*. Discuss how you might use any of the vocabulary words from Lessons 1–4 in the paragraphs for this lesson.

Day 2

1. Review your outline. If a note is unclear, fix it before you write your paragraphs.
2. With a teacher learn a new dress-up, the *who/which* clause, on page 40 and practice elements of style on page 41.
3. Use page 42 to learn how to create a title for your composition.
4. Study the checklist. Note that each paragraph needs both elements of style (an -ly adverb and a *who/which* clause). That is why there are two boxes to check in front of each.
5. Begin to write the paragraphs using only the outline and the style practice ideas to guide you. Try not to look back at the source text. *Write in your own words*. Follow the checklist.

Unit 2: Writing from Notes

Day 3

1. Finish writing your paragraphs, using your key word outline, your style practice ideas, and the checklist to guide you. Check off each item on the checklist when you are sure you have completed it. Let an editor proofread.

2. Review all vocabulary words learned thus far.

Day 4

1. Write or type a final draft, making any corrections your editor asked you to make.

2. Let an editor proofread again. He or she should check that all elements of structure and style are included and labeled as instructed on the checklist. Paperclip the checklist to your final draft to be turned in.

3. If you are making a Magnum Opus Notebook, revise your Anglo-Saxons paragraph from Lesson 2. (See Appendix II.) The chart of proofreaders' marks in the SRP may be helpful.

Lesson 4: Justinian the Great

Unit 2: Writing from Notes

Source Text

Justinian the Great

While the Western Roman Empire fell to barbarians, the Eastern Roman Empire withstood attacks. This was the Byzantine Empire. One of its mightiest emperors was Justinian the Great. When he came to power, laws in one part of the empire were different from laws in other parts. He made a just set of laws that would be the same everywhere. It was called the Justinian Code, and many of its laws are still used today. Since his name begins with the word *just*, it is easy to remember that he was the emperor who made just laws.

Justinian is famous for other things too. He rebuilt the capital city of Constantinople. When he did, he built the most beautiful church in the world, the Hagia Sophia (the Church of the Holy Wisdom). It has a huge marble dome that towers over several smaller domes. The inside is decorated with stunning mosaics and pure gold. Today the Hagia Sophia is a museum that awes visitors. Justinian also recaptured some of the lands that had been taken over by barbarians. Under Justinian the Great, the Byzantine Empire was at its largest, and it was strong and glorious.

Sample

Lesson 4: Justinian the Great

Key Word Outline

I. *W. Rom. Emp, ↓. E. Rom. Emp, withstood, attacks*

1. *= Byzantine Emp.*
2. *1, > emperors, Justinian the >*
3. *1st, laws, different, everywhere*
4. *Justinian, same, everywhere*
5. *Justinian Code, w/laws, still, 2day*
6. ***Just**inian, just, laws*

II. *Justinian, famous, more*

1. *rebuilt, cap., Constantinople*
2. *> beautiful, Hagia Sophia*
3. *>, marble, dome*
4. *inside, mosaics, gold*
5. *today, museum, awes*
6. *recaptured, lands, barbarians*
7. *under, J >, Byzantine Emp., >est*

Ask students to read the above sentences without the *who* or *which* clauses. They should read the following:

Justinian the Great desired to recapture Roman lands from the barbarians.

Constantinople was impressive.

New Style

Who/Which Clause Dress-Up

In this lesson you will learn to add another dress-up to your paragraphs: a *who/which* clause. A *who/which* clause (*w/w* clause) is a clause that begins with either the word *who* or the word *which* and tells more information about a person, place, thing, or idea.

A *who* clause tells more about a person.

A *which* clause tells more about a thing, place, or idea.

Here are some sentences containing *who/which* clauses:

Justinian the Great, who ruled the Eastern Roman Empire, desired to recapture Roman lands from the barbarians.

Constantinople, which was the capital of the Eastern Roman Empire, was impressive.

Notice that each *who/which* clause has a comma before it and either a comma or period after it. That is because it is added to a sentence that was already complete. You could take it out of the sentence and still have a complete sentence left. Try it and see.

Warning: You cannot just insert the word *who* or the word *which* into a sentence to make a *who/which* clause. If you do, you will create a fragment.

For example, if you begin with *Barbarians invaded Europe* and simply add the word *who*, notice what you have:

Barbarians, who invaded Europe

This is a fragment. You must now add more information to make a complete sentence:

Barbarians, who invaded Europe, caused the crumbling of the Western Roman Empire.

Indicate a *who/which* clause by underlining the word *who* or *which.*

Vocabulary words are in bold.

Style Practice

Who/Which Clause Dress-Up

Combine each pair of sentences into one sentence with a *who* or a *which* clause. Remember to underline the word *who* or the word *which*. Place a comma before and after each clause unless the clause is at the end of the sentence. In that case, only a comma before the clause is necessary.

Example: Justinian was a wise ruler. Justinian made fair laws.

Possible answer: Justinian, who was a wise ruler, made fair laws.

1. The Hagia Sophia was a beautiful church. The church was decorated with mosaics.

   The Hagia Sophia, which was decorated with mosaics, was a beautiful church.

2. Justinian recaptured land from barbarians. Justinian expanded the Byzantine Empire.

   Justinian, who recaptured land from barbarians, expanded the Byzantine Empire.

-ly Adverb Dress-Up

You will also be required to add an -ly adverb to each of your paragraphs. Practice by adding an -ly adverb to each of these sentences. You may write more than one option on each blank. When you write each paragraph, choose the -ly adverb you like best. (***Hint***: Many vocabulary words will work well. See the chart on pages 274–275.)

1. Justinian ruled *proudly, justly, competently, wisely,* ***astutely, resolutely, benevolently, nobly, earnestly, intrepidly***.

2. The walls and ceilings of the Hagia Sophia are *stunningly, elaborately, exquisitely, beautifully, masterfully, gorgeously, ornately,* ***opulently*** decorated.

3. The Justinian Code ensured that all laws were *fairly, justly,* ***uniformly*** enforced throughout the kingdom.

Unit 2: Writing from Notes

The Title Rule

The last thing you will add to your final draft of the Justinian the Great paragraphs is a title. We want a title that will grab the readers' attention and make them want to read the paragraph. Therefore, you should try to be a little creative with your titles.

The title should repeat one to three key words from the final sentence. For example, the source text ends with, "*Under Justinian the Great, the Byzantine Empire was at its largest, and it was strong and glorious*." The key words are underlined.

Here are some possible ways to repeat key words from the last sentence to form a title.

Justinian's Glorious Rule

A Great Emperor and Empire

Note: You may change your final sentence to help you create an intriguing title.

Remember the title rule:

Title repeats one to three key words from final sentence.

Write your own idea for a title.

Strong and Glorious

Byzantine's Great Ruler

Under the Great Justinian

Lesson 4: Justinian the Great

Unit 2 Composition Checklist

Lesson 4: Justinian the Great

Writing from Notes

Institute for Excellence in Writing
Listen. Speak. Read. Write. Think!

Name: ______________________________

STRUCTURE		
☐ MLA format (see Appendix I)	______	6 pts
☐ title centered and repeats 1–3 key words from final sentence	______	5 pts
☐ checklist on top, final draft, rough draft, key word outline	______	5 pts
STYLE (one of each in each paragraph)		
¶1 ¶2 Dress-Ups (underline)	(5 pts each)	
☐ ☐ -ly adverb	______	10 pts
☐ ☐ *who/which* clause	______	10 pts
MECHANICS		
☐ capitalization	______	1 pt
☐ end marks and punctuation	______	1 pt
☐ complete sentences (Does it make sense?)	______	1 pt
☐ spelling and usage	______	1 pt
VOCABULARY		
☐ vocabulary words - label *(voc)* in left margin or after sentence		
Total:	______	40 pts
Custom Total:	______	pts

Unit 2: Writing from Notes

Lesson 5: Beowulf

Structure: IEW Unit 3: Retelling Narrative Stories

Style: no new stylistic techniques

Writing Topic: Beowulf

Optional Student Reading Assignment: During Lessons 2–5, students may read an appropriate version of the tales of King Arthur. Please see Appendix IV.

Teaching Writing: Structure and Style

Watch the sections for Unit 3: Retelling Narrative Stories. At IEW.com/twss-help reference the TWSS Viewing Guides.

UNIT 3: RETELLING NARRATIVE STORIES

Lesson 5: Beowulf

Goals

- to be introduced to the Unit 3 Retelling Narrative Stories structural model
- to create a 3-paragraph key word outline using the Unit 3 Story Sequence Chart
- to write a 3-paragraph story about Beowulf
- to correctly use new vocabulary words: *fatally*, *hastily*, *brandish*, *spew*

Assignment Schedule

Note: Classes that meet weekly should complete Days 1 and 2 in class.

Day 1

1. Read the Review and Historical Information sections and the New Structure: The Story Sequence Chart section on pages 46–47.
2. Read "Beowulf" on page 48. Then, with the help of your teacher, complete the keyword outline on page 49. Do not take notes from each sentence. Simply answer the Story Sequence Chart questions. Your outline should be brief. You can add more details when you actually write your own version of the story.

   Note: Key words do not need to be placed on the line across from the questions they answer. For example, in Section I it does not matter whether you introduce the setting or the characters first. You may also need more than one line to answer one question. You may be able to answer two questions on one line.
3. Take turns telling back the story, using one line of the outline at a time.
4. Learn the new vocabulary words for Lesson 5: *fatally*, *hastily*, *brandish*, *spew*.

Day 2

1. Review your "Beowulf" story outline. Be sure you understand everything on it. If a note is unclear, fix it before you write your story.
2. With a teacher practice elements of style on pages 50–51.
3. Go over the checklist on page 52. Note that each of the three sections of the story should include both of the dress-ups you have learned.
4. Begin to write your own version of "Beowulf," using only your key word outline and the style practice ideas to guide you. *Write the new version in your own words*. Follow the checklist.

   Important note: Each Roman numeral on the outline should begin a new paragraph in your story.

Consider having a best title contest. Ask students to email their titles to you. Then, next week, write the titles anonymously on the whiteboard and let the class vote on their favorite. A title must follow the title rule to qualify.

Use this title rule:

Title repeats one to three key words from the final sentence.

Day 3

1. Finish writing your story. Check off each item on the checklist when you are sure you have completed it. Each paragraph needs both of the dress-ups. Let an editor proofread.
2. Review all vocabulary words learned thus far.

Day 4

1. Write or type a final draft, making any corrections your editor asked you to make.
2. Let an editor proofread again. He or she should check that all elements of structure and style are included and labeled as instructed on the checklist. Paperclip the checklist to your final draft to be turned in.
3. If you are making a Magnum Opus Notebook, revise your Monasteries paragraph from Lesson 3. (See Appendix II.)
4. If you are reading the suggested literature, obtain *One Thousand and One Arabian Nights* by Geraldine McCaughrean.

Review

How do you create an intriguing title?

Share the title of your Justinian paragraphs from Lesson 4.

Share a *who/which* clause in one of your Justinian paragraphs.

Play a vocabulary game from the Teacher's Manual.

Historical Information

The story you will retell in this lesson is a portion of one of the oldest literary works written in the Old English of the Anglo-Saxons. It is an epic poem called *Beowulf.* An epic poem is a very long poem that is usually about a hero who accomplishes many great feats. *Beowulf* is the longest poem written in Old English with about 3000 lines! We are not sure exactly when it was written, but most people think it was around AD 700. The story is about a prince and warrior, Beowulf, who sails to Denmark to fight a monster named Grendel. He defeats this monster as well as the monster's angry mother. He becomes king of the Geats, who lived in what is now southern Sweden, and he rules for many, many years. The source text is a simplified version of the end of the story.

Lesson 5: Beowulf

New Structure

The Story Sequence Chart

The next several lessons will focus on story writing. You will use a new method of note taking that will help you appreciate the important elements of a story. Every story, regardless of how long it is, contains the same basic elements.

Setting and Characters

Stories usually begin by introducing readers to the time and place of the story. This is called the *setting.* Think about the words you should choose to describe the setting of the story. For example, a sad story might begin with gray skies and fog. A suspenseful story might begin with booming thunder, howling wind, and creaking doors.

Also at their beginnings, stories must introduce their readers to the main people (or animals) of the story—the *characters*.

Conflict or Problem

Then, for a story to be captivating, it must move into the next important element—the *conflict.* This is the problem, want, or need of the main character(s). Stories without some sort of problem to overcome or need to be met are not very interesting. Most of the action of the story is simply how the conflict is dealt with—what the characters do, say, think, or feel with respect to the conflict.

Climax and Resolution

If there is a conflict or problem, there must be a way to solve it! We call the event that leads to the problem being solved the *climax* of the story. It is often the most exciting part of the story. We call the result of the climax (how the problem works out) the *resolution.*

Characters and the readers often learn something about truth in life from a story. This is called a moral or message. Common morals include ideas such as good overcomes evil and virtues such as courage, honesty, perseverance, and compassion are rewarded. A moral or message gives the story a sense of purpose. However, some stories do not have a clear moral. They are written just for fun, and that is fine.

Unit 3: Retelling Narrative Stories

Source Text

Beowulf

Long ago, in the fifth century, Beowulf was king of the Geats.* He had ruled wisely for many years, so the people were happy and the kingdom was peaceful. However, deep in a cave high on a cliff above the sea, a fierce dragon slept. He guarded a vast treasure. One day a runaway slave happened upon the chamber. At once he was both terrified of the dragon and astonished at the piles and piles of riches. As he turned to flee, he grabbed a golden goblet and was off. The dragon felt the loss of his goblet. He emerged from his lair, furious. He darted from village to village, spitting fire from his nostrils. All over the land fires blazed; then, the monster returned to his cave.

The king, Beowulf, though he was now old, knew he must stop the beast from terrorizing the villages again. He gathered his best warriors. As he and his men reached the dragon's den, flames blasted out from the opening. Beowulf called to the monster, and the sinister serpent roared and hissed as the ground quaked with his steps. As soon as they met, Beowulf and the dragon fought fiercely. All of the warriors ran from fear except for one youngster who fought alongside his king. Then, Beowulf's sword broke, and the dragon was able to seize him by the neck. The youngster climbed on the monster and stabbed at his throat until he finally dropped the king. The two men fought the beast until he was finally defeated and died. The town was now safe. However, Beowulf soon died from his wound. After he died, everyone remembered and honored him as their great hero.

*The Geats lived in what is now Sweden.

Sample

Lesson 5: Beowulf

Key Word Outline—Story Sequence Chart

Characters and Setting

When does the story happen?

Who is in the story?

What are they like?

Where do they live or go?

I. *5th century, land, Geats, ☺*

1. *Beowulf, [crown], wise*
2. *dragon, cave, zzzz, riches*
3. *slave, [eyes], took, ran*
4. *dragon, → villages, fire →*

Conflict or Problem

What does the main character need or want?

What do the characters do, say, think, and feel?

What happens before the climax?

II. *B-, knew, must, stop*

1. *gathered, warrior, →, [symbol], called*
2. *hiss, ground, quaked*
3. *fought, warriors, fled*
4. *1, young, stayed, help*

Climax and Resolution

What leads to the conflict being solved (the climax)?

What happens as a result?

What is learned? (message, moral)

III. *B-, sword, broke*

1. *dragon, grabbed, neck*
2. *young, climbed, stabbed, ↓, B-*
3. *B-, + young, XX, dragon* (*XX = kill, die*)
4. *B-, XX, remembered, hero*

Title repeats 1–3 key words from final sentence.

Style Practice

Who/Which Clause Dress-Up

Finish each sentence with a *who-clause* clause. Remember the comma after the clause. Remember to finish the sentence after the clause. Underline the word *who* or *which* as you will when you use a *who/which* clause in your story.

1. The dragon, who *felt the slave slip away, woke up.* ______________________________ .

Note: Use *who* to refer to animals only when they are characters in a story acting like people. If not, use *which.*

2. Beowulf, who *was wounded, continued to fight **tenaciously**.* ______________________________ .

-ly Adverb Dress-Up

You will be required to add an -ly adverb to each paragraph. Practice finding -ly adverbs to add to these sentences.

1. The dragon *suddenly* woke.
2. The slave *silently* slipped away.
3. Beowulf continued to fight although ***fatally*** wounded.
4. Beowulf fought ***tenaciously*** .

Vocabulary Practice

Open to the vocabulary chart on pages 274–275. How might you use some of these words in your story? Write ideas containing vocabulary words that could be used in your story. Begin with at least two Lesson 5 words.

*Beowulf was **fatally** wounded. The slave **hastily** grabbed a goblet.*

*The warriors **brandished** their swords. The dragon **spewed** fire.*

*the **fetid** dragon; the **massive** cave or beast*

*Beowulf was **astute** and **intrepid**. He fought **tenaciously**.*

*Beowulf **resolutely pursued** the monster.*

Offer students a ticket for each vocabulary word they can use correctly in a phrase that could be part of the Beowulf story. If they need help, read the phrases and sentences below without the vocabulary words. Can they guess the words?

Be sure students understand that both dress-ups have three boxes to check because each of the three paragraphs of the story must include both dress-ups.

Unit 3 Composition Checklist

Lesson 5: Beowulf

Retelling Narrative Stories

Institute for Excellence in Writing
Listen. Speak. Read. Write. Think!

Name: ______________________________

STRUCTURE

☐ MLA format (see Appendix I)	______	5 pts
☐ title centered and repeats 1–3 key words from final sentence	______	5 pts
☐ story follows Story Sequence Chart	______	6 pts
☐ each paragraph contains at least four sentences	______	6 pts
☐ checklist on top, final draft, rough draft, key word outline	______	5 pts
STYLE (one of each in each paragraph)		
¶1 ¶2 ¶3 Dress-Ups (underline)	(3 pts each)	
☐ ☐ ☐ -ly adverb	______	9 pts
☐ ☐ ☐ *who/which* clause	______	9 pts
MECHANICS		
☐ capitalization	______	1 pt
☐ end marks and punctuation	______	1 pt
☐ complete sentences (Does it make sense?)	______	1 pt
☐ spelling and usage	______	2 pts
VOCABULARY		
☐ vocabulary words - label *(voc)* in left margin or after sentence		
Total:	______	50 pts
Custom Total:	______	pts

If you will have a best title contest, have students note this on their checklists.

Teachers are free to adjust a checklist by requiring only the stylistic techniques that have become easy, plus one new one. "EZ+1."

Lesson 6: The Archbishop of Canterbury

Structure: IEW Unit 3: Retelling Narrative Stories

Style: strong verb

Writing Topic: The Archbishop of Canterbury (Augustine)

Optional Student Reading Assignment: During Lessons 6–8, students may read selected tales from *One Thousand and One Arabian Nights* by Geraldine McCaughrean.

UNIT 3: RETELLING NARRATIVE STORIES

Lesson 6: The Archbishop of Canterbury

Goals

- to practice the Unit 3 structural model
- to create a 3-paragraph key word outline using the Unit 3 Story Sequence Chart
- to write a 3-paragraph story about the Archbishop of Canterbury
- to correctly add a new dress-up: strong verb
- to ban weak verbs: *go/went, say/said*
- to correctly use new vocabulary words: *flee*, *extol*, *rebuke*, *intrigue*

Assignment Schedule

Note: Classes that meet weekly should complete Days 1 and 2 in class.

Day 1

1. Read the Review and Historical Information sections on page 55.
2. Read "The Archbishop of Canterbury" on page 56. Then, with the help of your teacher, complete the keyword outline on page 57.
3. Take turns telling back the story, using one line of the outline at a time.
4. Learn the new vocabulary words for Lesson 6: *flee*, *extol*, *rebuke*, *intrigue*.

Day 2

1. Review your key word outline. If a note is unclear, fix it.
2. With a teacher learn a new dress-up, the strong verb, on page 58 and practice elements of style on page 59.
3. Go over the checklist on page 60. Note that each of the three sections of the story should include all dress-ups.
4. Begin to write your own version of "The Archbishop of Canterbury," using only your key word outline and the style practice ideas to guide you. *Write in your own words*. Follow the checklist.

Day 3

1. Finish writing your story. Check off each item on the checklist when you are sure you have completed it. Let an editor proofread.
2. Review all vocabulary words learned thus far.

Unit 3: Retelling Narrative Stories

Day 4

1. Write or type a final draft, making any corrections your editor asked you to make.
2. Let an editor proofread again. He or she should check that all elements of structure and style are included and labeled as instructed on the checklist. Paperclip the checklist to your final draft to be turned in.
3. If you are making a Magnum Opus Notebook, revise your Justinian the Great paragraphs from Lesson 4. (See Appendix II.)

Study for Vocabulary Quiz 2. It will cover words from Lessons 1–6.

Literature Suggestion

With Lessons 6–8, read *One Thousand and One Arabian Nights* by Geraldine McCaughrean.

Review

Play a vocabulary game from Appendix VI of the Teacher's Manual in order to prepare for the quiz in Lesson 7.

Share the title of your Beowulf story. Does it repeat one to three key words from your final sentence?

Share your favorite element of style from your Beowulf story. This could include an -ly adverb, a *who/which* clause, or a vocabulary word.

Review the elements of the Story Sequence Chart. Fill in the blanks below.

I. When and where the story takes place ______ *setting* ______

Whom the story is about ______ *characters* ______

II. The problem, want, or need ______ *conflict* ______

III. What leads to the problem being solved? ______ *climax* ______

The end result ______ *resolution* ______

What can be learned ______ *message or moral* ______

If you had a best title contest for the Beowulf story, let the class vote. Put all titles on the whiteboard. When students know which one or two they will vote for, they should close their eyes and put their heads down. As you read each title, they should raise their hands for the one or two they want to vote for. Students may not vote for their own.

Historical Information

The dominant religion in Western Europe during the Middle Ages was Roman Catholicism. One man, called the pope, was the supreme ruler. Under him were archbishops, who ruled large regions, bishops, who oversaw local churches, and monks, who lived in monasteries and devoted their lives to God and the church. The story in this lesson tells how Catholicism reached England (part of Britain) and how a monk became a great archbishop.

Unit 3: Retelling Narrative Stories

Source Text

The Archbishop of Canterbury

It was a cool, misty morning. As Pope Gregory walked through Rome, crowds of people pushed and shoved him toward the slave auction block. There, a strange sight caught his eye. At the slave market three boys looked different from any he had ever seen. Their hair and skin were almost pure white.

"Where did you find these boys?" he asked the slave traders.

"On the island of Britain," they said. "They are Angles."

"They look like angels. I'll buy all three," the pope said as he reached for his money. "No one should have to be a slave."

Pope Gregory took the boys home with him and asked them about their land and their religion. He discovered that they knew nothing about the God of the Bible.

Pope Gregory became deeply saddened. He desired to send missionaries to England, so he sent for Augustine.

"Augustine," he said, "you must sail to Britain and tell the people about the Lord."

Augustine agreed and sailed with a group of monks. It was a long journey with many setbacks, but eventually they reached the south shore of Britain called Kent.

Augustine met with King Ethelbert, the king of the land.

"Who are you, and what is your purpose here?" he asked.

"We're Christians, here to tell your people about God," Augustine proclaimed.

Augustine told the king all about the God of the Bible, and the king became a Christian! "You may live in Canterbury and preach to my people," he stated.

Many Anglo-Saxons were converted. On Christmas Day of 597, Augustine baptized thousands. The pope sent more monks to help Augustine, and churches were built all over the land. The pope made Augustine the Archbishop of Canterbury, and today some people call him "The Apostle of England."

Sample

Lesson 6: The Archbishop of Canterbury

Key Word Outline—Story Sequence Chart

Characters and Setting

> When does the story happen?
>
> Who is in the story?
>
> What are they like?
>
> Where do they live or go?

I. *cool, misty, AM, Rome*

1. *Pope Gregory, kind, ☺*
2. *pushed, auction, 👁👁, 3 slaves*
3. *boys, white, A-Sax, Britain*
4. *bought, "Ø, should, slave"*

Conflict or Problem

> What does the main character need or want?
>
> What do the characters do, say, think, and feel?
>
> What happens before the climax?

II. *pope, boys, Ø, God*

1. *called, monk, Augustine*
2. *"go, Britain, preach"*
3. *Aug. + monks, long, journey*
4. *reached, south, Kent*

Climax and Resolution

> What leads to the conflict being solved (the climax)?
>
> What happens as a result?
>
> What is learned? (message, moral)

III. *met, ♛ Ethelbert, "purpose?"*

1. *Aug, told, ♛, ✝, ♛ → Christian*
2. *"live, Canterbury, preach"*
3. *> A. Sax, converted, 1000s baptized, Christmas 597*
4. *pope, → monks, built, ⛪s*
5. *made, Aug, "Archbishop of Canterbury"*

Title repeats 1–3 key words from final sentence.

Medieval History-Based Writing Lessons: Student Book 57

New Style

Strong Verb Dress-Up

In this lesson you will learn another IEW dress-up: *strong verb.*

Every sentence has a verb, but not all verbs are *strong* verbs. Strong verbs show action. The strongest verbs show action that is easy to picture. In each pair of sentences below, a verb is in italics. Circle the verb that is stronger because it is easier to picture.

1. The fog *went* into the city. — The fog *rolled* into the city.
2. "Slavery is not right," he *said.* — "Slavery is not right," he *boomed.*
3. The boys *ate* the bread. — The boys *devoured* the bread.

Notice how substituting a stronger verb makes each sentence clearer and more descriptive.

Which vocabulary words from Lesson 5 are strong verbs? spew, brandish

Which of the following sentences paint more vivid pictures in your mind?

1. The dragon *blew* fire upon the city. — The dragon *spewed* fire upon the city.
2. Beowulf *waved* his sword. — Beowulf *brandished* his sword.

Note: *Spewed* and *brandished* are the past tense forms of *spew* and *brandish.* You may use whichever form of a vocabulary word that works in your sentence.

Banned Words

Boring verbs should be avoided in writing. For this reason you will not be allowed to use certain verbs in the writing you do for this class. These will be called *banned words*. The first verbs we will ban are *go*, *went*, *say*, and *said.*

To help you avoid these banned words, there are lists of substitutes for them in the strong verbs section of the SRP. Look at some of those words.

On the Style Practice page of this lesson, you will practice finding stronger verbs to use in place of *said* and *went.*

Banned Words

go/went *say/said*

Teachers, provide sticky tabs or sticky notes. Instruct students to tab the verb section of their SRPs.

Style Practice

Strong Verb Dress-Up and -ly Adverb Dress-Up

Following each sentence, write at least two strong verbs that could replace the banned word in italics; then, write ideas for -ly adverbs to modify those verbs. Consider including some vocabulary words. See the chart on pages 274–275.

1. "Slavery is evil," *said* Pope Gregory.

   strong verbs *scolded, **rebuked**, insisted, commented, stated*

   -ly adverbs *sternly, **earnestly***

2. "You must sail to Britain to tell the people about God," *said* the pope.

   verbs *instructed, commanded, announced, **proclaimed***, declared, resolved*

   -ly adverbs *enthusiastically, firmly, confidently, **resolutely***

3. Augustine *went* to Britain.

   verbs *sailed, journeyed, traveled, set sail*

   -ly adverbs *obediently, confidently, willingly, **earnestly, benevolently***

Who/Which Clause Dress-Up

Write a sentence that you could use in your paragraph that includes a *who/which* clause. Remember to set off the clause with commas and underline the word *who* or *which*.

Pope Gregory, who wanted to convert the Anglo-Saxons, sent for Augustine.

**Proclaim* is a vocabulary word for Lesson 7. Allow students to look ahead on the vocabulary word chart if they would like to.

Unit 3 Composition Checklist

Lesson 6: The Archbishop of Canterbury

Retelling Narrative Stories

Institute for Excellence in Writing

Name: ______________________

STRUCTURE		
☐ MLA format (see Appendix I)	______	5 pts
☐ title centered and repeats 1–3 key words from final sentence	______	5 pts
☐ story follows Story Sequence Chart	______	6 pts
☐ each paragraph contains at least four sentences	______	6 pts
☐ checklist on top, final draft, rough draft, key word outline	______	5 pts
STYLE (one of each in each paragraph)		
¶1 ¶2 ¶3 Dress-Ups (underline)	(3 pts each)	
☐ ☐ ☐ -ly adverb	______	9 pts
☐ ☐ ☐ *who/which* clause	______	9 pts
☐ ☐ ☐ strong verb	______	9 pts
☐ banned words: go/went, say/said (-1 for each use)	______	pts
MECHANICS		
☐ capitalization	______	1 pt
☐ end marks and punctuation	______	1 pt
☐ complete sentences (Does it make sense?)	______	2 pts
☐ spelling and usage	______	2 pts
VOCABULARY		
☐ vocabulary words - label *(voc)* in left margin or after sentence		
Total:	______	60 pts
Custom Total:	______	pts

Teachers are free to adjust a checklist by requiring only the stylistic techniques that have become easy, plus one new one. "EZ+1."

Lesson 7: Mohammed

Structure: IEW Unit 3: Retelling Narrative Stories

Style: *because* clause

Writing Topic: Mohammed

Optional Student Reading Assignment: During Lessons 6–8, students may read selected tales from *One Thousand and One Arabian Nights* by Geraldine McCaughrean.

UNIT 3: RETELLING NARRATIVE STORIES

Lesson 7: Mohammed

Goals

- to practice the Unit 3 structural model
- to create a 3-paragraph key word outline using the Unit 3 Story Sequence Chart
- to write a 3-paragraph story about Mohammed
- to correctly add a new dress-up: *because* clause
- to correctly apply the comma rule for the *because* clause
- to take Vocabulary Quiz 2
- to correctly use new vocabulary words: *proclaim*, *retreat*, *embellish*, *deduce*

Assignment Schedule

Note: Classes that meet weekly should complete Days 1 and 2 in class.

Day 1

1. Begin class with Vocabulary Quiz 2.
2. Read the Historical Information on page 62.
3. Read "Mohammed" on page 64. Write a keyword outline of the story on page 65. When you outline, remember that you need just the bare-bones key ideas to answer each Story Sequence Chart question. You can add details as you practice style and write.
4. Take turns telling back the story, using one line of the outline at a time.
5. Learn the new vocabulary words for Lesson 7: *proclaim, retreat, embellish, deduce.*

Day 2

1. Review your key word outline. If a note is unclear, fix it.
2. With a teacher learn a new dress-up, the *because* clause, on page 66 and practice elements of style on pages 67–68.
3. Begin to write your own version of the Mohammed story, using only the outline and the style practice ideas to guide you. *Write the new version in your own words*. Follow the checklist.

Day 3

1. Finish writing your story. Check off each item on the checklist when you are sure you have completed it. Let an editor proofread.
2. Review all vocabulary words learned thus far.

Day 4

1. Write or type a final draft, making any corrections your editor asked you to make.
2. Let an editor proofread again. He or she should check that all elements of structure and style are included and labeled as instructed on the checklist. Paperclip the checklist to your final draft to be turned in.
3. If you are making a Magnum Opus Notebook, revise the Beowulf story from Lesson 5. (See Appendix II.)

Historical Information

Roman Catholicism was the dominant religion of Europe in the Middle Ages, but another religion began during this time—Islam, which means "submission" or "surrender." Islam is the religion of the Muslims. It is based on the claims of a man named Mohammed (also spelled Muhammed). After he died, his teachings were collected in a book called the Koran (Quran). Islam spread through the Middle East and across Africa as Mohammed's followers, led by a warrior and leader named Abu Bakr, conquered surrounding lands. Today Islam is a major world religion.

The following story is a legend that developed about Mohammed's flight to Medina. This flight is called the Hegira, and it begins the Islamic calendar. Like most legends, the story is based on real events, but it is embellished quite a bit. (See vocabulary for Lesson 7 to find out what *embellished* means.)

Lesson 7: Mohammed

Source Text

Mohammed

Mohammed did not like the busy, dirty city of Mecca during the early 600s. He did not like the many greedy merchants or the travelers who poured in. He did not like the many temples built for so many different gods and idols. Sometimes he went to the desert to be alone.

One day he claimed that while he was in a cave, an angel, surrounded by light, appeared to him. He said that the angel told him that he was to be Allah's messenger. He was to tell the people to stop worshiping idols and serve the god called Allah.

When Mohammed began to preach this, some people listened, but others did not. He made many enemies because merchants made money from their idols. Soon Mohammed learned that his enemies were going to kill him. He and his friend decided to escape in the night. They left the city. They climbed the rocky hills and eventually rested in a cave.

Suddenly they heard voices and footsteps. It was an angry mob searching for them. They were coming closer and closer. Mohammed and his friend sat still and quiet. Just as they thought the angry men were coming in, they heard one say, "Look, there's a spider web across the entrance, so they can't be in there, or they would have broken it." The men went on, and Mohammed made the journey to Medina safely. There, many people believed and followed him.

Sample

Key Word Outline—Story Sequence Chart

Characters and Setting

When does the story happen? Who is in the story? What are they like? Where do they live or go?	I. *600s, Mecca, busy, dirty* 1. *Mohammed, Ø, like, greedy* 2. *Ø, like, travelers, idols* 3. *→ desert, , claimed, , angel* 4. *Allah's, messenger, , ppl, Ø, idols*

Conflict or Problem

What does the main character need or want? What do the characters do, say, think, and feel? What happens before the climax?	II. *preaching, → enemies, b/c idols, = $$* 1. *learned, enemies, wanted, XX* 2. *M-, + friend, escaped, hills* 3. *heard, footsteps, enemies* 4. *sat, still, quiet*

Climax and Resolution

What leads to the conflict being solved (the climax)? What happens as a result? What is learned? (message, moral)	III. *"Look, spider's web . . .* 1. *Ø, inside, b/c broken."* 2. *men, left, M-, → Medina* 3. *> ppl, Medina, followed* 4. *= beginning, Islam*

Title repeats 1–3 key words from final sentence.

= said or told (It is a speech bubble.)

New Style

Because Clause Dress-Up

The *because* clause is a clause (a group of words with a subject and a verb) that begins with the word *because*. Even though a *because* clause has a subject and a verb, it is not a complete sentence. Adding the word *because* to a sentence makes it an incomplete thought:

Mohammed did not like the busy city. (a sentence)

Because Mohammed did not like the busy city (not a sentence)

An entire *because* clause must be added to a sentence that is already complete. It may be added before or after the complete sentence.

Remember the comma rules:

If the *because* clause is at the beginning of the sentence, follow the entire clause with a comma.

Do not put a comma before a *because* clause.

To check that you have a complete sentence, remove the word *because*. You should have *two* sentences left. What are the two sentences in the samples below?

Mohammed did not like the busy city because it was noisy and dirty.

Because it was noisy and dirty, Mohammed did not like the busy city.

The Two Sentences

Mohammed did not like the busy city. It was noisy and dirty.

A *because* clause helps add more detail to a sentence. It also helps explain *why* something happens or something is true. Try to add a *because* clause in each paragraph you write. When you do, underline the word *because* and remember the comma rules.

Practice

Write a sentence with a *because* clause. It can be about anything. Underline the word *because*. That is how you will indicate it in your paragraphs.

The student was ready for the quiz because he had studied hard.

Lesson 7: Mohammed

Style Practice

Because Clause Dress-Up

Add a *because* clause to the ideas below. Underline the word *because*.

1. Mohammed made many enemies in Mecca. ______________________________

   Mohammed made many enemies in Mecca because he preached against the city's idols.

2. Mohammed and his friend decided to escape Mecca. ______________________________

   Mohammed and his friend decided to escape Mecca because their enemies wanted to kill them.

3. "They cannot be in this cave," the man stated. ______________________________

   "They cannot be in this cave because the web would have been broken," the man stated.

Who/Which Clause Dress-Up

Fill in each blank with a *who/which* clause. Remember to separate the clause from the rest of the sentence with commas.

1. Mohammed *, who did not like the noise of Mecca,* retreated to the desert.

2. The merchants *, who made money from selling idols,* wanted to kill Mohammed.

3. The spider's web *, which was across the cave's entrance,* saved Mohammed.

Unit 3: Retelling Narrative Stories

Strong Verb Dress-Up and -ly Adverb Dress-Up

Write strong verbs that could replace each of the banned words below. Use the SRP for help. Can you add -ly adverbs to the strong verbs? Try to include some strong verbs and -ly adverbs using your vocabulary words too. See the chart on pages 274–275.

1. He went to a cave to be alone.

   strong verbs *__retreated__, headed, escaped, climbed, trudged, ambled*

   -ly adverbs *frequently, __earnestly__*

2. He said that the angel told him that he was to be Allah's messenger.

   strong verbs *claimed, __proclaimed__, insisted, declared*

   -ly adverbs *__earnestly, tenaciously, resolutely__, excitedly*

3. They went out of the city.

   strong verbs *__fled__, bolted, snuck, crept, slipped*

   -ly adverbs *slyly, __hastily, astutely__*

4. "The web would be broken if they entered the cave," they heard one soldier say.

   strong verbs *whisper, reason, conclude, deduce, decide*

   -ly adverbs *logically, impatiently, __astutely, hastily__*

Lesson 7: Mohammed

Unit 3 Composition Checklist

Lesson 7: Mohammed

Retelling Narrative Stories

IEW Institute for Excellence in Writing
Listen. Speak. Read. Write. Think!

Name: ______________________________

STRUCTURE

☐ MLA format (see Appendix I)	______	5	pts
☐ title centered and repeats 1–3 key words from final sentence	______	5	pts
☐ story follows Story Sequence Chart	______	6	pts
☐ each paragraph contains at least four sentences	______	6	pts
☐ checklist on top, final draft, rough draft, key word outline	______	5	pts
STYLE (one of each in each paragraph)			
¶1 ¶2 ¶3 Dress-Ups (underline)	(3 pts each)		
☐ ☐ ☐ -ly adverb	______	9	pts
☐ ☐ ☐ *who/which* clause	______	9	pts
☐ ☐ ☐ strong verb	______	9	pts
☐ ☐ ☐ *because* clause	______	9	pts
☐ banned words: go/went, say/said (-1 for each use)	______		pts
MECHANICS			
☐ capitalization	______	1	pt
☐ end marks and punctuation	______	1	pt
☐ complete sentences (Does it make sense?)	______	2	pts
☐ spelling and usage	______	3	pts
VOCABULARY			
☐ vocabulary words - label *(voc)* in left margin or after sentence			
Total:	______	70	pts
Custom Total:	______		pts

Teachers are free to adjust a checklist by requiring only the stylistic techniques that have become easy, plus one new one. "EZ+1."

Unit 3: Retelling Narrative Stories

Lesson 8: The Sword in the Stone

Structure: IEW Unit 3: Retelling Narrative Stories

Style: no new stylistic techniques

Writing Topic: The Sword in the Stone (The Legend of King Arthur)

Optional Student Reading Assignment: During Lessons 6–8, students may read selected tales from *One Thousand and One Arabian Nights* by Geraldine McCaughrean.

UNIT 3: RETELLING NARRATIVE STORIES

Lesson 8: The Sword in the Stone

Goals

- to practice the Unit 3 structural model
- to create a 3-paragraph key word outline using the Unit 3 Story Sequence Chart
- to write a 3-paragraph story about King Arthur
- to correctly use new vocabulary words: *disclose, contritely, scowl, dislodge*

Assignment Schedule

Note: Classes that meet weekly should complete Days 1 and 2 in class.

Day 1

1. Read the Review and Historical Information on page 72.
2. Read "The Sword in the Stone" on pages 73–74. Write a key word outline of the story on page 75. When you outline, remember that you need just the bare-bones key ideas to answer each Story Sequence Chart question. You can add details as you write.
3. Take turns telling back the story, one line of the outline at a time.
4. Learn the new vocabulary words for Lesson 8: *disclose, contritely, scowl, dislodge*.

Day 2

1. Review your key word outline. If a note is unclear, fix it.
2. With a teacher practice elements of style on pages 76–77.
3. Begin to write your own version of the story, using only the outline and the style practice ideas to guide you. *Write the new version in your own words*. Follow the checklist.

Day 3

1. Finish writing your story. Check off each item on the checklist when you are sure you have completed it. Let an editor proofread.
2. Review all vocabulary words learned thus far.

Day 4

1. Write or type a final draft, making any corrections your editor asked you to make.
2. Let an editor proofread again. He or she should check that all elements of structure and style are included and labeled as instructed on the checklist. Paperclip the checklist to your final draft to be turned in.
3. If you are making a Magnum Opus Notebook, revise The Archbishop of Canterbury story from Lesson 6. (See Appendix II.)
4. If you are reading the suggested literature, obtain *The King's Shadow* by Elizabeth Alder or *Wulf the Saxon* by G.A. Henty for Lessons 9–12.

If the *because* clause is at the beginning of the sentence, follow the entire clause with a comma. Do not put a comma before a *because* clause.

Sentence Stretching

Instruct the students to write the sentence on a sheet of paper turned sideways with spaces between words. Then, direct them to do the following, one at a time:

1. Change the banned verb to a strong verb. (You may use the SRP for help.) Underline the strong verb.

2. Add a *because* clause. Underline the word *because*.

3. Add a *who/which* clause. Remember the commas. Underline the *who* or *which*.

4. Add an -ly adverb. Underline it.

5. Try to add a vocabulary word. Write it in all capital letters.

Example: The EXTOLLED knights, who RESOLUTELY promised to win the princess because she was so kind and beautiful, paraded proudly to the tournament.

Review

Share a strong verb and a *because* clause from your Mohammed story.

When and where do you use a comma with a *because* clause?

Stretch the following sentence by adding each element of style as your teacher instructs. (Use the space around, above, and below the sentence to add elements to it.)

The knights went to the tournament.

Historical Information

The story you will write in this lesson is probably one of the most famous medieval stories. It is part of the legend of King Arthur.

Lesson 8: The Sword in the Stone

Source Text

The Sword in the Stone

It was a cold Christmas morning in London. The streets were filled with people heading for the church, but instead of Christmas cheer, all seemed gloomy. England had been without a king for many years, and this had caused much fighting in the land. Sir Ector, an elderly but respected knight, and his two sons, Sir Kay and Arthur, were sitting solemnly in the church. Sir Kay was a young, handsome knight, and 18-year-old Arthur was his squire. More and more people filed in. Suddenly there was a great noise, and a burst of light blazed through the stained-glass windows. Everyone rushed outside. To their surprise, a white marble stone sat in the churchyard. In it was a glorious, jeweled sword. The archbishop slowly approached the curious sight. He read the words inscribed in the stone:

WHOSO PULLETH THE SWORD OUT
OF THIS STONE IS RIGHTWISE
BORN KING OF ENGLAND

Of course, every knight present tried to pull the sword from the stone, but all failed.

"Our king is not here," announced the archbishop. "We must tell every knight in the land about the sword in the stone. We must find the one who can pull the sword from the stone!"

It was decided that on New Year's Day all the great knights of England would come to London for a great tournament. After the tournament each would

Unit 3: Retelling Narrative Stories

attempt to remove the sword from the stone. So, on New Year's Day, Sir Ector, Sir Kay, and Arthur headed for London once again. They checked into the inn and headed for the tournament. As Kay's turn to fight neared, Arthur helped him with his armor.

"Now hand me my sword," he said.

"The sword!" Arthur gasped. "It's not here. It must be back at the inn."

"How can I fight without my sword?" Kay growled. "Go fetch it!"

Arthur jumped on his horse and prayed for help. On the way to the inn, he passed the churchyard and saw the sword in the stone. *I'll just grab that sword*, he thought. He hopped off his horse and hastily pulled the sword from the stone. He rode to the tournament in time for the match and handed Kay the sword.

"That's not my sword!" Kay roared. Then he looked at it. "It's the sword from the stone!" he exclaimed. "How did you get this?"

Arthur explained what he had done. Everyone gathered around.

"The boy is lying," some said.

So the crowd took Arthur back to the old churchyard. They told Arthur to put the sword back into the stone, which he did easily. Knight after knight tried to pull it back out, but it would not budge.

"Okay, boy. Now you try," demanded Kay.

Arthur reached for the sword and effortlessly pulled it from the stone. At that, all bowed down to him. "Hail to King Arthur," they said. Happiness was restored to the land that now had its rightful king.

Sample

Lesson 8: The Sword in the Stone

Key Word Outline—Story Sequence Chart

Characters and Setting

> When does the story happen?
>
> Who is in the story?
>
> What are they like?
>
> Where do they live or go?

I. *Christmas AM, ppl, ➔*

1. *☹, b/c, Ø, ➔ fighting*
2. *, Sir Ector, elderly, knight*
3. *sons, Sir Kay, knight*
4. *Arthur, 18 yr., squire*

Conflict or Problem

> What does the main character need or want?
>
> What do the characters do, say, think, and feel?
>
> What happens before the climax?

II. *> noise, light, burst*

1. *ppl, ➔, , sword, stone*
2. *"Whoso, pulleth, ... , Eng."*
3. *knights, tried, failed*
4. *planned, tournament, NY Day*

Climax and Resolution

> What leads to the conflict being solved (the climax)?
>
> What happens as a result?
>
> What is learned? (message, moral)

III. *Ector, K-, Arthur, ➔ tourn.*

1. *Arthur, forgot, K-, sword*
2. *➔ get, , sword, , grabbed*
3. *K-, "Not mine! Where?"*
4. *Arthur, explained, ppl, ➔, ,*
5. *only, A-, pull, ppl, bowed,*

Title repeats 1–3 key words from final sentence.

Note: Names of people, such as Sir Ector, count as one word.

Unit 3: Retelling Narrative Stories

Style Practice

Strong Verb Dress-Up and -ly Adverb Dress-Up

Write strong verbs that could replace each of the banned words below. Use the SRP for help. Can you add -ly adverbs to the strong verbs?

1. A burst of light went into the church. ____

   strong verbs *poured, flooded, blasted, exploded, flashed*

   -ly adverbs *suddenly, brightly, radiantly, blindingly*

2. The people went outside to see what had made the crash. ____

   strong verbs *fled, rushed, hurried, scurried, bolted, charged*

   -ly adverbs ***hastily**, curiously, anxiously*

3. "Get my sword!" Kay said. ____

   strong verbs *growled, roared, bellowed, yelled, exclaimed, rebuked*

   -ly adverbs *angrily, furiously, crossly, **brazenly***

4. "Hail to King Arthur," they said. ____

   strong verbs *chorused, repeated, chanted, **proclaimed***

   -ly adverbs ***reverently**, happily, excitedly*

Lesson 8: The Sword in the Stone

Because **Clause Dress-Up**

Add a *because* clause to the ideas below. Underline the word *because*.

1. It was decided that a great tournament must be held in London. *It was decided that a tournament be held in London because no knight could pull the sword from the stone.*

2. Sir Kay was irate. *Sir Kay was irate because Arthur had forgotten his sword.*

3. Everyone bowed to Arthur. *Everyone bowed to Arthur because he was their new king.*

Vocabulary Practice

Look at the vocabulary chart on pages 274–275. How might you use some of these words in your story? Write phrases containing vocabulary words that could be used in your story. Include at least one of the strong verbs for Lesson 8.

Offer students a ticket for each vocabulary word they can use correctly in a phrase that could be part of the story. If they need help, read the sentences below without the vocabulary words. Can they guess the words?

Here are some ideas:

The sword was **opulently embellished** with sparkling jewels.

Arthur **hastily fled** to **pursue** finding a sword for Kay.

The **perturbed** knights **scowled** at Arthur when he claimed to have **dislodged** the sword.

Everyone **uniformly extolled** Arthur when the sword in the stone **disclosed** that he was their new king.

Kay **contritely** bowed to his brother.

Unit 3: Retelling Narrative Stories

Unit 3 Composition Checklist

Lesson 8: The Sword in the Stone

Retelling Narrative Stories

Institute for Excellence in Writing

Name: ______________________

STRUCTURE

☐ MLA format (see Appendix I)	______	5 pts
☐ title centered and repeats 1–3 key words from **final** sentence	______	5 pts
☐ story follows Story Sequence Chart	______	6 pts
☐ each paragraph contains at least four sentences	______	6 pts
☐ checklist on top, final draft, rough draft, key word outline	______	5 pts

STYLE (one of each in each paragraph)

¶1 ¶2 ¶3 Dress-Ups (underline)	(3 pts each)	
☐ ☐ ☐ -ly adverb	______	9 pts
☐ ☐ ☐ *who/which* clause	______	9 pts
☐ ☐ ☐ strong verb	______	9 pts
☐ ☐ ☐ *because* clause	______	9 pts
☐ banned words: go/went, say/said (-1 for each use)	______	pts

MECHANICS

☐ capitalization	______	1 pt
☐ end marks and punctuation	______	1 pt
☐ complete sentences (Does it make sense?)	______	2 pts
☐ spelling and usage	______	3 pts

VOCABULARY

☐ vocabulary words - label *(voc)* in left margin or after sentence

Total:	______	70 pts
Custom Total:	______	pts

Teachers are free to adjust a checklist by requiring only the stylistic techniques that have become easy, plus one new one. "EZ+1."

Lesson 9: Charlemagne

Structure: IEW Unit 4: Summarizing a Reference
the topic-clincher relationship

Style: no new stylistic techniques

Writing Topic: Charlemagne

Optional Student Reading Assignment: During Lessons 9–12, students may read *The King's Shadow* by Elizabeth Alder or *Wulf the Saxon* by G.A. Henty.

Teaching Writing: Structure and Style

Watch the sections for Unit 4: Summarizing a Reference. At IEW.com/twss-help reference the TWSS Viewing Guides.

UNIT 4: SUMMARIZING A REFERENCE

Lesson 9: Charlemagne

Goals

- to be introduced to the Unit 4 Summarizing a Reference structural model
- to memorize and correctly use the topic-clincher rule
- to create a key word outline
- to write a 1-paragraph report about Charlemagne
- to correctly use new vocabulary words: *reform, restrain, apprehend, renowned*

Assignment Schedule

Note: Classes that meet weekly should complete Days 1 and 2 in class.

ONE paragraph

Day 1

1. With a teacher read the Review and Historical Information and the New Structure: Summarizing a Reference section on pages 80–81.
2. Read "Charlemagne" on page 82. You will have to limit the facts you want from it in order to write ONE summary paragraph. As you read, put an asterisk (*) by the facts you believe are most important or most interesting.
3. On the top line of the blank KWO, page 83, write key words that will help you write a topic sentence. What will your paragraph be about?
4. Next, reread the source text and look for at least five but *no more than seven* of the most important or most interesting facts. You cannot write everything there is in the source text in one summary paragraph. *You will have to leave some information out. You are summarizing.*

   To help you remember each fact you choose, write no more than three key words on one line of the blank outline.
5. Without looking at the source text, tell the meaning of each line of your notes. It may take more than one sentence to tell the meaning of a line of notes. If you do not understand one of your notes, fix it so you do.
6. Learn the new vocabulary words for Lesson 9: *reform, restrain, apprehend, renowned.*

Day 2

1. Review your key word outline. If a note is unclear, fix it before you write your paragraph.
2. With a teacher practice elements of structure and style on pages 84–85.
3. Look at the checklist on page 86. Note that you must highlight or bold two or three key words that repeat or reflect in both the topic and clincher sentences.
4. Begin to write ONE paragraph using only your key word outline and style practice ideas to guide you. *Write the new version in your own words.* Follow the checklist.

Important to Point Out to Teachers

You will most likely have to help students quite a bit at first. Most students find limiting their notes difficult until they see it modeled. See the sample key word outline for help. Many details in the source text are unnecessary. Let students choose the ones they think are the most important or the most interesting, but limit them. Ask them which facts they could do without.

Day 3

1. Finish writing your paragraph. Check off each item on the checklist when you are sure you have completed it. Let an editor proofread.
2. Review all vocabulary words learned thus far.

Day 4

1. Write or type a final draft, making any corrections your editor asked you to make.
2. Let an editor proofread again. He or she should check that all elements of structure and style are included and labeled as instructed on the checklist. Paperclip the checklist to your final draft to be turned in.
3. If you are making a Magnum Opus Notebook, revise your Mohammed story from Lesson 7. (See Appendix II.)

Literature Suggestion

With Lessons 9–12, read *The King's Shadow* by Elizabeth Alder or *Wulf the Saxon* by G.A. Henty.

Review

Play a vocabulary game from Appendix VI of the Teacher's Manual.

Historical Information

The report you will write for this lesson is about the grandson of Charles the Hammer, Charlemagne. Follow the instructions on the assignment page closely.

New Structure

Summarizing a Reference

In this lesson you will learn to write a report by summarizing a reference. Reports do not have the same structure as stories, so the key word outlining method you will use will be different from the methods you have used thus far.

When you write a short report, most often you turn to an encyclopedia, textbook, or Internet article for information. These sources may have much more information than you need. In Lessons 9–12, you will read fairly lengthy sources and look for only enough information to create a summary. It is important to understand that you will not try to note every fact from your source text. You only want to look for the most important or most interesting facts. Remember, you will be "SOME-a-rizing."

Topic Sentence

When you write a report, your facts must be organized into paragraphs. Every paragraph must have a clear topic. A topic is what the paragraph is about. Begin each paragraph with a *topic sentence* that reveals its topic.

A topic sentence should not say anything like, "In this paragraph I will tell you about ... " or "The topic of this paragraph is ... ." It should simply make a statement about the topic.

Clincher Sentence

It is also a good technique to end a paragraph by reminding the reader of the topic. You do this by repeating or reflecting (using words that mean the same thing) two or three key words from the topic sentence in the final sentence. We will call this last sentence the *clincher*.

> **Remember the topic-clincher rule:**
> The topic sentence and the clincher sentence MUST repeat or reflect two or three key words.

Read the following paragraph. Pay close attention to the first and last sentence. These are the topic sentence and clincher sentence. Highlight the words that are repeated or reflected in these. Do they tell what the paragraph is about?

> Charles Martel, called Charles the Hammer, ruled the Franks from 719 to 741. He received this nickname because of his persistent determination. He won the throne despite many enemies attempting to stop him—even throwing him in jail. When he was ruler, Islamic armies conquered Spain and planned to take his kingdom as well. However, Charles defeated the invading armies and repeatedly attacked them in the famous Battle of Tours. Thus, he was given the title by which he is remembered: Charles the Hammer.

The paragraph tells how Charles Martel received his nickname, "Charles the Hammer." The repeated and reflected words (Charles the Hammer, called, and title) hint at this.

Topic Sentence

Ask students what subjects interest them. Choose one idea to break into topics. For example, if they are interested in sharks, ask what topics this subject could be broken into (kinds, teeth, other physical characteristics, habitat, shark attacks, and the like). So, if I begin a paragraph with this sentence: "Shark attacks are frightening but rare," what will this paragraph be about? How could you begin a paragraph about shark teeth?

Clincher Sentence

For the above topic sentence about shark attacks, a clincher could be this:

Most swimmers do not need to fear a shark attack.

Use quotations?

Unit 4: Summarizing a Reference

Source Text

Charlemagne

Charlemagne, whose name means "Charles the Great," is one of the most famous rulers of the Middle Ages. He was born in A.D. 742. He was the son of King Pepin the Short and the grandson of Charles the Hammer. From them he inherited the kingdom of the Franks. The Franks lived in what is now France and part of Germany.

Charlemagne was a deeply religious man. He wanted to recapture lands taken by barbarians in order to spread his idea of the Christian faith everywhere. For thirty years he fought many wars. By 800, his empire covered almost all of western Europe. There had not been an empire so large since ancient Rome. In his zeal to spread his faith, he forced those he conquered to be baptized. In addition, all across his empire he made reforms to improve the lives of his people. He made uniform laws, and he hired loyal men to keep law and order. In exchange for their service, he gave them land. This was the beginning of knighthood. He built roads so people, especially priests and teachers, could travel more easily. He established many schools, the most famous one being in his palace. For these schools he sought the best teachers from all over the world. He believed that education should be free for all who wanted it. Charlemagne had such a huge impact on so much of Europe that he is sometimes called "the Father of Europe."

Sample

Key Word Outline

I. Topic: *Charlemagne, = "Charles the Great," renowned*

1. *inherited, kingdom, Franks*
2. *religious, wanted, spread, †*
3. *fought, 30 yrs, conquered, >, W. Europe*
4. *reforms, improve, lives*
5. *= laws, hired, ♂ keep*
6. *roads, schools, > teachers, 🌍*
7. *> impact, = "Father of Europe"*

Clincher

Unit 4: Summarizing a Reference

Structure Practice

Topic and Clincher Sentences

Write an idea for a topic sentence for this paragraph. Use the key words that you wrote on the topic line of your key word outline (or synonyms of those words) to write a sentence that tells the topic of the paragraph. Highlight them as you will in your paragraph.

Note: Be careful not to copy the first sentence of the source text exactly. For example, what other words for *famous*, *ruler*, and *Middle Ages* might you use? (You could use a vocabulary word from this lesson.)

Charlemagne, who was known as "Charles the Great," was a ***renowned*** *medieval monarch.*

Now, write a possible clincher to match the above topic sentence. Highlight the two or three key words that you repeat or reflect.

Charlemagne lived up to his name and was a great king.

Style Practice

Strong Verb Dress-Up

On the line following each sentence, write at least two strong verbs that could replace the boring or banned words in italics. Can you add an -ly adverb to them?

1. Charlemagne *wanted* to spread his idea of Christianity.

   desired, hoped, strove, aspired ***earnestly****, fervently, zealously, strongly*

2. He *got* the best teachers from around the world. ***pursued****, hired, apprehended, scoured the land for, hunted for* ***tenaciously****, determinedly, astutely*

3. Charlemagne *made* many reforms. *implemented, executed, introduced, devised, forced*

   wisely, consistently, justly, ***astutely***

Note: The vocabulary word *reform* can be used as a noun, meaning *a beneficial change*, or as a strong verb, meaning *to change for the better*. Because Charlemagne made many reforms in his kingdom, we can say he *reformed* his land and his people.

Lesson 9: Charlemagne

-ly Adverb Dress-Up

Add an -ly adverb to each sentence. (You may write several ideas on each blank and then choose your favorite to add to your paragraph.)

1. Charlemagne fought *bravely, **intrepidly, tenaciously, resolutely**, confidently, interminably* .

2. Charlemagne is ***reverently**, frequently, respectfully, admiringly* remembered as "the Father of Europe."

***Who/Which* Clause Dress-Up**

Add a *who/which* clause to this sentence. Remember to set it off with commas.

Charlemagne, *who **earnestly** desired to spread his faith,* conquered much of Europe.

***Because* Clause Dress-Up**

Expand the sentence below by adding a *because* clause to it. Underline the word *because*.

Charlemagne established many schools throughout his empire.

Charlemagne established many schools throughout his empire because he desired his people to be educated.

Remember the comma rules:

If the *because* clause is at the beginning of the sentence, follow the entire clause with a comma. Do not put a comma before a *because* clause.

Unit 4 Composition Checklist

Lesson 9: Charlemagne

Summarizing a Reference

Institute for Excellence in Writing
Listen. Speak. Read. Write. Think!

Name: ______________________________

STRUCTURE

☐ MLA format (see Appendix I)	______	2 pts
☐ title centered and repeats 1–3 key words from final sentence	______	3 pts
☐ topic-clincher sentences repeat or reflect 2–3 key words (highlight or bold)	______	3 pts
☐ checklist on top, final draft, rough draft, key word outline	______	1 pt
STYLE (one of each in each paragraph)		
¶1 Dress-Ups (underline)	(3 pts each)	
☐ -ly adverb	______	3 pts
☐ *who/which* clause	______	3 pts
☐ strong verb	______	3 pts
☐ *because* clause	______	3 pts
☐ banned words: go/went, say/said (-1 for each use)	______	pts
MECHANICS		
☐ capitalization	______	1 pt
☐ end marks and punctuation	______	1 pt
☐ complete sentences (Does it make sense?)	______	1 pt
☐ spelling and usage	______	1 pt
VOCABULARY		
☐ vocabulary words - label *(voc)* in left margin or after sentence		
Total:	______	25 pts
Custom Total:	______	pts

Teachers are free to adjust a checklist by requiring only the stylistic techniques that have become easy, plus one new one. "EZ+1."

Lesson 10: Vikings

Structure: IEW Unit 4: Summarizing a Reference

Style: quality adjective

Writing Topic: Vikings

Optional Student Reading Assignment: During Lessons 9–12, students may read *The King's Shadow* by Elizabeth Alder or *Wulf the Saxon* by G.A. Henty.

UNIT 4: SUMMARIZING A REFERENCE

Lesson 10: Vikings

Goals

- to practice the Unit 4 structural model
- to create a key word outline
- to write a 1-paragraph report about Vikings
- to correctly add a new dress-up: quality adjective
- to ban weak adjectives: *good/bad, big/little*
- to correctly use new vocabulary words: *wanton, merciless, imminent, unrivaled*

Assignment Schedule

Note: Classes that meet weekly should complete Days 1 and 2 in class.

Day 1

1. With a teacher read the Review section on page 88.
2. Read "Vikings" on page 90. As you read, put an asterisk (*) by the facts you believe are the most important or most interesting.
3. On the blank outline on page 91, write key words for a topic. What about Vikings will your paragraph focus on?
4. Reread the source text. Below the topic line, note five to seven facts you wish to include. Remember to use no more than three key words for each.
5. In your own words tell the meaning of each line of your notes.
6. Learn the new vocabulary words for Lesson 10: *wanton, merciless, imminent, unrivaled.*

Day 2

1. Review your key word outline. If a note is unclear, fix it before you write your paragraph.
2. With a teacher learn a new dress-up, the quality adjective, on pages 92–93 and practice elements of structure and style on pages 93–95.
3. Begin to write ONE paragraph about Vikings using your key word outline and style practice ideas to guide you. *Write in your own words*. Follow the checklist.

Be sure to save time to play a vocabulary game at the end of class. Lesson 11 will begin with Vocabulary Quiz 3.

Review

See Appendix VI for instructions for No-Noose Hangman. Use the phrase TOPIC CLINCHER RULE. Once solved, ask, "What is the topic-clincher rule?"

Day 3

1. Finish writing your paragraph. Remember to highlight or bold two or three key words in your topic and clincher sentences that tell the topic of the paragraph. Check off each item on the checklist when you are sure you have completed it. Let an editor proofread.
2. Review all vocabulary words learned thus far.

Day 4

1. Write or type a final draft, making any corrections your editor asked you to make.
2. Let an editor proofread again. He or she should check that all elements of structure and style are included and labeled as instructed on the checklist. Paperclip the checklist to your final draft to be turned in.
3. If you are making a Magnum Opus Notebook, revise The Sword in the Stone story from Lesson 8. (See Appendix II.)

Study for Vocabulary Quiz 3. It will cover words from Lessons 1–10.

Review

Play No-Noose Hangman from the Teacher's Manual.

Read the topic and clincher sentences from your Charlemagne report. Did you remember to highlight or bold two or three key words that repeat or reflect in each?

Lesson 10: Vikings

Unit 4: Summarizing a Reference

Source Text

Vikings

The Norsemen lived in Scandinavia where the land was very cold and harsh. Norse warriors, also known as Vikings, were feared by much of Europe. They were fierce. They attacked and looted other European countries from 700–1100. They killed women and children as well as men. Monasteries were especially targeted because they were usually stocked with provisions and valuables.

The most savage of the Viking warriors were called *berserkers*. They were like raging madmen. The term *berserk*, which now is used to describe someone who is acting wildly, originated from this name for Viking warriors. The Vikings were so feared that churches in Europe had a special prayer for protection: "God deliver us from the fury of the Norsemen."

Sometimes the warriors wanted to take over land. To do this, they sent several hundred huge warships. The sight of such a massive fleet heading for shore must have been terrifying. From these attacks, the Vikings were able to gain and settle parts of England and France. For example, when Vikings came to France in 911, King Charles the Simple did not even fight. He gave them a piece of land in northern France. This land was then called Northmen's Land, or Normandy. Everywhere they went, Viking warriors struck fear in people.

Sample

Key Word Outline

I. Topic: *Vikings, feared, much, Eur.*

1. *lived, Scandinavia, raided, Eur, 700s–1100*
2. *XX, all, looted*
3. *> savage, berserkers, ➔ berserk*
4. *take, land, 100s, warships, ➔*
5. *settled, parts, Fr, Eng.*
6. *ex: 👑 Charles (Fr), Ø, fight*
7. *gave, N. Fr, North♂♂'s land = Normandy*

Clincher

New Style

Quality Adjective Dress-Up

As you write your paragraph, you will need to add all of the dress-ups you have learned. In addition, look for a place to add a new dress-up: the quality adjective.

An adjective is a word that describes a noun—a person, place, thing, or idea. Adjectives tell things like *what color, what size, what shape, what kind, what emotion, how many*. Most adjectives can be put into phrases like this:

the __________________ pen the __________________ person

Can you think of some adjectives to describe the things you see around you?

Banned Words

Descriptive words like adjectives make writing more enjoyable; however, there are some adjectives that are overused or boring. You do not want to use these. When you write, you should use *quality* adjectives, which are adjectives that are clear and specific. They paint clear pictures in your readers' minds.

Look at the pairs of sentences below. The adjectives are in italics. Underline the *quality* adjectives.

1. He was a *good* ruler.

   He was a *noble* ruler.

2. It was a *bad* time in Europe.

   It was a *dismal* time in Europe.

Good and *bad* are vague adjectives because they do not include in what way something is *good* or *bad*. For example, is the ruler *good* because he is a man of moral character, because he is kind, or because he is strong and powerful? We do not know simply from the word *good*.

The best adjectives are the adjectives that are the most specific and descriptive. Which vocabulary word from Lesson 9 is a quality adjective? Which sentence is more specific and descriptive? *renowned*

He was a *good* ruler. He was a *renowned* ruler.

Lesson 10: Vikings

Four adjectives that you may not use when you write for this class are listed below.

Banned Words
good/bad *big/little*

The above adjectives are banned because they are vague. They do not paint clear pictures in your readers' minds. Take out your SRP. Look for quality adjectives that you can substitute for these banned words.

Structure Practice

Topic and Clincher Sentences

Write an idea for a topic sentence for this paragraph. Use the key words that you wrote on the topic line of your key word outline (or synonyms of those words) to write a sentence that tells the topic of the paragraph. Highlight the key words as you will in your paragraph.

Note: The source text began with the fact that the Norsemen lived in Scandinavia, but this will not be the focus of your paragraph, so do not use this fact as your topic sentence. What will your paragraph focus on regarding Vikings?

*Much of Europe **feared** the **Vikings** during the Middle Ages.*

Now write a possible clincher to match the above topic sentence. Highlight the two or three key words that you repeat or reflect.

***Vikings** were **fierce** warriors.*

Unit 4: Summarizing a Reference

Style Practice

Quality Adjective Dress-Up

What quality adjectives could you use to replace the following banned adjectives? You may use the SRP for help.

1. Vikings were good warriors. ______

   unrivaled, *fierce, unbeatable, invincible, unequaled, burly, savage*

2. The land in Scandinavia was not good, so Vikings raided other lands. ______

   fertile, lush, productive, fruitful

3. Vikings were feared for their bad attacks on Europe. ______

   wanton, merciless, *savage, fierce, ruthless*

4. To conquer a land, Vikings sailed in big boats. ______

   massive, enormous, daunting, intimidating

Strong Verb Dress-Up

In this paragraph there are many references to Vikings coming to other lands in order to steal from them or conquer them. What strong verbs could you use to say they *came* to other lands? Write at least three ideas that suggest they are coming to steal or conquer.

raided, invaded, attacked, stormed, ransacked, looted

-ly Adverb Dress-Up

What -ly adverbs might you add to the above ideas for strong verbs?

brazenly, mercilessly, *ruthlessly, viciously, savagely*

Because Clause Dress-Up

Add a *because* clause to this basic sentence.

Vikings were greatly feared.

Vikings were greatly feared because they were so fierce.

Vocabulary Practice

Can you fill in these blanks with vocabulary words from Lessons 1–10? Use the vocabulary chart on pages 274–275 for help. Remember that you may use any form of a vocabulary word. For example, some of the -ly adverbs may be changed to adjectives by removing the -ly.

1. Vikings were *intrepid, tenacious, brazen, unrivaled* warriors. (Lesson 1, 2, or 10)
2. Vikings *brandished* deadly weapons. (Lesson 5)
3. When Viking ships were spotted, an attack was *imminent*. (Lesson 10)
4. Vikings desired to *apprehend* all the land and valuables that they could. (Lesson 9)
5. The *wanton* attacks were *merciless*. (Lesson 10)

Play a vocabulary game such as Around the World or Lightning to prepare for the quiz next week.

See Appendix VI.

Unit 4 Composition Checklist

Lesson 10: Vikings

Summarizing a Reference

Institute for Excellence in Writing

Name: ______________________________

STRUCTURE

☐ MLA format (see Appendix I)	______	2 pts
☐ title centered and repeats 1–3 key words from final sentence	______	3 pts
☐ topic-clincher sentences repeat or reflect 2–3 key words (highlight or bold)	______	5 pts
☐ checklist on top, final draft, rough draft, key word outline	______	1 pt
STYLE (one of each in each paragraph)		
¶1 Dress-Ups (underline)	(3 pts each)	
☐ -ly adverb	______	3 pts
☐ *who/which* clause	______	3 pts
☐ strong verb	______	3 pts
☐ *because* clause	______	3 pts
☐ quality adjective	______	3 pts
☐ banned words: go/went, say/said, good/bad, big/little (-1 for each use)	______	pts
MECHANICS		
☐ capitalization	______	1 pt
☐ end marks and punctuation	______	1 pt
☐ complete sentences (Does it make sense?)	______	1 pt
☐ spelling and usage	______	1 pt
VOCABULARY		
☐ vocabulary words - label *(voc)* in left margin or after sentence		
Total:	______	30 pts
Custom Total:	______	pts

Teachers are free to adjust a checklist by requiring only the stylistic techniques that have become easy, plus one new one. "EZ+1."

Lesson 11: Alfred the Great

Structure: IEW Unit 4: Summarizing a Reference

Style: *www.asia* clause

Writing Topic: Alfred the Great

Optional Student Reading Assignment: During Lessons 9–12, students may read *The King's Shadow* by Elizabeth Alder or *Wulf the Saxon* by G.A. Henty.

UNIT 4: SUMMARIZING A REFERENCE

Lesson 11: Alfred the Great

Goals

- to practice the Unit 4 structural model
- to create a key word outline
- to write a 1-paragraph report about Alfred the Great
- to correctly add a new dress-up: *www.asia* clause
- to correctly apply the comma rule for the *www.asia* clause
- to take Vocabulary Quiz 3
- to correctly use new vocabulary words: *prominent, myriad, virtuous, bestow*

Assignment Schedule

Note: Classes that meet weekly should complete Days 1 and 2 in class.

Day 1

1. Begin class with Vocabulary Quiz 3.
2. With a teacher read the Review section on page 98.
3. Read "Alfred the Great" on page 100. As you read, put an asterisk (*) by the facts you believe are the most important or most interesting.
4. On the blank outline on page 101, write key words for a topic.
5. Reread the source text. Below the topic line, note five to seven facts you wish to include.
6. In your own words tell the meaning of each line of your notes.
7. Learn the new vocabulary words for Lesson 11: *prominent, myriad, virtuous, bestow*.

Day 2

1. Review your key word outline. Be sure you understand everything on it. If a note is unclear, fix it before you write your summary paragraph.
2. With a teacher learn a new dress-up, the *www.asia* clause, on page 102 and practice elements of structure and style on page 103.
3. Begin to write ONE paragraph about Alfred the Great, using your key word outline and structure and style practice ideas to guide you. *Write in your own words*. Follow the checklist. Watch out for banned words!

Unit 4: Summarizing a Reference

Day 3

1. Finish writing your paragraph. Check off each item on the checklist when you are sure you have completed it. Let an editor proofread.
2. Review all vocabulary words learned thus far.

Day 4

1. Write or type a final draft, making any corrections your editor asked you to make.
2. Let an editor proofread again. He or she should check that all elements of structure and style are included and labeled as instructed on the checklist. Paperclip the checklist to your final draft to be turned in.
3. If you are making a Magnum Opus Notebook, revise your Charlemagne report from Lesson 9. (See Appendix II.)

Review

Share a quality adjective from your Vikings report from Lesson 10.

Lesson 11: Alfred the Great

Unit 4: Summarizing a Reference

Source Text

Alfred the Great

Alfred the Great is probably the most famous ruler of the Anglo-Saxons in England. He was king of the West Saxons in Wessex from 871–899. He had four brothers who were king before him, but they all died. The crown, therefore, passed to him when he was only twenty-one years old. He is the only ruler in England to be called "the Great." He is best remembered for his clever, persistent fighting against Viking raiders. Vikings had conquered all of the regions surrounding Wessex, but Alfred withstood their attacks. Alfred was eventually able to defeat and make peace with the Vikings. In fact, he helped convert their king to Christianity.

Alfred is also remembered as the king who burned a peasant's cakes. A famous legend tells of a time when he was fleeing from Vikings and came upon a woman's cottage. She took him in as a stranger and asked him to watch her cakes while she tended to her animals. His mind was so busy planning an attack on the Vikings that the cakes burned, and she scolded him. How horrified she must have been when she discovered that she had rebuked her king!

Alfred ruled his kingdom well. He was kind and fair. He worked hard to make his kingdom prosperous. Some historians have called him "the most perfect character in history." Alfred was, indeed, a great ruler.

Sample

Lesson 11: Alfred the Great

Key Word Outline

I. Topic: *Alfred, >, , West Saxons, 871–899*

1. *only, , Eng., called, "the>"*
2. *remembered, fighting, Vikings*
3. *Vik, conquered, land, , , Wessex*
4. *, defeated, peace, w/Vikings*
5. *legend, burned, peasants,*
6. *kind, fair, diligent*
7. *kingdom, prospered*

Clincher

New Style

www.asia Clause Dress-Up

You have been using a *because* clause for a while. Now you will learn to form the same type of clause with other words. This acronym will help you remember them: *www.asia*. Each letter is the first letter of one of the words shown below that can begin a clausal dress-up:

when, while, where, as, since, if, although

A *www.asia* clause helps you add more detail to a sentence. Memorize these words. You can also find them in the SRP.

> ***Example***: *Alfred became king when his brothers died.*

Always check that a sentence with this dress-up is composed of two sentences plus the *www.asia* word. In the example above, if you remove the word *when*, you will see two sentences. What are they? *Alfred became king. His brothers died.*

> **Remember the comma rules:**
>
> If the *www.asia* clause is at the beginning of the sentence, follow the entire clause with a comma. We do not usually put a comma before a *www.asia* clause.

Structure Practice

Topic and Clincher Sentences

Write an idea for a topic sentence for this paragraph. Use the key words that you wrote on the topic line of your key word outline (or synonyms of those words) to write a sentence that tells the topic of the paragraph. Highlight the key words as you will in your paragraph.

Alfred the Great ruled the West Saxons from 871–899.

____

Now write a possible clincher to match the above topic sentence. Highlight the two or three key words that you repeat or reflect.

Alfred will always be remembered as a great ruler in England.

____

Style Practice

www.asia Clause Dress-Up

Add a *www.asia* clause to complete these sentences. Do not use the word *because*; use one of the new *www.asia* words. Remember to follow the comma rules.

1. Alfred was known for standing strong *when Vikings tried to invade*.

2. Alfred burned the cakes *while he was thinking about how to defeat the Vikings*.

Who/Which Clause Dress-Up

Write an idea for a *who/which* clause you could add to this sentence.

Alfred, *who ruled wisely and justly*, is remembered as a great leader.

Quality Adjective Dress-Up

Write ideas for quality adjectives that could replace the banned adjectives in these sentences.

1. Alfred was a *good* Anglo-Saxon king.

just, courageous, ***noble, prominent, proficient, virtuous, astute, benevolent,*** *diligent*

2. Alfred stopped the *bad* Vikings from conquering his land.

evil, ***brazen,*** *savage, ruthless, sinister, bloodthirsty*

Vocabulary Practice

Take out the vocabulary chart on pages 274–275. How could some of the words be used in this story?

See bold words above. Here are other ideas:

Alfred ruled ***capably*** *and* ***benevolently.***

He ***resolutely*** *stood against the raiders and* ***restrained*** *them.*

Alfred was ***renowned*** *and* ***extolled*** *by having the title "the Great"* ***bestowed*** *upon him.*

The peasant ***scowled*** *at Alfred, and he was* ***contrite.*** *Alfred's character was* ***impeccable.***

If students have trouble with ideas, read some of the sample sentences without the vocabulary words. Can they guess which words would fill in the blanks?

Teachers are free to adjust a checklist by requiring only the stylistic techniques that have become easy, plus one new one. "EZ+1."

Unit 4 Composition Checklist
Lesson 11: Alfred the Great

Summarizing a Reference

Name: ______________________________

Institute for Excellence in Writing

STRUCTURE

☐ MLA format (see Appendix I)	______	2 pts
☐ title centered and repeats 1–3 key words from final sentence	______	3 pts
☐ topic-clincher sentences repeat or reflect 2–3 key words (highlight or bold)	______	2 pts
☐ checklist on top, final draft, rough draft, key word outline	______	1 pt
STYLE (one of each in each paragraph)		
¶1 Dress-Ups (underline)	(3 pts each)	
☐ -ly adverb	______	3 pts
☐ *who/which* clause	______	3 pts
☐ strong verb	______	3 pts
☐ *because* clause	______	3 pts
☐ quality adjective	______	3 pts
☐ *www.asia* clause	______	3 pts
☐ banned words: go/went, say/said, good/bad, big/little (-1 for each use)	______	pts
MECHANICS		
☐ capitalization	______	1 pt
☐ end marks and punctuation	______	1 pt
☐ complete sentences (Does it make sense?)	______	1 pt
☐ spelling and usage	______	1 pt
VOCABULARY		
☐ vocabulary words - label *(voc)* in left margin or after sentence		

Total:	______	30 pts
Custom Total:	______	pts

Lesson 12: The Battle of Hastings

Structure: IEW Unit 4: Summarizing a Reference

Style: #2 prepositional opener

Writing Topic: The Battle of Hastings

Optional Student Reading Assignment: During Lessons 9–12, students may read *The King's Shadow* by Elizabeth Alder or *Wulf the Saxon* by G.A. Henty.

UNIT 4: SUMMARIZING A REFERENCE

Lesson 12: The Battle of Hastings

Goals

- to practice the Unit 4 structural model
- to create two key word outlines from a single reference
- to write a 2-paragraph report about the Battle of Hastings
- to be introduced to variety in sentence openers
- to correctly add a new sentence opener: #2 prepositional opener
- to correctly use new vocabulary words: *endure*, *smug*, *proficient*, *treacherous*

Assignment Schedule

Note: Classes that meet weekly should complete Days 1 and 2 in class.

Day 1

1. With a teacher read the Review section on page 106.
2. In this lesson you will write a 2-paragraph report from one source text. Before you begin taking notes, you must know the topics of each of your paragraphs. I will choose your two topics for this lesson. Scan "The Battle of Hastings" on pages 107–108.
3. The first paragraph you write will be about the famous historical Battle of Hastings. Next to Roman numeral I on the Key Word Outline write *Battle of Hastings, famous, history*. The second paragraph you write will be about the results of the Battle of Hastings that changed England. Next to Roman II write, *Battle of Hastings, changed, England.*
4. Read "The Battle of Hastings" again. As you read, put an asterisk (*) by the interesting or important facts that tell about events that occurred during the battle. These are the facts you will use to in your first paragraph. Because the topic of this paragraph is the famous battle, you should only gather facts related to the battle.
5. Below the first topic line on the Key Word Outline, note five to seven facts you wish to include.
6. In your own words tell the meaning of each line of notes.
7. Learn the new vocabulary words for Lesson 11: *prominent, myriad, virtuous, bestow*.

Day 2

1. Review your key word outline for your first paragraph. If a note is unclear, fix it before you write your paragraph.
2. With a teacher read about sentence openers on page 111 and learn the new #2 prepositional opener on page 112.
3. Practice elements of structure and style on pages 110, 113, and 114.

4. Look at the checklist on page 115. Notice the addition of the #2 prepositional opener, which must be numbered, not underlined.
5. Write the rough draft of your first paragraph using only your key word outline and style practice ideas to guide you. Write in your own words. Follow the checklist.

Day 3

1. Today you will write your second paragraph about the results of the Battle of Hastings.
2. Read "The Battle of Hastings" again. As you read, put an asterisk (*) by the interesting or important facts that tell about the lasting results of the battle. Because the topic of this paragraph is the results of the battle, you should only gather facts that indicate what happened after the battle.
3. Below Roman numeral II, the second topic line on the Key Word Outline, note five to seven facts you wish to include.
4. In your own words tell the meaning of each line of notes. If a note is unclear, fix it.
5. Write the rough draft of your second paragraph using only your key word outline. Remember to add the dress-ups listed on the checklist.
6. Check off each item on the checklist when you are sure you have completed it. Let an editor proofread.

Day 4

1. Write or type a final draft, making any corrections your editor asked you to make.
2. Let an editor proofread again. He or she should check that all elements of structure and style are included and labeled as instructed on the checklist. Paperclip the checklist to your final draft to be turned in.
3. If you are making a Magnum Opus Notebook, revise your Vikings report from Lesson 10. (See Appendix II.)
4. If you are reading the suggested literature, obtain *Robin Hood* by J. Walker McSpadden (or other version for children) for Lessons 13–15.

Review

Play a review game such as Tic-Tac-Toe or 21 Questions from the Teacher's Manual.

Lesson 12: The Battle of Hastings

Source Text

The Battle of Hastings

The year 1066 is a famous year in history because in it the Battle of Hastings was fought. It was a battle over the throne of England. It was fought because William, the Duke of Normandy in France, claimed that King Edward had made him his heir. They were cousins. However, after the king died, the archbishop of York crowned Harold Godwinson, who was the king's brother-in-law. He had served beside the king for several years. When William heard the news, he headed for England with his army. Harold prepared for battle. He had his men build barricades of tree trunks. Then the soldiers armed themselves with double-edged axes and spears and lined up on the hillside. On October 14, William's forces met Harold's forces on a hill near the town of Hastings. A long and difficult battle followed. It lasted all day until an arrow struck and killed Harold. Some legends say the arrow struck him in the eye. The Normans won the battle, and William headed to London. He was crowned King of England on the following Christmas Day. Harold, therefore, was the last Anglo-Saxon king of England. That great battle of 1066 gave England a Norman king and changed the line of royalty there forever.

William had to be a powerful ruler. Many Englishmen were not happy about a Norman king ruling England, and for five years there were revolts. To stop these revolts, William was ruthless. For example, William had his soldiers destroy the region by burning down farms, killing livestock, and destroying food. Thousands of Englishmen died. He also took land away from the Saxon nobles and granted it to those who supported him. Most of these noblemen were Normans. They became William's barons. Barons controlled large areas of land. They had to swear an oath of loyalty to the king. They also provided soldiers (knights) for the king, and they collected taxes from the people. Thus, William began the feudal system in England. William also had castles built to help maintain order. The most famous of these was the Tower of London. The castles he built across England served as fortresses and prisons. They were reminders of his power.

Sample

Key Word Outline

I. Topic: *Battle of Hastings, famous, history*

1. *Eng. 1066, over, throne, England*
2. *Will, Dk. Normandy, claimed, ♔, →, heir*
3. *♔, XX, Archbp. York, crowned, Harold Godwinson*
4. *Will, →, England, w/army*
5. *Oct. 14, fought, Harold, XX*
6. *Will, →, London*
7. *crowned, Christmas, 1066*

Clincher

II. Topic: *Battle of Hastings, changed, history*

1. *Dk. Normandy, rule, England*
2. *Eng, ☹, revolts, 5 yrs*
3. *W., ruthless, squashed*
4. *took, lands, Saxons → Norms*
5. *prom, loyalty, provided, soldiers*
6. *→ feudal system, England*
7. *+ castles, show, power*

Clincher

Structure Practice

Topic and Clincher Sentences

1. Write an idea for the topic sentence for the first paragraph. Use the key words (or synonyms of those words) that you wrote next to Roman numeral I on the key word outline to write a sentence that tells the topic of the paragraph. Highlight the key words as you will in your paragraph.

   The Battle of Hastings is one of the most famous battles in England's history.

2. Now write a possible clincher to match the above topic sentence. Highlight the two or three key words you repeat or reflect.

   England's history was significantly changed when William won the Battle of Hastings.

3. Write an idea for the topic sentence for the second paragraph. This time you will use the key words (or synonyms of those words) that you wrote on the Roman numeral II line to write a sentence that tells the topic of the second paragraph. Highlight the key words as you will in your paragraph.

   After the Battle of Hastings, significant changes occurred in England because the country was now ruled by a king from Normandy.

4. Now write a possible clincher to match the above topic sentence. Highlight the two or three key words you repeat or reflect.

   Numerous changes occurred in England because of the results of the battle of 1066.

New Style

Sentence Openers

In this lesson you will learn a new type of element of style. To help you appreciate it, read the following two versions of part of a report about William the Conqueror. What is the difference between them? Which sounds better?

Version 1

William the Conqueror took the throne of England in 1066. He began feudalism there. Feudalism is a social structure and system of rule. The king was at the top. He was the technical owner and ruler of all the land. Nobles and knights were given land to maintain and defend. Peasants, called serfs, worked the land or were craftsmen. They gave most of what they produced to the noble. Each class served the class above it.

Version 2

In 1066 William the Conqueror took the throne of England. He began feudalism there, which is a social structure and system of rule. At the top was the king. Technically he was the owner and ruler of all the land; however, nobles and knights were given land to maintain and defend. Peasants, called serfs, farmed the land. They gave most of the produce to the noble. Each class served the class above it.

In the paragraphs above you should have noticed that in Version 1 all the sentences begin with the subject and are about the same length. This makes the paragraph boring to read.

Two ways to make your writing more sophisticated are to begin some of your sentences with something other than the subject and to use sentences of differing lengths—some short, some medium, and some long. Can you see how Version 2 accomplished both of these things?

In Version 2 the phrase *In 1066* is placed in front of the sentence. Then, the next two sentences are combined into one sentence using a *who/which* clause. This is followed by a sentence that begins with the phrase *At the top*. The next sentence begins with an -ly adverb.

Guide students to see that a prepositional phrase begins with a preposition, ends with a noun, and never has a verb in it. A prepositional phrase follows this pattern: preposition + noun (no verb).

#2 Prepositional Opener

In this lesson learn the #2 prepositional opener that begins a sentence with a prepositional phrase. So that you can indicate it when you use it, it is given a number. (You will learn more sentence openers later that will be given other numbers.)

Here are two sample #2 prepositional openers from Version 2 of the previous page:

[2] In 1066 William the Conqueror took the throne of England.

[2] At the top was the king.

Note that a #2 sentence is a sentence that *begins* with a prepositional phrase.

A prepositional phrase always consists of a preposition plus a noun. A prepositional phrase never contains a verb.

There might be other words between the preposition and the noun, but there is never a verb in a prepositional phrase. Here are some examples of prepositional phrases: *in the land, across the river, during the night.*

If your prepositional phrase has five words or more, follow it with a comma. A comma is optional but usually not recommended with shorter phrases.

Some Prepositions

about	above	across	around	at	after	by	because of	during
for	from	in	inside	into	near	of	off	on
outside	over	past	through	to	under	up	with	without

Practice

Write a sentence with a #2 prepositional opener. It can be about anything. Label it by writing a 2 in the left margin across from it or a [2] right before the sentence. Do *not* underline the sentence openers.

Note: You can find a longer list of prepositions in the SRP behind the Sentence Openers tab.

[2] Without variety in sentence structure, writing is boring.

Tell students that these words show a relationship between one object and another. Then, on the whiteboard, you could draw two rabbits (Mr. and Mrs.), some trees, a river, and a large rock with a hole in it. Have students look at the list of prepositions and create sentences that begin with a preposition, explaining how Mr. Rabbit relates to the other things. (Examples: Near the rock Mr. Rabbit sits. Over the rock he jumps. To Mrs. Rabbit he hops. Across the river he swims. During the day Mr. Rabbit plays.)

Have fun with this. It is OK if students use things not in your picture.

Style Practice

#2 Prepositional Opener

Add a #2 prepositional opener to each sentence. Label each by placing a 2 in the left margin or a [2] right before the sentence. If your prepositional phrase has five words or more, follow it with a comma.

1. *During the battle, Despite his valiant efforts, To the horror of England's army,*

   Harold was struck by an arrow.

2. *In 1066, After the battle, To the dismay of the English, In triumph, Because of his victory,*

   William was crowned king.

Who/Which Clause Dress-Up and *www.asia* Clause Dress-Up

Add a *who/which* clause to this sentence. Remember the commas.

William, *who was the king's cousin,* believed he had a right to the throne.

Add a *www.asia* clause to this sentence.

William won the battle *when an arrow struck Harold*.

Strong Verb Dress-Up and -ly Adverb Dress-Up

Replace the banned verb and add an -ly adverb in the sentence below.

William *went* *rushed, stormed, headed for, sailed* *immediately, boldly, fearlessly, greedily*

to England to take the throne.

Quality Adjective Dress-Up

Describe the following with quality adjectives:

1. William *__tenacious__, angry, irate, ruthless, __brazen, smug, merciless__*
2. the battle *grueling, __fatal__, brutal, long, __renowned__, significant*

Let students offer ideas. Give a ticket for each word they use correctly.

If students have trouble with ideas, read some of the sample sentences without the vocabulary words. Can they guess which words would fill in the blanks?

Vocabulary Practice

Take out the vocabulary chart on pages 274–275. How could some of the words be used in this story? Remember that you may use any form or tense of a vocabulary word.

Here are a few ideas to get you started. Try to add a few of your own.

1. When King Edward died, the archbishop of York ___*bestowed*___ the crown upon Harold. (Lesson 11)
2. When Harold was ___*fatally*___ struck by an arrow, the English army could no longer ___*endure*___ . (Lessons 5, 12)

*William sailed to **resolutely pursue** the throne.*

*The battle was **treacherous**.*

*William **proclaimed** that he should be king.*

Lesson 12: The Battle of Hastings

Unit 4 Composition Checklist

Lesson 12: The Battle of Hastings

Summarizing a Reference

Institute for Excellence in Writing

Name: ______________________

STRUCTURE

☐ MLA format (see Appendix I)	_____	1 pt
☐ title centered and repeats 1–3 key words from final sentence	_____	2 pts
☐ topic-clincher sentences repeat or reflect 2–3 key words (highlight or bold)	_____	6 pts
☐ checklist on top, final draft, rough draft, key word outline	_____	5 pts
STYLE (one of each in each paragraph)		
¶1 ¶2 Dress-Ups (underline)	(3 pts each)	
☐ ☐ -ly adverb	_____	6 pts
☐ ☐ *who/which* clause	_____	6 pts
☐ ☐ strong verb	_____	6 pts
☐ ☐ *because* clause	_____	6 pts
☐ ☐ quality adjective	_____	6 pts
☐ ☐ *www.asia* clause	_____	6 pts
☐ banned words: go/went, say/said, good/bad, big/little (-1 for each use)	_____	pts
¶1 ¶2 Sentence Opener (number)		
☐ ☐ [2] prepositional	_____	6 pts
MECHANICS		
☐ capitalization	_____	1 pt
☐ end marks and punctuation	_____	1 pt
☐ complete sentences (Does it make sense?)	_____	1 pt
☐ spelling and usage	_____	1 pt
VOCABULARY		
☐ vocabulary words - label *(voc)* in left margin or after sentence		
Total:	_____	60 pts
Custom Total:	_____	pts

Teachers are free to adjust a checklist by requiring only the stylistic techniques that have become easy, plus one new one. "EZ+1."

Unit 4: Summarizing a Reference
116
Institute for Excellence in Writing

Lesson 13: The Samurai and the Dragon

Structure: IEW Unit 5: Writing from Pictures

Style: no new stylistic techniques

Writing Topic: The Samurai

Optional Student Reading Assignment: During Lessons 13–15, students may read *Robin Hood* by J. Walker McSpadden.

Teaching Writing: Structure and Style

Watch the sections for Unit 5: Writing from Pictures. At IEW.com/twss-help reference the TWSS Viewing Guides.

UNIT 5: WRITING FROM PICTURES

Lesson 13: The Samurai and the Dragon

Goals

- to be introduced to the Unit 5 Writing from Pictures structural model
- to create a key word outline from a series of three pictures: The Samurai and the Dragon
- to write a 3-paragraph composition from the key word outline
- to ask questions to get ideas for writing
- to correctly use new vocabulary words: *relish*, *scramble*, *bewildered*, *anguish*

Assignment Schedule

Note: Classes that meet weekly should complete Days 1 and 2 in class.

Day 1

1. With a teacher read the Review section on page 118.

   In this lesson you will not have a source text from which you can take notes. Instead, you will have three pictures to guide you. With a teacher read page 119.

2. Look at the three pictures on page 120. On the top blank next to the first picture, write what is happening in the picture (the central fact) in key words.

   On the other lines by the first box, you will explain in more detail what is happening by answering questions about the pictures. Here are some sample questions: *What is happening in the picture? Why? What are the characters doing, saying, thinking, or feeling? Where is it happening? What would be seen, heard, or felt around the scene in the picture? What happened before what you see in the picture? Why? What will happen next?* In a class setting, outline together. Do not copy the ideas that your teacher writes on the whiteboard because you will do your own outline later.

   Note: See page 119 for ideas for samurai names.

   The paragraph should end with a clincher that repeats or reflects two or three key words from your central fact sentence. For example, if the central fact of the first picture is that two **samurai** were **practicing** their **swordsmanship**, the middle of the paragraph could tell where and why they were practicing, what they were thinking and feeling, and other background details that occurred until they heard a cry for help. The clincher could include that **they** left their **swordsmanship practice** to answer the call. (Notice that the words in bold are repeated or reflected.)

3. Repeat the above step for the remaining two pictures.
4. Begin orally composing a class version of the story you outlined together.
5. Learn the new vocabulary words for Lesson 13: *relish*, *scramble*, *bewildered*, *anguish*.

words + ideas from brain

– no source text → 3 pics

– event description

– TOPIC / CLINCHER relationship

See the sample key word outline for help, especially in discussing central fact and clincher ideas.

Day 2

1. Look at the pictures on page 120 again. Begin writing your own key word outline. Use the question words to help you.
2. With a teacher practice elements of style on page 121.
3. Begin to write your story using only your key word outline and style practice ideas to guide you. *Write in your own words*. Follow the checklist.
4. Each paragraph should begin with the central fact of one of the pictures and end with a clincher that repeats or reflects two or three words from this. Highlight or bold the repeated or reflected key words.

Day 3

1. Finish writing your 3-paragraph story. Check off each item on the checklist when you are sure you have completed it. Let an editor proofread.
2. Review all vocabulary words learned thus far.

Day 4

1. Write or type a final draft, making any corrections your editor asked you to make.
2. Let an editor proofread again. He or she should check that all elements of structure and style are included and labeled as instructed on the checklist. Paperclip the checklist to your final draft to be turned in.
3. If you are making a Magnum Opus Notebook, revise your Alfred the Great paragraph from Lesson 11. (See Appendix II.)

Literature Suggestion

Read *Robin Hood* by J. Walker McSpadden (or any children's version of this story) with Lessons 13–15.

Review

Play a vocabulary game from the Teacher's Manual.

Share the #2 prepositional opener in your Battle of Hastings paragraph from Lesson 12. Did you remember to label it with a *[2]* rather than an underline?

Before collecting the students' papers, check that each student has added and numbered a sentence that begins with a preposition. Help those who did not.

Lesson 13: The Samurai and the Dragon

Historical Information

The pictures for this lesson include medieval Japanese samurai. Samurai were professional Japanese soldiers who served the shoguns (rulers) and their lords. They followed a strict code called *bushido*, which means "way of the warrior." This code required loyalty to their masters and virtuous behavior. The samurai wore armor in battle. However, their armor looked quite different from European armor as it was made to allow them to move easily. Samurai fought mostly with swords. They always carried a long sword called a *katana* and a short sword called a *wakizashi* in their belts so that they would be ready to fight at all times.

New Structure

Writing from Pictures

When writing from pictures, if you are stuck about what to say, try asking yourself questions about each picture. There are "brain-helping" questions in the margin next to the blank key word outline to help you think of what to write.

> *Who? What? Where? How? Why? When? Thinking? Feeling? Doing? Saying? Before? After? Outside or around the picture? Description?*

You do not have to use all of the question words, and you do not have to use them in the order in which they are listed. They are simply there to help you ask questions about the pictures in order to give you ideas for what to write in your story.

To write your story for this lesson, follow the assignment instructions.

Here are some samurai names you could use for your characters. If you do not like these, research other possible names.

Yuki Hideyasu

Oka Dokan

Hojo Soun

Otomo Sorin

Toki Takato

Shima Sokon

Mori Yoshinari

Niimi Nishiki

Sample

Key Word Outline

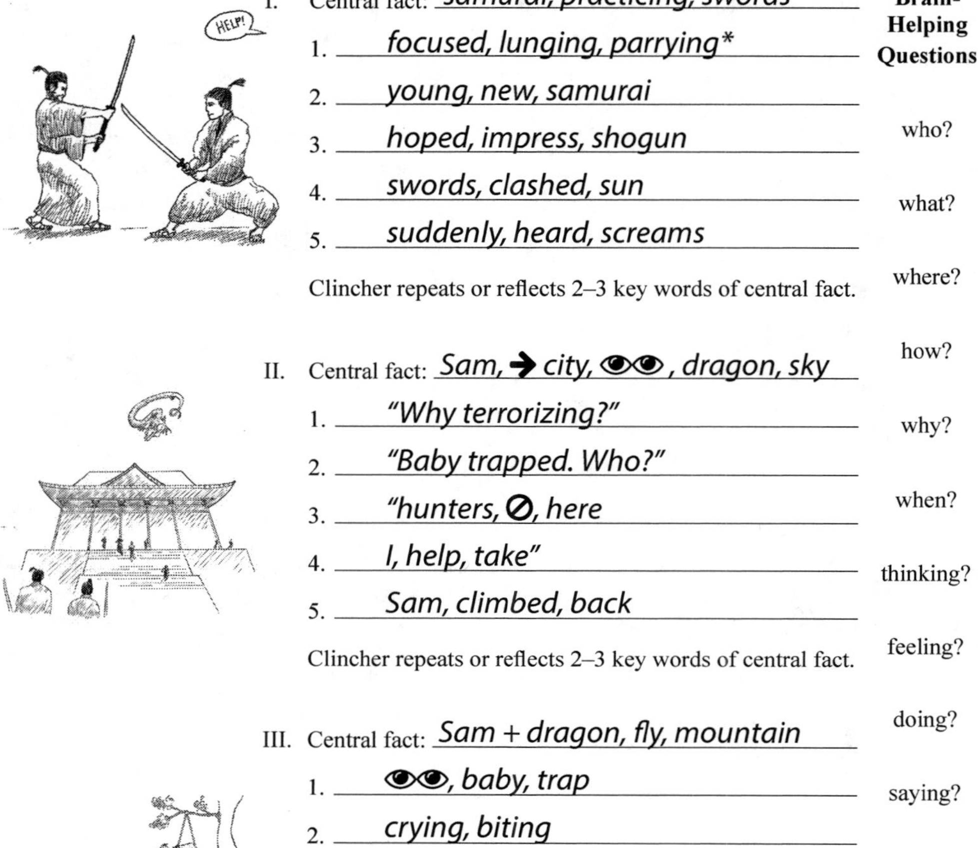

I. Central fact: *samurai, practicing, swords*
1. *focused, lunging, parrying**
2. *young, new, samurai*
3. *hoped, impress, shogun*
4. *swords, clashed, sun*
5. *suddenly, heard, screams*

Clincher repeats or reflects 2–3 key words of central fact.

II. Central fact: *Sam, → city, 👀, dragon, sky*
1. *"Why terrorizing?"*
2. *"Baby trapped. Who?"*
3. *"hunters, ⊘, here*
4. *I, help, take"*
5. *Sam, climbed, back*

Clincher repeats or reflects 2–3 key words of central fact.

III. Central fact: *Sam + dragon, fly, mountain*
1. *👀, baby, trap*
2. *crying, biting*
3. *Sam, "Don't worry"*
4. *took, katana, freed*
5. *mom, ☺, BFF, w/Sam*

Clincher repeats or reflects 2–3 key words of central fact.
Title repeats 1–3 key words from final sentence.

Brain-Helping Questions

who?
what?
where?
how?
why?
when?
thinking?
feeling?
doing?
saying?
before?
after?
outside?

120 Institute for Excellence in Writing

Discuss ideas for a clincher. For example, to reflect the words in the central fact above, one possibility is this: The **two samurai** clutched their **swords** and ran to the city. (The words in bold are reflected from the central fact.)

Discuss ideas for a clincher. For example, to reflect the words in the central fact above, one possibility is this: The **dragon** and the **samurai** soared into the **sky**. (The words in bold are reflected from the central fact.)

Discuss ideas for a clincher. For example, to reflect the words in the central fact above, one possibility is this: Though they did not see each other often, whenever they looked at the **mountain**, they remembered **they** had a special friend in the other. (The words in bold are reflected from the central fact.)

*You may want to teach students the word *parry*—to evade or dodge, especially a thrust, stroke, or weapon.

Lesson 13: The Samurai and the Dragon

Style Practice

#2 Prepositional Opener

Write an idea for a #2 prepositional opener to begin each of these sentences. Label each by placing a 2 in the left margin or a [2] right before the sentence. Do not underline.

1. *With much intensity, In preparation for the visit of the Shogun, Outside the city,*

   the two samurai were practicing their swordsmanship.

2. *In much despair, With much pleading, Above the temple*

   the dragon asked for help.

3. *In the trap, For hours, In great fear, During the night and the morning,*

   the baby dragon had been crying.

Quality Adjective Dress-Up

Describe these nouns. Use a thesaurus to find words that create strong image or feeling.

1. the dragon *massive, desperate, fiery red, fierce, distraught, relieved, thankful*
2. the baby dragon ***frantic, bewildered**, sad, helpless, hopeless, terrified*

Strong Verb Dress-Up and -ly Adverb Dress-Up

Use strong verbs to tell what the people did as they ran from the mother dragon and what the baby dragon did while he was trapped. Add -ly adverbs if you can.

1. the people ***scrambled frantically**, screamed hysterically, **fled***
2. the baby dragon trapped on the hill *whimpered softly, sobbed hysterically, **cowered** fearfully, **feebly** attempted to break the chains*

Note: Cower is a vocabulary word in Lesson 14. It is all right for students to look ahead and use future words.

Unit 5 Composition Checklist

Lesson 13: The Samurai and the Dragon

Writing from Pictures

IEW Institute for Excellence in Writing
Listen. Speak. Read. Write. Think!

Name: ______________________________

STRUCTURE

☐ MLA format (see Appendix I)	______	1 pt
☐ title centered and repeats 1–3 key words from final sentence	______	2 pts
☐ clincher sentences repeat or reflect 2–3 key words of central fact (highlight or bold)	______	6 pts
☐ checklist on top, final draft, rough draft, key word outline	______	5 pts
STYLE (one of each in each paragraph)		
¶1 ¶2 ¶3 Dress-Ups (underline)	(2 pts each)	
☐ ☐ ☐ -ly adverb	______	6 pts
☐ ☐ ☐ *who/which* clause	______	6 pts
☐ ☐ ☐ strong verb	______	6 pts
☐ ☐ ☐ *because* clause	______	6 pts
☐ ☐ ☐ quality adjective	______	6 pts
☐ ☐ ☐ *www.asia* clause	______	6 pts
☐ banned words: go/went, say/said, good/bad, big/little (-1 for each use)	______	pts
¶1 ¶2 ¶3 Sentence Opener (number)		
☐ ☐ ☐ [2] prepositional	______	6 pts
MECHANICS		
☐ capitalization	______	1 pt
☐ end marks and punctuation	______	1 pt
☐ complete sentences (Does it make sense?)	______	1 pt
☐ spelling and usage	______	1 pt
VOCABULARY		
☐ vocabulary words - label *(voc)* in left margin or after sentence		
Total:	______	60 pts
Custom Total:	______	pts

Teachers are free to adjust a checklist by requiring only the stylistic techniques that have become easy, plus one new one. "EZ+1."

Lesson 14: Llama Saves the Day

Structure: IEW Unit 5: Writing from Pictures

Style: no new stylistic techniques

Writing Topic: The Inca

Optional Student Reading Assignment: During Lessons 13–15, students may read *Robin Hood* by J. Walker McSpadden.

UNIT 5: WRITING FROM PICTURES

Lesson 14: Llama Saves the Day

Goals

- to practice the Unit 5 structural model
- to create a key word outline from a series of three pictures: Llama Saves the Day
- to write a 3-paragraph composition from the key word outline
- to correctly use new vocabulary words: *din, cower, brim, frantically*

Assignment Schedule

Note: Classes that meet weekly should complete Days 1 and 2 in class.

Day 1

1. With a teacher read the Review and Historical Information on page 124.
2. Look at the three pictures on page 125. On the top blank next to the first picture, write what is happening in the picture (the central fact) in key words.

   On the other lines by the first box, you will explain in more detail what is happening by answering questions about the pictures. Here are some sample questions: *What happened before what you see in the picture? Why? What will happen next? What are the characters doing, saying, thinking, or feeling? Where is it happening? What would be seen, heard, or felt around the scene in the picture?* In a class setting, outline together. Do not copy the ideas that your teacher writes on the whiteboard because you will do your own outline later.

   The paragraph should end with a clincher that repeats or reflects two or three key words from your central fact sentence. For example, if the central fact of the first picture is the Inca were sitting around the fire enjoying their **lively music**, the middle of the paragraph could describe the night and the fire, tell why the people were there, and what the people were thinking and feeling. The clincher could include that the **music** was so **loud** that they could not hear the calls for help. (Notice that the words in bold are repeated or reflected.)
3. Repeat the above step for the remaining two pictures.
4. Begin orally composing a class version of the story you outlined together.
5. Learn the new vocabulary words for Lesson 14: *din, cower, brim, frantically.*

Day 2

1. Look at the pictures on page 125 again. Begin writing your own outline. Use the question words to help you.
2. With a teacher practice elements of style on pages 126–127.
3. Begin to write your story. Follow the checklist. Each paragraph should begin with the central fact of one of the pictures and end with a clincher that repeats or reflects two or three words from this. Highlight or bold the repeated or reflected words.

See the sample key word outline for help, especially in discussing central fact and clincher ideas.

Day 3

1. Finish writing your 3-paragraph story. Check off each item on the checklist when you are sure you have completed it. Let an editor proofread.
2. Review all vocabulary words learned thus far.

Day 4

1. Write or type a final draft, making any corrections your editor asked you to make.
2. Let an editor proofread again. He or she should check that all elements of structure and style are included and labeled as instructed on the checklist. Paperclip the checklist to your final draft to be turned in.
3. If you are making a Magnum Opus Notebook, revise your Battle of Hastings paragraph from Lesson 12. (See Appendix II.)

Study for Vocabulary Quiz 4. It will cover words from Lessons 1–14.

Review

Share a #2 prepositional opener from the story you wrote for Lesson 13. Then play Preposition Round Robin from the Teacher's Manual.

Historical Information

The pictures for this story are of the Inca (also spelled *Inka*) people. The Inca established a great empire in the Andes Mountains of South America. At its height the empire covered almost the entire length of the west coast of the continent. Because they lived on the mountainsides, they cut large terraces on which to live and farm. They also built roads, bridges, and aqueducts. They had a strong government that harshly punished crime, so there were few criminals.

The Inca worshiped many gods, but the sun god, called Inti, was their most important god. The word *Inca* means "people of the sun," and the "Temple of the Sun" had walls covered in pure gold.

The Inca liked music and made pan pipes (an instrument with several pipes of different sizes that they blew into), flutes, and drums. The most important animal to the Inca was the llama. It is related to a camel. Requiring very little water, llamas can travel long distances carrying heavy loads. They are also able to travel well on the slopes of mountains.

Note: When you write your story, you should give your characters Incan names. Here are a few ideas.

Boys: Amaru, Asto, Atik, Hakan, Kumya, Kunak, Manko, Raymi, Samin

Girls: Asiri, Kayara, Koya, Rimak, Sisa, Pacha, Quri, Taki, Wayta

Preposition Round Robin

Give students one minute to study the list of prepositions on page 112 or the list in the SRP behind the Sentence Openers tab. Then, have them all stand. In turn, each student has 10 seconds to name a preposition. As each preposition is named, write it on the whiteboard and give the student who said it a ticket (or point). Students who are successful remain standing; however, if a student cannot think of a preposition, gives a word that is not a preposition, or gives a preposition already on the whiteboard, he or she must sit down. Continue until only one student remains standing. If you get down to two or three students and none can give you another preposition, they tie. Winners get 5 extra tickets.

Hint: Rather than handing the tickets out, place a stack of tickets near each group of students. Let them simply take one when they name a preposition. This will help the game flow smoothly as you write the prepositions on the whiteboard.

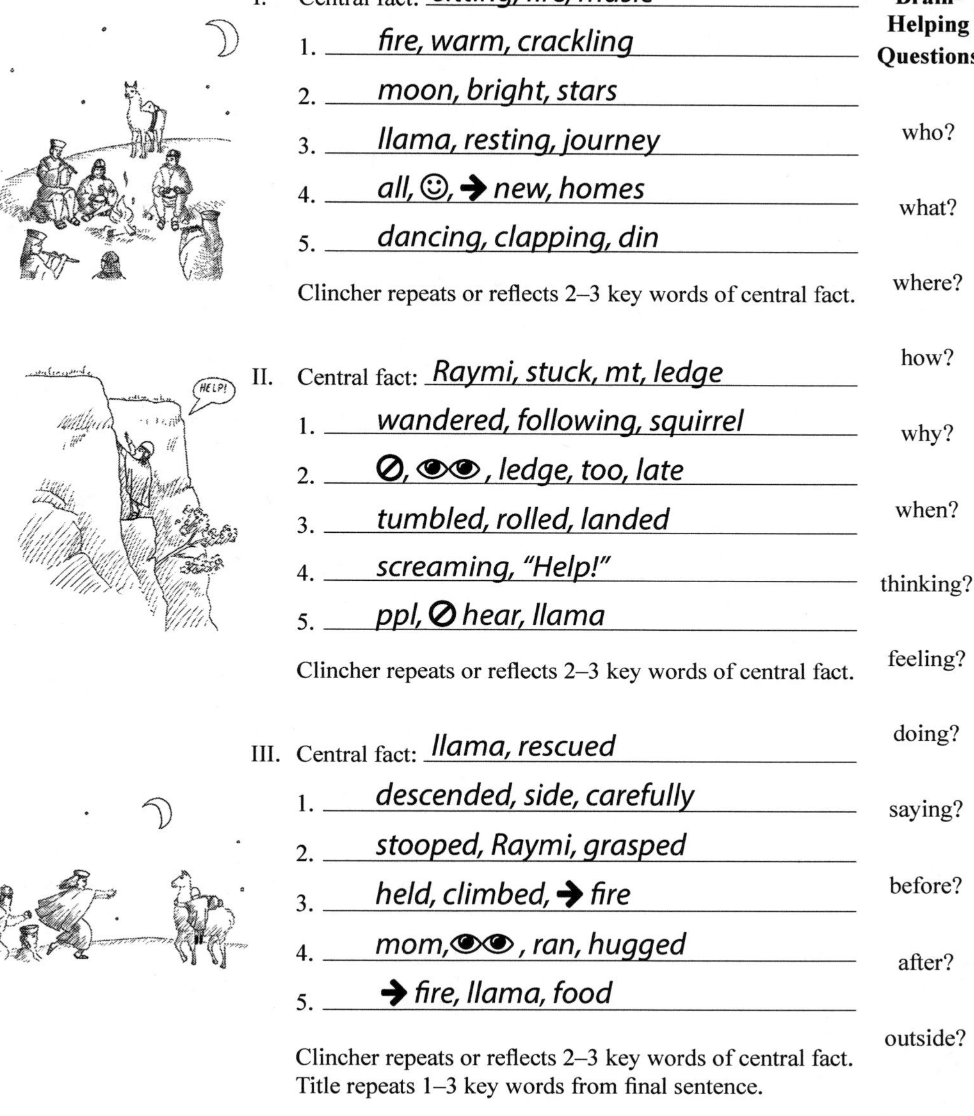

Sample

Lesson 14: Llama Saves the Day

Key Word Outline

		Brain-Helping Questions
I.	Central fact: *sitting, fire, music*	
1.	*fire, warm, crackling*	
2.	*moon, bright, stars*	
3.	*llama, resting, journey*	who?
4.	*all, ☺, ➔ new, homes*	what?
5.	*dancing, clapping, din*	
	Clincher repeats or reflects 2–3 key words of central fact.	where?
		how?
II.	Central fact: *Raymi, stuck, mt, ledge*	
1.	*wandered, following, squirrel*	why?
2.	*⊘, 👁👁, ledge, too, late*	
3.	*tumbled, rolled, landed*	when?
4.	*screaming, "Help!"*	thinking?
5.	*ppl, ⊘ hear, llama*	
	Clincher repeats or reflects 2–3 key words of central fact.	feeling?
		doing?
III.	Central fact: *llama, rescued*	
1.	*descended, side, carefully*	saying?
2.	*stooped, Raymi, grasped*	
3.	*held, climbed, ➔ fire*	before?
4.	*mom, 👁👁, ran, hugged*	after?
5.	*➔ fire, llama, food*	
	Clincher repeats or reflects 2–3 key words of central fact. Title repeats 1–3 key words from final sentence.	outside?

Medieval History-Based Writing Lessons: Student Book 125

Discuss ideas for a clincher. For example, to reflect the words in the central fact above, one possibility is this: Everyone was so mesmerized by the **music** and the **fire** that they did not notice Raymi was missing. (The words in bold are reflected from the central fact.)

Discuss ideas for a clincher. For example, to reflect the words in the central fact above, one possibility is this: **Raymi's** llama headed to the **ledge**. (The words in bold are reflected from the central fact.)

Discuss ideas for a clincher. For example, to reflect the words in the central fact above, one possibility is this: Everyone rejoiced to see that the **llama** had **saved** Raymi. (The words in bold are reflected from the central fact.)

Unit 5: Writing from Pictures

Style Practice

Quality Adjective Dress-Up

Use adjectives to describe the following things that will likely be in your story. Consider what they would look like, sound like, and feel like.

1. the fire *warm, crackling, flickering, glowing, dancing*
2. the music *merry, loud, lively, spirited*
3. the mountainside ***treacherous**, steep, dangerous, rocky, slick*

Strong Verb Dress-Up and -ly Adverb Dress-Up

Use strong verbs to tell what the following might do in different parts of the story. Can you add an -ly adverb to some of your strong verbs?

1. pan pipes *sang, rang, whistled loudly, melodiously, enchantingly*
2. the boy *stumbled, rolled rapidly, uncontrollably* ***scrambled** wildly*
   yelled, cried, hollered desperately, frantically gripped, grasped, hugged tightly
3. the llama *climbed adeptly, carefully, **resolutely***
   stooped lovingly

www.asia Clause Dress-Up

Write a sentence that includes a *www.asia* clause that you could use in your story.

Raymi slipped when he stepped too near the edge.

Because Clause Dress-Up

Write a sentence that includes a *because* clause that you could use in your story.

Raymi's mom was relieved because her son returned safely.

#2 Prepositional Opener

Write a sentence that begins with a #2 prepositional opener that you could use in your story. Remember to label it with a [2].

[2] With the noise of the music, no one heard Raymi's cries.

Vocabulary Practice

Prepare for the vocabulary quiz with Lesson 15. Turn to the vocabulary chart on pages 274–275. How could some of the words be used in this story?

Here are some ideas:

*The Inca **relished** their music.*

*The **din** of the music drowned out his cries.*

*The slope was **treacherous**.*

*From the **brim** of the cliff, he **frantically** cried for help.*

*Mom **rebuked** Raymi for wandering off, and he was **contrite**.*

*Raymi was too **hasty** in **pursuing** the critter, so he did not see the edge of the cliff until too late.*

*Mom was **bewildered** when she saw Raymi's llama; then, she **extolled** it.*

If students have trouble with ideas, read some of the sample sentences without the vocabulary words. Can they guess which words would fill in the blanks?

Unit 5 Composition Checklist

Lesson 14: Llama Saves the Day

Writing from Pictures

Name: ______________________________

Institute for Excellence in Writing

STRUCTURE

☐ MLA format (see Appendix I)	______	1 pt
☐ title centered and repeats 1–3 key words from final sentence	______	2 pts
☐ clincher sentences repeat or reflect 2–3 key words of central fact (highlight or bold)	______	6 pts
☐ checklist on top, final draft, rough draft, key word outline	______	5 pts
STYLE (one of each in each paragraph)		
¶1 ¶2 ¶3 Dress-Ups (underline)	(2 pts each)	
☐ ☐ ☐ -ly adverb	______	6 pts
☐ ☐ ☐ *who/which* clause	______	6 pts
☐ ☐ ☐ strong verb	______	6 pts
☐ ☐ ☐ *because* clause	______	6 pts
☐ ☐ ☐ quality adjective	______	6 pts
☐ ☐ ☐ *www.asia* clause	______	6 pts
☐ banned words: go/went, say/said, good/bad, big/little (-1 for each use)	______	pts
¶1 ¶2 ¶3 Sentence Opener (number)		
☐ ☐ ☐ [2] prepositional	______	6 pts
MECHANICS		
☐ capitalization	______	1 pt
☐ end marks and punctuation	______	1 pt
☐ complete sentences (Does it make sense?)	______	1 pt
☐ spelling and usage	______	1 pt
VOCABULARY		
☐ vocabulary words - label *(voc)* in left margin or after sentence		
Total:	______	60 pts
Custom Total:	______	pts

Teachers are free to adjust a checklist by requiring only the stylistic techniques that have become easy, plus one new one. "EZ+1."

Lesson 15: The Magic Lamp

Structure: IEW Unit 5: Writing from Pictures

Style: no new stylistic techniques

Writing Topic: The Magic Lamp

Optional Student Reading Assignment: During Lessons 13–15, students may read *Robin Hood* by J. Walker McSpadden.

UNIT 5: WRITING FROM PICTURES

Lesson 15: The Magic Lamp

Goals

- to practice the Unit 5 structural model
- to create a key word outline from a series of three pictures: The Magic Lamp
- to write a 3-paragraph composition from the key word outline
- to take Vocabulary Quiz 4
- to correctly use new vocabulary words: *gravely, fatigued, insolent, scorn*

Assignment Schedule

Note: Classes that meet weekly should complete Days 1 and 2 in class.

Day 1

1. Begin class with Vocabulary Quiz 4.
2. With a teacher read the Review Section on page 130.
3. Look at the three pictures on page 131. Note that these pictures are set in Arabia. On the top blank next to the first picture, write what is happening in the picture (the central fact) in key words. On the other lines by the first box, you will explain in more detail what is happening by answering questions about the pictures. If you understand the process, it will not be necessary for your teacher to model an outline for you.
4. Repeat the above step for the remaining two pictures.
5. Learn the new vocabulary words for Lesson 15: *gravely, fatigued, insolent, scorn.*

Day 2

1. Look at the pictures on page 131 again. Begin writing your own outline. Use the question words to help you.
2. With a teacher practice elements of style on pages 132–133.
3. Begin to write your story. Follow the checklist. Each paragraph should begin with the central fact of one of the pictures and end with a clincher that repeats or reflects two or three words from this. Highlight or bold the repeated or reflected words.

Day 3

1. Finish writing your 3-paragraph story. Check off each item on the checklist when you are sure you have completed it. Let an editor proofread.
2. Review all vocabulary words learned thus far.

Day 4

1. Write or type a final draft, making any corrections your editor asked you to make.
2. Let an editor proofread again. He or she should check that all elements of structure and style are included and labeled as instructed on the checklist. Paperclip the checklist to your final draft to be turned in.
3. If you are making a Magnum Opus Notebook, revise your Samurai and Dragon paragraph from Lesson 13. (See Appendix II.)

Literature Suggestions

Elementary students who are reading the suggested literature should obtain *The Door in the Wall* by Marguerite de Angeli for Lessons 16–18.

Junior high and high school students should obtain *Winning His Spurs: A Tale of the Crusades* by G.A. Henty for Lessons 16–20. *Winning His Spurs* is available at *LibriVox*. This is a wonderful book to listen to.

Review

Stretch the following sentence by adding each element of style as your teacher instructs. (Use the space around, above, and below the sentence to add elements to it.)

Ali went into the cave.

Sentence Stretching

Put each of the following dress-ups on the whiteboard, one at a time. Each time, instruct the students to add the element to the sentence above using a ^. Explain that while they will not usually add all the dress-ups to a single sentence, this exercise gives them practice. It is also fun!

who/which clause

www.asia clause

because clause

strong verb (Replace *went.*)

-ly adverb

quality adjective

vocabulary word (This may be your -ly adverb, strong verb, or quality adjective as well.)

Sample: Ali, who feared for his life, scrambled frantically into the cold, creepy cave when he spied the invaders because there was no place else to hide. (voc x2)

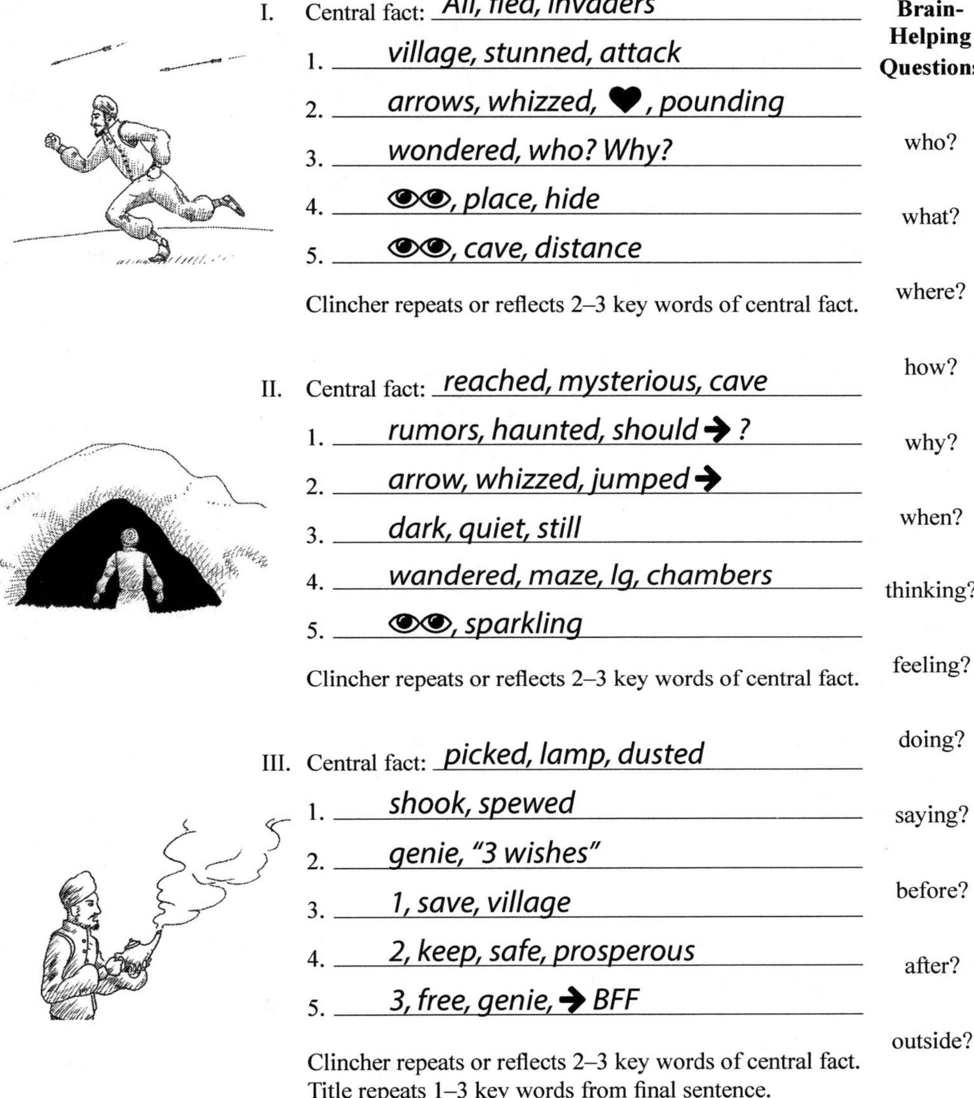

Sample

Lesson 15: The Magic Lamp

Key Word Outline

I. Central fact: *Ali, fled, invaders*
1. *village, stunned, attack*
2. *arrows, whizzed, ♥, pounding*
3. *wondered, who? Why?*
4. *👀, place, hide*
5. *👀, cave, distance*

Clincher repeats or reflects 2–3 key words of central fact.

II. Central fact: *reached, mysterious, cave*
1. *rumors, haunted, should → ?*
2. *arrow, whizzed, jumped →*
3. *dark, quiet, still*
4. *wandered, maze, lg, chambers*
5. *👀, sparkling*

Clincher repeats or reflects 2–3 key words of central fact.

III. Central fact: *picked, lamp, dusted*
1. *shook, spewed*
2. *genie, "3 wishes"*
3. *1, save, village*
4. *2, keep, safe, prosperous*
5. *3, free, genie, → BFF*

Clincher repeats or reflects 2–3 key words of central fact.
Title repeats 1–3 key words from final sentence.

Brain-Helping Questions

who?
what?
where?
how?
why?
when?
thinking?
feeling?
doing?
saying?
before?
after?
outside?

Medieval History-Based Writing Lessons: Student Book 131

Discuss ideas for a clincher. For example, to reflect the words in the central fact above, one possibility is this: **Ali dashed** toward the cave, hoping to hide from the **invaders**. (The words in bold are reflected from the central fact.)

Discuss ideas for a clincher. For example, to reflect the words in the central fact above, one possibility is this: The **mysterious** treasure in the **cave** intrigued him. (The words in bold are reflected from the central fact.)

Discuss ideas for a clincher. For example, to reflect the words in the central fact above, one possibility is this: Ali was glad he **picked up** the **lamp**. (The words in bold are reflected from the central fact.)

Unit 5: Writing from Pictures

Style Practice

Quality Adjective Dress-Up

Use quality adjectives to describe the following things in this story. Consider what each would look like, sound like, or feel like (sense of touch). When describing people, think about how they would feel (emotions).

1. arrows *sharp, fast, deadly, **treacherous**, numerous, horrifying, frightening*
2. the man (in each scene) *terrified, panicked, relieved, curious, cautious, stunned, doubtful*
3. cave *dark, cool, hidden, **serene**, quiet, remote, creepy, damp*
4. lamp *dusty, golden, exquisite, dented, radiant, sleek, stunning, odd, peculiar*

Strong Verb Dress-Up and -ly Adverb Dress-Up

Use strong verbs with -ly adverbs to tell what each of the following would be doing.

1. arrows *whooshed and whizzed, flew, pierced wildly, relentlessly, unceasingly*
2. the man (in each scene) ***fled**, panted; gazed, beheld, studied, explored curiously;*

   *rubbed, hoped quickly, **hastily**, rapidly*
3. lamp *sat, tantalized, sparkled, glowed silently, eerily, elegantly, radiantly, gloriously*

www.asia Clause Dress-Up

Write a sentence containing a *www.asia* clause that you could use in your story.

Ali fled when he saw the soldiers.

Because Clause Dress-Up

Write a sentence containing a *because* clause that you could use in your story.

Ali crept into the cave because there was no other place to hide.

#2 Prepositional Opener

Write a sentence that begins with a #2 prepositional opener that you could use in your story. Remember to label it with a [2].

[2] In the corner of the cave, Ali spotted an intriguing object.

Vocabulary Practice

Take out the vocabulary chart on pages 274–275. How could some of the words be used in this story? Here are some ideas to get you started. Fill in the blanks. Remember that you may use any tense or form of a vocabulary word.

1. Ali *hastily/frantically* (Lessons 5 or 14) *fled* (Lesson 6) through the *fetid* (Lesson 1) garbage-filled streets.

2. Ali *cowered* (Lesson 14) in the corner, *bewildered* (Lesson 13) and in *anguish* (Lesson 13).

3. After all that running, he was *fatigued* (Lesson 15) and could not *restrain* (Lesson 9) his tears.

Can you think of others?

*A cloud of blue **spewed** from the lamp.*
*Ali had **brazenly apprehended** the cheese.*
*Now the **merciless** merchant's men were pursuing him.*
*"Come back here, you **insolent** imp," they shouted.*
*The cave was **embellished** with **opulent** treasure.*

If students have trouble with ideas, read some of the sample sentences without the vocabulary words. Can they guess which words would fill in the blanks?

Unit 5 Composition Checklist

Lesson 15: The Magic Lamp

Writing from Pictures

IEW Institute for Excellence in Writing

Name: ______________________

STRUCTURE

☐ MLA format (see Appendix I)	______	1 pt
☐ title centered and repeats 1–3 key words from final sentence	______	1 pt
☐ clincher sentences repeat or reflect 2–3 key words of central fact (highlight or bold)	______	6 pts
☐ checklist on top, final draft, rough draft, key word outline	______	6 pts
STYLE (one of each in each paragraph)		
¶1 ¶2 ¶3 Dress-Ups (underline)	(2 pts each)	
☐ ☐ ☐ -ly adverb	______	6 pts
☐ ☐ ☐ *who/which* clause	______	6 pts
☐ ☐ ☐ strong verb	______	6 pts
☐ ☐ ☐ *because* clause	______	6 pts
☐ ☐ ☐ quality adjective	______	6 pts
☐ ☐ ☐ *www.asia* clause	______	6 pts
☐ banned words: go/went, say/said, good/bad, big/little (-1 for each use)	______	pts
¶1 ¶2 ¶3 Sentence Opener (number)		
☐ ☐ ☐ [2] prepositional	______	6 pts
MECHANICS		
☐ capitalization	______	1 pt
☐ end marks and punctuation	______	1 pt
☐ complete sentences (Does it make sense?)	______	1 pt
☐ spelling and usage	______	1 pt
VOCABULARY		
☐ vocabulary words - label *(voc)* in left margin or after sentence		
Total:	______	60 pts
Custom Total:	______	pts

Teachers are free to adjust a checklist by requiring only the stylistic techniques that have become easy, plus one new one. "EZ+1."

Lesson 16: Medieval Cathedrals

Structure: IEW Unit 6: Summarizing Multiple References

Style: #3 -ly adverb opener

Writing Topic: Medieval Cathedrals

Optional Student Reading Assignment: Elementary students: With Lessons 16–18 read *The Door in the Wall* by Marguerite de Angeli. Junior high and high school students: With Lessons 16–20 read *Winning His Spurs: A Tale of the Crusades* by G.A. Henty.

Teaching Writing: Structure and Style

Watch the sections for Unit 6: Summarizing Multiple References. At IEW.com/twss-help reference the TWSS Viewing Guides.

UNIT 6: SUMMARIZING MULTIPLE REFERENCES

Lesson 16: Medieval Cathedrals

Goals

- to be introduced to the Unit 6 Summarizing Multiple References structural model
- to create source outlines from multiple references
- to create a fused outline
- to write a 1-paragraph report about medieval cathedrals
- to correctly add a new sentence opener: #3 -ly adverb opener
- to correctly use new vocabulary words: *grandiose*, *serene*, *toil*, *contrive*

Assignment Schedule

Note: Classes that meet weekly should complete Days 1 and 2 in class.

Day 1

1. With a teacher read the New Structure: Summarizing Multiple References section on page 136.
2. Read Source 1, "Grandiose Structures," on page 137. On your own paper, formatted like page 139, write three key words to help you remember each of the facts you think are the most interesting or most important. You only need to choose four or five facts from each source. Notice that words for the topic line have been filled in for you for the assigned topic: medieval cathedrals.
3. Repeat step 2 with Source 2, "Awe-Inspiring Cathedrals," on page 138. Do not note facts that you already noted from the first source. Notice that the words on the topic line are the same as the words on the Source 1 topic line because both outlines are gathering facts for the same topic.
4. Once you have source outlines, you will have to organize them into one fused outline on the bottom of page 139. Remember that report paragraphs need topic sentences. Notice that *medieval cathedrals* has been filled in on the topic sentence line, but now you must refine your idea for a topic sentence. What main idea about cathedrals is supported by your details? Write one or two additional words for your topic sentence on the top line of the fused outline.
5. Under the topic line, write no more than seven facts from your source outlines. Arrange the notes in an order that makes sense.
6. Use the fused outline to tell back in complete sentences the ideas you will include in your paragraph.

Using their own paper will allow students to have their notes next to the source text; they will not have to flip pages back and forth.

Day 2

1. Review your fused outline.
2. Use the top of page 140 to create a topic and a clincher sentence.

3. Learn and practice the new #3 -ly adverb opener on page 140 and practice vocabulary on page 141.
4. Begin to write one paragraph about Medieval Cathedrals from your fused outline. Follow the checklist. Remember that you will need one -ly adverb as a dress-up in the middle of a sentence (underlined) and another -ly adverb at the beginning of a sentence that is not underlined. It will be labeled with a [3] for #3 -ly adverb opener.

Day 3

1. Finish writing your paragraph. Check off each item on the checklist when you are sure you have completed it. Let an editor proofread.
2. Learn the new vocabulary words for Lesson 16: *grandiose*, *serene*, *toil*, *contrive*.

Day 4

1. Write or type a final draft, making any corrections your editor asked you to make. Check off each item on the checklist that you have completed and indicated as instructed.
2. Let an editor proofread again. He or she should check that all elements of structure and style are included and labeled as instructed on the checklist. Paperclip the checklist to your final draft to be turned in.
3. Review all vocabulary words learned thus far.
4. If you are making a Magnum Opus Notebook, revise your "Llama Saves the Day" story from Lesson 14. (See Appendix II.)

Literature Suggestions

Elementary students: With Lessons 16–18 read *The Door in the Wall* by Marguerite de Angeli.

Junior high and high school students: With Lessons 16–20 read *Winning His Spurs: A Tale of the Crusades* by G.A. Henty. *Winning His Spurs* is available as an audiobook at *LibriVox*.

New Structure

Summarizing Multiple References

When you are asked to write a research report, your teacher will require that you use several sources from which to gather facts. In this lesson you will write a 1-paragraph report, but you will have more than one source text. This means that you will first make a key word outline from each source; then, you will pick and choose the notes you would like to put into a fused outline from which you will write the paragraph. The topic for this lesson is "Medieval Cathedrals." Follow the steps in the Assignment Schedule.

Lesson 16: Medieval Cathedrals

Source Text 1

Grandiose Structures

A prominent symbol of the Middle Ages was the cathedral. Cathedrals symbolized the importance of religion and the power of the church during the Middle Ages. They were large churches that served as the headquarters of a bishop. In fact, the word *cathedral* came from a Greek word that meant *seat* because the bishop's seat or throne was inside the cathedral. Between 1000 and 1540 hundreds of huge cathedrals were built all across Europe. Each was a monumental undertaking that required hundreds of workers and over a hundred years to complete. They were larger than castles and far more glorious. Cathedrals were often built in the shape of a cross with very high ceilings, and they were filled with awe-inspiring art and architecture. Cathedrals were used for daily church services, religious ceremonies, and public meetings. A city's public life centered around its cathedral. These magnificent structures reminded the people of the power and authority of the church and the glory of God.

Source Text 2

Awe-Inspiring Cathedrals

During the Middle Ages enormous and splendid churches were erected to inspire people to faith. These churches were called cathedrals. The cathedrals were the largest structures in cities. They were built for the glory of God. They impressed upon the people the power and majesty of God. They were built from millions of pounds of carved stones. They were adorned with magnificent sculptures, paintings, tapestries, murals, and stained glass windows. These works of art often depicted scenes and events from the Bible or from church history to help peasants who could not read remember them. Since the cathedral was for the glory of God, everything in it, including seemingly insignificant things such as doorknobs and hinges, had to be beautiful. Building a cathedral took the efforts and money of an entire community and could take centuries to build. People who began work on a cathedral knew they would not see it finished in their lifetime. Cities took great pride in their cathedrals and often competed with other cities to have the tallest spire. The building of the cathedrals helped advance art and architecture in an otherwise dark time. Today hundreds of medieval cathedrals across Europe continue to awe visitors.

Sample

Source Outlines

Make key word outlines on your own paper formatted like this.

Topic: Medieval Cathedrals

Source 1: "Grandiose Structures"

I. Topic: medieval, cathedrals

1. *= lg, , HQ, bishop*
2. *A.D. 1000–1540, 100s, built, Europe*
3. *100s workers, 100s, yrs, build*
4. *>castles, >glorious*
5. *w/, art, architecture*

Source 2: "Awe-Inspiring Cathedrals"

I. Topic: medieval, cathedrals

1. *for, glory, God*
2. *millions, carved, stones*
3. *cities, >, pride*
4. *competed, spire*
5. *today, 100s, , awe, visitors*

Choose some of the notes you took from both sources and put them in a logical order.

Fused Outline

I. Topic: medieval, cathedrals, *=, power, , Mid-A*

1. *lg, , = HQ, bishop*
2. *A.D. 1000–1540, 100s, built, Europe*
3. *took, 100s workers, 100s yrs, build*
4. *millions, carved, stones*
5. *> castles, more, glorious*
6. *built, glory, God*
7. *cities, >pride, competed,*

Clincher

Help your students finish the Topic line for the fused outline. What is the main idea about cathedrals in this paragraph?

Structure Practice

Topic and Clincher Sentences

Paragraphs in Unit 6 compositions must follow the topic-clincher rule: The topic sentence and the clincher sentence must repeat or reflect two or three key words.

A topic sentence should tell the main idea of the paragraph. Write an idea for a clear topic sentence for your paragraph about medieval cathedrals. Highlight the key words as you will in your paragraph.

Majestic cathedrals built during the Middle Ages symbolize the power of the church during that time.

____

Write an idea for a clincher that repeats or reflects two or three key words from your topic sentence. Highlight the two or three key words you repeat or reflect.

These grandiose structures still stand to remind us of medieval times.

____

New Style

#3 -ly Adverb Opener

Before you write a paragraph from your fused outline, learn a new sentence opener: the #3 -ly adverb opener. The #3 -ly adverb opener is an -ly adverb placed at the beginning of a sentence.

Here is an example:

[3] Fundamentally, cathedrals were the headquarters of bishops.

An -ly adverb as the first word of a sentence cannot count as an -ly dress-up anymore. It will be your #3 sentence opener. You will now, therefore, need to have two -ly adverbs in each paragraph you write—one at the beginning of a sentence (#3 opener) and one in the middle of a sentence (dress-up).

The -ly adverb opener should not be underlined, but the dress-up should be. A *3* in the left margin or a [3] right before the sentence is the indicator for the -ly opener.

Add a #3 -ly adverb opener to the sentences below. Indicate each with a *3* in the left margin or a [3] right before the sentence.

1. *[3] Majestically* ______________ cathedrals towered over all other structures.

2. *[3] Proudly* ______________ cities competed to have the tallest spire.

Lesson 16: Medieval Cathedrals

Vocabulary Practice

Take out the vocabulary chart on pages 274–275. How could some of the words be used in this paragraph? Here are a few ideas to get you started. Can you add others? Remember that you may use any tense or form of a vocabulary word.

1. People of different cities ___contrived___ to have the tallest spire. *(Lesson 16)*

2. The cathedral was the most ___prominent/opulent/grandiose___ structure in a medieval city. *(Lesson 11, 4, or 16)*

3. Cathedrals were ___embellished___ with ___opulent___ art and architecture. *(Lessons 7, 4)*

4. Cathedrals have ___endured___ even until today and continue to ___intrigue___ tourists. *(Lessons 12, 6)*

Give a ticket for each word a student can use correctly in another sentence that could be in this paragraph. Here are some ideas:

Cathedrals were **grandiose** structures.

Workers **toiled** for over one hundred years on a cathedral.

Cities **reverently** constructed cathedrals for the glory of God.

Unit 6 Composition Checklist

Lesson 16: Medieval Cathedrals

Summarizing Multiple References

Name: ______________________________

Institute for Excellence in Writing
Listen. Speak. Read. Write. Think!

STRUCTURE

☐ MLA format (see Appendix I)	______	2 pts
☐ title centered and repeats 1–3 key words from final sentence	______	2 pts
☐ topic-clincher sentences repeat or reflect 2–3 key words (highlight or bold)	______	6 pts
☐ checklist on top, final draft, rough draft, key word outline	______	5 pts
STYLE (one of each in each paragraph)		
¶1 Dress-Ups (underline)	(2 pts each)	
☐ -ly adverb	______	2 pts
☐ *who/which* clause	______	2 pts
☐ strong verb	______	2 pts
☐ *because* clause	______	2 pts
☐ quality adjective	______	2 pts
☐ *www.asia* clause	______	2 pts
☐ banned words: go/went, say/said, good/bad, big/little (-1 for each use)	______	pts
¶1 Sentence Openers (number)		
☐ [2] prepositional	______	2 pts
☐ [3] -ly adverb	______	2 pts
MECHANICS		
☐ capitalization	______	1 pt
☐ end marks and punctuation	______	1 pt
☐ complete sentences (Does it make sense?)	______	1 pt
☐ spelling and usage	______	1 pt
VOCABULARY		
☐ vocabulary words - **label** *(voc)* in left margin or after sentence		
Total:	______	35 pts
Custom Total:	______	pts

Teachers are free to adjust a checklist by requiring only the stylistic techniques that have become easy, plus one new one. "EZ+1."

Lesson 17: Knights, Part 1

Structure: IEW Unit 6: Summarizing Multiple References

Style: #6 very short sentence (vss)

Writing Topic: Knights

Optional Student Reading Assignment: Elementary students: With Lessons 16–18 read *The Door in the Wall* by Marguerite de Angeli. Junior high and high school students: With Lessons 16–20 read *Winning His Spurs: A Tale of the Crusades* by G.A. Henty.

UNIT 6: SUMMARIZING MULTIPLE REFERENCES

Lesson 17: Knights, Part 1

Goals

- to practice the Unit 6 structural model
- to create source outlines from multiple references
- to create a fused outline
- to write a 1-paragraph report about knights
- to correctly add a new sentence opener: #6 vss
- to correctly use new vocabulary words: *primarily, elite, allegiance, impeccable*

Assignment Schedule

Note: Classes that meet weekly should complete Days 1 and 2 in class.

Day 1

1. With a teacher read the Review section on page 144.

   In the next two lessons, you will again use more than one source of information to help you write a 2-paragraph report. On pages 145–149 there are three different articles about knights. You are going to choose some of the information in these articles and use it to write your report, one paragraph at a time.

2. Before you begin taking notes, you must know the topics of each of your paragraphs. To choose your topics, first scan the paragraphs in each source to determine the topics covered in them. Looking at the first and last sentence of each paragraph should give you a good clue. *Write the topic of each paragraph in the margin.*
3. Choose a topic that is covered in at least two sources.
4. Write the topic of your choice at the top of its own sheet of paper formatted like page 150.
5. Make key word outlines from all sources for the first topic on your first piece of paper by reading about the topic you have chosen.
6. Once you have two key word outlines from the sources that cover your topic, organize them into one fused outline on page 151. Begin by refining the words for a topic sentence. *What about the topic you have chosen can you say that is supported by your details?* Then choose the facts from your key word outlines that you want in your paragraph and write them in an order that makes sense. End with a clincher that repeats or reflects the topic.
7. Tell back the facts in complete sentences to be sure you understand them. Fix any notes you do not understand.

Teachers should model this process using duties of knights as a topic.

Day 2

1. Review your fused outline.
2. Use the top of page 152 to create a topic and a clincher sentence.
3. Learn a new element of style, the #6 very short sentence on page 152.
4. Complete page 153 to practice sentence openers you could include in your paragraph.
5. Begin to write a paragraph about the topic that you chose on Day 1 from your fused outline, using the style practice ideas to guide you. Follow the checklist.

Day 3

1. Finish writing your paragraph. Check off each item on the checklist when you are sure you have completed it. Let an editor proofread.
2. Learn the new vocabulary words for Lesson 17: *primarily, elite, allegiance, impeccable*.

Day 4

1. Write or type a final draft, making any corrections your editor asked you to make. Check off each item on the checklist that you have completed and indicated as instructed.
2. Let an editor proofread again. He or she should check that all elements of structure and style are included and labeled as instructed on the checklist. Paperclip the checklist to your final draft to be turned in.
3. Review all vocabulary words learned thus far.
4. If you are making a Magnum Opus Notebook, revise your Magic Lamp story from Lesson 15. (See Appendix II.)

Review

What is a fused outline?

What must a fused outline begin with? End with?

A fused outline combines selected notes from multiple sources into one outline.

It begins with notes for the topic. Details that follow are sorted into a logical flow. End with a clincher that repeats or reflects two or three key words from the topic.

Source Text 1

Knights

When you think of the Middle Ages, do knights come to mind? Knights were the armored, horse-mounted soldiers of the Middle Ages. There are two explanations for the origin of the term. The first says that it came from the Anglo-Saxon word for boy: *cniht*, because the early knights were not much more than boys hired to serve a nobleman. The other explanation says the term came from the Old English word *cnight*, which means household retainer. This is what the English called the Norman soldiers of William the Conqueror who were in their land to squash revolts against the new king. Regardless of the origin of the term, *knight* is a word that is well-known even today.

Topic: *origin of term "knight"*

Knights had many duties in service to the nobles (called lords) they pledged to serve. They were first and foremost soldiers. They protected their lord's land from invaders. Often they went off to battle for their lord. In exchange, they were given large amounts of land. When they were not in battle, they kept law and order in the land and managed the affairs of the estate. Knights also practiced a variety of combat skills like jousting, hand-to-hand combat, and archery in tournaments. Hundreds of knights would come together for such tournaments, which kept them fit and provided great entertainment for the people. Knights were loyal, well-trained, respected soldiers.

Topic: *duties*

Knights followed the Code of Chivalry. At that time, *chivalry* meant "horse soldiers." Because these soldiers all agreed to live by the same code,

(continued on next page)

Topic: *Code of Chivalry*

chivalry became the word used to describe the behavior and ethics of the knights. Above all else, knights were supposed to love and protect the church and its teachings, honor their lord, and fight for their country. They were also supposed to protect women and the feeble. If they fell in love with a lady, they had to do any task she gave them to do. Loyalty, courtesy, courage, and honor were the main virtues the code expected in all knights.

Topic: *armor*

Knights would not be knights without their shining armor. Early armor was made of chain mail, but that only stopped simple arrows. So blacksmiths made metal plates to put over the chain mail to protect knights from crossbow arrows, sword blows, and battle axes. Over the years armor became more sophisticated. For example, blacksmiths made plated gloves with metal spikes soldered onto the knuckles for hand-to-hand combat. The armor also became heavy. A helmet could weigh fifty pounds. A sword could weigh twenty-five to thirty pounds. Every knight depended upon his armor in battle.

Topic: *knights of Crusades*

The most famous knights were the knights of the Crusades. These were the knights who traveled to Jerusalem and the Middle East to recapture the Christian holy lands invaded by Muslims. These knights also hoped to gain land for themselves. The first crusade was the most successful; it recaptured Jerusalem in 1099, but not for long. For the next two hundred years, Christian knights fought Muslims for control of Jerusalem, and power changed hands many times. In 1244, Muslims conquered and retained it for the rest of the Middle Ages.

Bibliography (fictitious)

"Knights." *Verstegen's Encyclopedia of the Middle Ages*, 2010.

Lesson 17: Knights, Part 1

Source Text 2

The Age of Knights

"The Age of Knights" began about A.D. 900 and lasted until the 1500s. Knights were one kind of soldier at this time. The other soldiers were archers and foot soldiers. On the battlefield knights were like the tanks of today. They were clad in armor and rode horses that were also covered in armor. They could plow through ranks of foot soldiers. Knights were expected to protect their king, their lord, and the church. Knights were also the wealthiest soldiers. For their services they were usually paid a large amount of land. This was necessary for them to be able to raise enough money for their horses and armor, which were very expensive. A war horse could cost as much as a small airplane would cost today. Knights, therefore, were part of a wealthy, elite class of warriors.

Topic: *soldiers (duties)*

People of the Middle Ages believed knighthood was a holy calling, so knights were bound by the Code of Chivalry. This was a set of standards that controlled their behavior. In war a chivalrous knight was to be brave, loyal to his lord, and willing to sacrifice himself for the greater good. At home a knight promised to defend the weak, to serve God and his king at all times, and never to boast. Toward noble ladies he was to be gracious and gentle. In reality these standards were not always followed. Many knights broke rules to gain power or wealth. Some even became "robber knights" and turned to organized crime. Others plundered villages. Still, knighthood is known for the ideal of the Code of Chivalry.

Topic: *Code of Chivalry*

Knights are also known for their protective armor. Early armor was made of chain mail, which was thousands of tiny metal rings woven together. When the

(continued on next page)

Topic: *armor*

crossbow was invented, chain mail did not protect knights well enough. So a suit of metal plates was invented. It became so complicated that it took two men to put it on a knight. It was so cumbersome that if a knight was knocked from his horse, it was very difficult for him to fight. The main weapon of a knight was his sword. It could be twice as long as his arm and weigh as much as a bicycle. Armor was expensive, hot, and heavy!

Topic: *training*

Training for knighthood began at age seven. Boys this young were called pages. They learned to ride and care for horses, fight with a sword, wrestle, and hunt with a falcon. They also played games like chess to learn battle strategies. At around age twelve to fifteen, a page could become a squire. As a squire he served under one knight. He took care of the knight's armor, weapons, and horses. Sometimes he even followed him into battle. He was also the only one allowed to help his master in a tournament. At as early as age sixteen, a squire could be knighted by a knight. Sometimes this happened on the battlefield, but usually it was a formal ceremony. The squire would kneel before the knight. The knight would then tap his shoulder with his sword and say, "I dub you knight."

Topic: *knights of today*

Today in many countries like England, there are still knights. They do not ride horses and wear shining armor. Instead, knighthood is an honor bestowed on someone who does something outstanding for his country. A knight today is given the title "Sir" if he is a man. A woman can be knighted too. A female knight is called "Dame." This knighthood is very different from the knighthood of the Middle Ages.

Bibliography (fictitious)

Doe, Jane. *The Age of Knights*. ABC Publishers, 2006.

Lesson 17: Knights, Part 1

Source Text 3

Becoming a Knight

Many boys of the Middle Ages probably dreamed of becoming knights. While technically anyone could become a knight by proving himself in battle, knighthood was generally only for the wealthy, noble class. That is because a knight's armor, weapons, and horses were extremely expensive.

Topic: *who*

When a nobleman decided his son was to be a knight, the boy was sent to live with a knight as one of his pages when he was about seven years old. At this stage the boy was a servant to the knight and learned proper behavior and good manners. Pages also studied the arts, music, and battle strategies. It was basically like being in school, with the teacher being the knight's squire. Eventually pages would practice sword fighting with wooden swords and shields and horseback riding with lances.

Topic: *page*

Around fifteen years of age, after fighting skills were proficient, a page advanced to squire, which means "shield bearer." A squire cared for his knight's horses, cleaned his armor and weapons, and followed him into battle. Squires continued to practice their fighting skills with real weapons and by jousting. Young men were usually squires for five or six years.

Topic: *squire*

Once a squire proved his skill and bravery in battle, he could become a knight in a ceremony called a dubbing. He was to spend the entire night before the dubbing alone in prayer. At the ceremony the squire knelt in front of the king or knight, who then tapped him on the shoulder with his sword. The new knight would take an oath to honor and protect the king and the church.

Topic: *dubbing*

Bibliography (fictitious)

Verstegen, Lori. "Becoming a Knight." *Medieval Highlights*, 20 May 2015, medievaleurope.mrsv.org/knights.html.

Sample

Source Outlines

Make key word outlines on your own paper formatted like this. Each topic for Lessons 17 and 18 needs its own paper. Every topic line will contain the same exact key words. These key words indicate the topic of the paragraph you are writing about. For example, if you chose to write about the Duties of Knights, then the topic lines of the source outlines and the fused outline would have the same topic words: knights, duties.

Notes Topic A: *Duties of Knights*

Source 1: "Knights" (quote marks because it is an article)

I. Topic A: *knights, duties*

1. *protect, land, invaders*
2. *➔ battle, paid, w/land*
3. *home, law, order*
4. *+ practiced, skills, tournaments*
5. *loyal, respected*

Source 2: *The Age of Knights* by Doe (italics because it is a book)

I. Topic A: *knights, duties*

1. *1, kind, soldier*
2. *like, tanks, w/armor*
3. *+ horse, w/armor*
4. *protected, ♛, lord, ⛪*
5. *$$$, elite, class*

Source 3: "Becoming a Knight" by Verstegen
(***Note***: This source will be used only for a paragraph about knights' training.)

I. Topic A: ________

1. *This sample KWO is blank because this source did not contain*
2. *information about the duties of knights.*
3.
4.
5.

Sample

Fused Outline

The topic line for the fused outline may be refined with added word(s).

I. Topic A: *knights, duties >, soldiers*

1. *1st, protect, lord's, land*
2. *+ protect, ♔, ⛪*
3. *often, → battle*
4. *w/armor, + horse, lk, tanks*
5. *home, law, order*
6. *+ practiced, skills, tournaments*
7. *paid, w/land, → $$$*

Clincher

Help your students finish the Topic line for the fused outline. What is the main idea about the duties of knights in this paragraph?

Structure Practice

Topic and Clincher Sentences

Paragraphs in Unit 6 compositions must follow the topic-clincher rule: The topic sentence and the clincher sentence must repeat or reflect two or three key words.

A topic sentence should tell the main idea of the paragraph. Write an idea for a clear topic sentence about the topic you chose. Highlight the key words as you will in your paragraph.

Knights were elite soldiers who had many duties.

Write an idea for a clincher that repeats or reflects two or three key words from your topic sentence. Highlight the two or three key words you repeat or reflect.

A knight was always working for his lord and the king.

New Style

#6 Vss Opener

Before you write from your fused outline, learn a new sentence opener: the #6 very short sentence. This is simply a sentence with at least two words but no more than five words. Remember that variety in sentence structure and length is important to good writing. In each paragraph you should have some sentences that are long, some that are of medium length, and some that are short. With all of the dress-ups and openers you have learned, you may end up with too many long sentences. Purposely adding a very short sentence will solve this problem.

A very short sentence is best placed in a spot you would like to emphasize because it will stand out. Here are some samples from *Robin Hood* by J. Walker McSpadden. Note that they are labeled with a [6]. Notice how each stands out among longer sentences.

> "A yeoman am I, from Lockesley town. [6] Men call me Robin Hood."

> His clothes were coated with dirt, one of his hosen had slipped halfway down from his knee, the sleeve of his jerkin was split, and his face was streaked with sweat and blood. [6] Little John eyed him drolly.

Lesson 17: Knights, Part 1

Style Practice

Sentence Openers

The checklist will require you to include all sentence openers you have learned thus far. Write an idea for one of each type of sentence that you could use in your paragraph about duties of knights.

[2] *In battle knights towered over foot soldiers.*

[3] *Loyally knights served their lords.*

[6] *Knights were soldiers.*

Unit 6 Composition Checklist

Lesson 17: Knights, Part 1

Summarizing Multiple References

Institute for Excellence in Writing

Name: ______________________

STRUCTURE

☐ MLA format (see Appendix I)	______	2 pts
☐ topic-clincher sentences repeat or reflect 2–3 key words (highlight or bold)	______	2 pts
☐ checklist on top, final draft, rough draft, key word outline	______	2 pts
STYLE (one of each in each paragraph)		
¶1 Dress-Ups (underline)	(2 pts each)	
☐ -ly adverb	______	2 pts
☐ *who/which* clause	______	2 pts
☐ strong verb	______	2 pts
☐ *because* clause	______	2 pts
☐ quality adjective	______	2 pts
☐ *www.asia* clause	______	2 pts
☐ banned words: go/went, say/said, good/bad, big/little (-1 for each use)	______	pts
¶1 Sentence Openers (number)		
☐ [2] prepositional	______	2 pts
☐ [3] -ly adverb	______	2 pts
☐ [6] vss	______	2 pts
MECHANICS		
☐ capitalization	______	1 pt
☐ end marks and punctuation	______	2 pts
☐ complete sentences (Does it make sense?)	______	1 pt
☐ spelling and usage	______	2 pts
VOCABULARY		
☐ vocabulary words - label *(voc)* in left margin or after sentence		
Total:	______	30 pts
Custom Total:	______	pts

Teachers are free to adjust a checklist by requiring only the stylistic techniques that have become easy, plus one new one. "EZ+1."

Lesson 18: Knights, Part 2

Structure: IEW Unit 6: Summarizing Multiple References

Style: no new stylistic techniques

Writing Topic: Knights

Optional Student Reading Assignment: Elementary students: With Lessons 16–18 read *The Door in the Wall* by Marguerite de Angeli. Junior high and high school students: With Lessons 16–20 read *Winning His Spurs: A Tale of the Crusades* by G.A. Henty.

Lesson 18: Knights, Part 2

UNIT 6: SUMMARIZING MULTIPLE REFERENCES

Lesson 18: Knights, Part 2

Goals

- to practice the Unit 6 structural model
- to create source outlines from multiple references
- to create a fused outline
- to write a second paragraph about knights
- to correctly add a bibliography
- to correctly use new vocabulary words: *agile, devoted, feeble, clad*

Assignment Schedule

Note: Classes that meet weekly should complete Days 1 and 2 in class.

Day 1

1. With a teacher read the Review section on page 157.

   In this lesson we will complete the 2-paragraph report about knights using the source texts provided in Lesson 17. Then, you will add a bibliography page.

   Since you will be adding to your paragraph from Lesson 17, do not turn that in yet.

2. Choose your second topic about knights and write it at the top of its own sheet of paper formatted like page 159. Choose a topic that is covered in at least two of the source texts.
3. On your paper make key word outlines for your chosen topic. Do this by writing key word outlines from all sources that cover this topic. Remember to begin each outline with words that tell the topic.
4. Once you have outlines from the sources that cover your chosen topic, organize them into one fused outline on page 160. Begin the fused outline with words for a topic sentence that repeat the words on the topic line of the source outline. You may add 1 or 2 words in order to refine an idea for a topic sentence. Then choose the facts from your source outlines that you want in your paragraph and write them on the fused outline in an order that makes sense. End with a clincher that repeats or reflects the topic.
5. Tell back the facts in complete sentences to be sure you understand them. Fix any notes you do not understand.

Teachers should model the process using armor as a topic.

See page 159 for sample outlines.

Day 2

1. Review your fused outline.
2. Use page 161 to create a topic and a clincher sentence.
3. See pages 157–158 to learn how to add a bibliography to your report.
4. Begin to write a bibliography.
5. Begin to write a paragraph about your second topic of choice from your fused outline.

Unit 6: Summarizing Multiple References

Day 3

1. Finish writing your paragraph using the fused outline. Follow the checklist and check off each item when you are sure you have completed it. Let an editor proofread.
2. Finish writing a complete bibliography.
3. Learn the new vocabulary words for Lesson 18: *agile, devoted, feeble, clad.*

Day 4

1. Write or type a final draft, making any corrections your editor asked you to make. Check off each item on the checklist that you have completed and indicated as instructed.
2. Add your second paragraph about knights to the paragraph you wrote in Lesson 17 so that you have a 2-paragraph report. Follow it with the bibliography page. Follow the checklists for both Lesson 17 and 18.
3. Let an editor proofread again. He or she should check that all elements of structure and style are included and labeled as instructed on both checklists (Lessons 17 and 18). Paperclip both checklists to your final draft to be turned in.
4. Review all vocabulary words learned thus far.
5. If you are making a Magnum Opus Notebook, revise your Medieval Cathedrals paragraph from Lesson 16. (See Appendix II.)
6. Be sure to save this 2-paragraph report. You will use it again in Lesson 25.

Study for Vocabulary Quiz 5. It will cover words from Lessons 1–18.

Note: Next week you will be writing a report about King Richard. One source will be provided for you. You must find two other sources of your own from either the library or the Internet. Bring these sources to class next week.

Important: Choose fairly short and simple sources. History textbooks, Internet articles (especially those labeled "for kids"), encyclopedia articles, and short children's books will make the best sources. The difficulty of this lesson will be determined largely upon the level of difficulty of the sources you find. Parents or teachers should strive to help students find short, simple sources. If you go to the library, ask the librarian for help. Learning to use the library is a valuable skill in and of itself.

Lesson 18: Knights, Part 2

Review

Play a vocabulary review game from the Teacher's Manual to prepare for the quiz in Lesson 19.

Read the topic and clincher sentences of your paragraph from Lesson 17. Did you remember to tell the topic and highlight or bold the two or three key words that you repeated or reflected?

Bibliography

A bibliography is a list of the sources that were used to write a research report. It is placed as the last page of the report. See the SRP for instructions on how to format a bibliography. (These are behind the MLA and Citation tab.) Here are some general guidelines:

- Double-space the entire page.
- Center the title (Bibliography) at the top of the page.
- List sources in alphabetical order. (Use the first word of each entry, but ignore *A*, *An*, *The*.)
- Do not indent the first line of each entry.
- If you run out of room on a line, indent second and other lines of the same entry ½ inch from left.

In order to practice listing various types of sources, pretend that you actually used the fictitious sources given at the bottom of each source text.

Books

The source text that is on page 148 is a book. Copy its bibliography information exactly as it is into your bibliography on page 158. Note that the book title is in italics. (If it were handwritten, it would be underlined.)

In future reports, you can use this bibliography entry to guide you in entering other books into other bibliographies.

Encyclopedia Articles

The source text that is on pages 145–146 is an example of an encyclopedia article without an author. Copy its bibliography information exactly as it is into your bibliography on page 158.

In future reports if you use an encyclopedia, use the bibliography entry on page 146 to guide you in entering other articles. If the article has an author, simply add his or her name to the beginning: Last name, First name.

Websites

The source text that is on page 149 is an example of an Internet article with an author's name. If no author had been given, this entry would have started with the title of the article.

Internet articles can be tricky to list. Often websites have an icon that says, "Cite." If you click on this, it might provide you with the information you need. Here is how to format information from a website:

Author's last name, first name. [If no author given, check the website for any "how to cite" information.] "Title of Article." [in quotes] *Title of website, [in italics]* Publisher or sponsor, Day Month Year the article was posted, URL.

(If the article is not dated, list the date accessed after the URL: Accessed Day Month Year.)

For other types of sources, refer to the SRP.

Begin Your Bibliography

Use the lines below to write the entries for the source texts on pages 145–149 in alphabetical order.

- Begin by centering the title, Bibliography, on the top line.
- Double-space.
- Do not indent the first line of each entry; however, if an entry requires an additional line, indent it ½ inch.

Bibliography

Doe, Jane. *The Age of Knights*. ABC Publishers, 2006.

"Knights." *Verstegen's Encyclopedia of the Middle Ages*, 2010.

Verstegen, Lori. "Becoming a Knight." *Medieval Highlights*, 20 May 2015, medievaleurope.mrsv.org/knights.html.

Sample

Source Outlines

Make key word outlines on your own paper formatted like this. Place the key words for the chosen topic of this paragraph on the Topic lines for all sources that you use.

Notes Topic B: *knights' armor*

Source 1: "Knights" (quote marks because it is an article)

II. Topic B: *knights' armor*

1. *early, chain, mail*
2. *only, stopped, arrows*
3. *later, metal, plates*
4. *became, complicated, heavy*
5. *helmet, 50 lbs., sword, 25–30 lbs.*

Source 2: *The Age of Knights* by Doe (italics because it is a book)

II. Topic B: *knights' armor*

1. *chain = 1000s, metal, O's, woven*
2. *plates, 2 men, dress, kn-*
3. *knocked, horse, difficult*
4. *sword, 2x arm, length*
5. *armor, $$$, hot, heavy*

Source 3: "Becoming a Knight" by Verstegen
(***Note***: This source will be used only for a paragraph about knights' training.)

II. Topic B: *Source 3 does not have information for this topic.*

1. __________
2. __________
3. __________
4. __________
5. __________

Sample

(Use this outline only after you have taken notes from the sources on pages 145–149 on your own paper, formatted like page 159.) The topic line for the fused outline may be refined with added word(s).

Fused Outline

II. Topic B: *armor, protected, kn-, battle*

1. *chain, mail, 1000s, met, O's*
2. *only, stopped, arrows*
3. *later, metal, plates*
4. *became, complicated, heavy*
5. *helmet, 50 lbs, sword 25–30 lbs, + 2x arm*
6. *took, 2, men, dress, kn-*
7. *knocked, horse, difficult*

Clincher

Lesson 18: Knights, Part 2

Structure Practice

Topic and Clincher Sentences

Paragraphs in Unit 6 compositions must follow the topic-clincher rule: The topic sentence and the clincher sentence must repeat or reflect two or three key words.

A topic sentence should tell the main idea of the paragraph. Write an idea for a clear topic sentence about the armor of knights or your topic of choice. Highlight the key words as you will in your paragraph.

Knights wore armor to protect them in battle.

Write an idea for a clincher that repeats or reflects two or three key words from your topic sentence. Highlight the two or three key words you repeat or reflect.

Armor protected a knight, but it was not comfortable.

Unit 6 Composition Checklist

Lesson 18: Knights, Part 2

Summarizing Multiple References

Institute for Excellence in Writing

Name: ______________________

STRUCTURE

☐ MLA format (see Appendix I)	______	2 pts
☐ title centered and repeats 1–3 key words from final sentence	______	2 pts
☐ topic-clincher sentences repeat or reflect 2–3 key words (highlight or bold)	______	2 pts
☐ insert paragraph(s) from last lesson	______	2 pts
☐ checklist on top, final draft, rough draft, key word outline		

STYLE (one of each in each paragraph)

¶2 Dress-Ups (underline)	(2 pts each)	
☐ -ly adverb	______	2 pts
☐ *who/which* clause	______	2 pts
☐ strong verb	______	2 pts
☐ *because* clause	______	2 pts
☐ quality adjective	______	2 pts
☐ *www.asia* clause	______	2 pts
☐ banned words: go/went, say/said, good/bad, big/little (-1 for each use)	______	pts
¶2 Sentence Openers (number)		
☐ [2] prepositional	______	2 pts
☐ [3] -ly adverb	______	2 pts
☐ [6] vss	______	2 pts

MECHANICS

☐ capitalization	______	1 pt
☐ end marks and punctuation	______	1 pt
☐ complete sentences (Does it make sense?)	______	1 pt
☐ spelling and usage	______	1 pt

VOCABULARY

☐ vocabulary words - label *(voc)* in left margin or after sentence

Total:	______	30 pts
Custom Total:	______	pts

Teachers are free to adjust a checklist by requiring only the stylistic techniques that have become easy, plus one new one. "EZ+1."

Lesson 19: King Richard

Structure: IEW Unit 6: Summarizing Multiple References

Style: no new stylistic techniques

Writing Topic: King Richard

Optional Student Reading Assignment: Junior high and high school students: With Lessons 16–20 read *Winning His Spurs: A Tale of the Crusades* by G.A. Henty.

UNIT 6: SUMMARIZING MULTIPLE REFERENCES

Lesson 19: King Richard

Goals

- to practice the Unit 6 structural model
- to create source outlines from multiple references
- to create a fused outline
- to write a 1-paragraph report about King Richard
- to take Vocabulary Quiz 5

Assignment Schedule

Note: Classes that meet weekly should complete Days 1 and 2 in class.

Day 1

1. Begin class with Vocabulary Quiz 5.
2. With a teacher read the Review section on page 164.

   This assignment will provide more practice creating source outlines from multiple references and will add library (or Internet) research. Prepare a paper for note taking. Format it like page 166. The topic of this paragraph has been chosen for you: King Richard the Lionhearted.
3. Read the source text on page 165. Put an asterisk (*) by the facts you think are most important or most interesting.
4. Reread the source text and use key words to note 5–7 of the most important or most interesting facts.
5. Bring your two additional sources about King Richard to class for use on Day 2.

Day 2

1. On the Source Outlines page, take notes from two other sources about King Richard. (Do not lose the sources. You will need to create a bibliography.)
2. Use all of your source notes to create a fused outline on page 167.
3. With a teacher practice elements of structure and style on pages 168–169.
4. If your class meets weekly, read instructions for Days 3–4 with your teacher to be sure you understand what to do on your own.

Day 3

1. Write a paragraph about King Richard using the fused outline. Follow the checklist and check off each item when you are sure you have completed it. Let an editor proofread.
2. Write or type a complete bibliography. In alphabetical order, list all the sources you used. See pages 157–158 for help.
3. There are no new vocabulary words for Lesson 19. Review all previous words. Try to use some in your paragraph.

Day 4

1. Write or type a final draft of your paragraph, making any corrections your editor asked you to make. Check off each item on the checklist that you have completed and indicated as instructed.
2. Let an editor proofread again. He or she should check that all elements of structure and style are included and labeled as instructed on the checklist.
3. If you are an elementary student reading the suggested literature, obtain *Adam of the Road* by Elizabeth Janet Gray for Lessons 20–22. Junior high and high school students, continue reading *Winning His Spurs*.

A bibliography is a list of the sources you read to help you write your paper. It is placed at the end of the paper on a page by itself.

Sources should be listed in alphabetical order.

Before you collect the homework, help students check that they completed the bibliography correctly.

Review

What is a bibliography? Where is it placed?
In what order should your sources be listed?

Lesson 19: King Richard

Source Text

King Richard

If you have seen Walt Disney's *Robin Hood* or read any of the stories about Robin Hood, you have heard of King Richard and his evil brother, Prince John. They were sons of King Henry II. Richard I was the king of England from 1189–1199. He was called "Coeur de Lion," meaning lionhearted, because he was valiant in battle. Richard was loved by the people of England, and he was thought of as a hero. However, he was rarely in his country. He actually spent less than one year out of the ten that he was king in England. Instead, he was off fighting battles, like the Third Crusade to recapture the Holy Land in Palestine. He did not win this crusade, but he was able to make a truce with the Muslim leader Saladin. This truce allowed Christians to go to Jerusalem. While King Richard was away, John tried to rule in his place, but he was greedy and was not liked by the people. He was not like his brother Richard. In 1199 Richard was killed in a battle in France, so John became king.

Bibliography

Verstegen, Lori. "King Richard." *Medieval History-Based Writing Lessons*, Institute for Excellence in Writing, 2015, p. 165.

Sample

Source Outlines

Make key word outlines on your own paper formatted like this.

King Richard

Source 1: "King Richard" (Verstegen)

I. Topic: *King Richard, "lionhearted"*

1. *[crown], England, 1189–1199, ppl, hero*
2. *often, →, battles, 1 yr/10, home*
3. *→ Holy Land, 3rd Crusade*
4. *truce, allowed, †, → Jerusalem*
5. *XX, battle, France, 1199*

Source 2:

I. Topic: *King Richard, "lionhearted"*

1. _____
2. *Notes for Sources 2 and 3 will come from sources students find.*
3. _____
4. _____
5. _____

Source 3:

I. Topic: *King Richard, "lionhearted"*

1. _____
2. _____
3. _____
4. _____
5. _____

Sample

Fused Outline

Fill out this outline using the notes you took from page 165 plus notes from two other sources.

I. Topic: *King Richard, "lionhearted"*

1.
2. *Key word facts for this outline will vary because students*
3. *will have used different source texts.*
4.
5.
6.
7.

Clincher

Structure Practice

Topic and Clincher Sentences

Paragraphs in Unit 6 compositions must follow the topic-clincher rule: The topic sentence and the clincher sentence must repeat or reflect two or three key words.

A topic sentence should tell the main idea of the paragraph. Write an idea for a clear topic sentence about King Richard. Highlight the key words as you will in your paragraph.

Because of his bravery King Richard is often referred to as King Richard the Lionhearted.

Write an idea for a clincher that repeats or reflects two or three key words from your topic sentence. Highlight the two or three key words you repeat or reflect.

King Richard died a heroic warrior with a lion's heart.

Style Practice

Dress-Ups

List quality adjectives to describe King Richard:

*valiant, brave, strong, **impeccable, renowned, intrepid, noble***

Cross out the boring verb that is in italics and replace it with a stronger verb; then, add an -ly adverb in front of it:

The people *affectionately nicknamed; worthily dubbed* ~~*called*~~ their king "Richard the Lionhearted."

Write a sentence containing a *www.asia* clause that you could include in your paragraph.

The truce Richard the Lionhearted made with the Muslims allowed Christians to travel to Jerusalem although he did not win the Third Crusade

#2 Prepositional Opener and #3 -ly Adverb Opener

Add either a #2 prepositional or #3 -ly adverb opener to the sentences below. Use at least one of each opener. Be sure to label each with either a [2] or [3].

1. *[2] From 1189–1199* *[3] Nobly*

   King Richard ruled England.

2. *[2] In order to fight in battles,* *[3] Unfortunately*

   King Richard often left the country.

3. *[2] During a great battle* *[3] Sadly*

   King Richard died in France.

Vocabulary Practice

Open to the chart of vocabulary words on pages 274–275. Write ideas for using some of these words in your paragraph about King Richard.

Vocabulary Practice

Let students offer ideas. Give a ticket for each word they use correctly.

Unit 6: Summarizing Multiple References

Unit 6 Composition Checklist

Lesson 19: King Richard

Summarizing Multiple References

Institute for Excellence in Writing

Name: ______________________________

STRUCTURE		
☐ MLA format (see Appendix I)	______	2 pts
☐ title centered and repeats 1–3 key words from final sentence	______	2 pts
☐ topic-clincher sentences repeat or reflect 2–3 key words (highlight or bold)	______	2 pts
☐ checklist on top, final draft, rough draft, key word outline	______	2 pts
STYLE (one of each in each paragraph)		
¶1 Dress-Ups (underline)	(2 pts each)	
☐ -ly adverb	______	2 pts
☐ *who/which* clause	______	2 pts
☐ strong verb	______	2 pts
☐ *because* clause	______	2 pts
☐ quality adjective	______	2 pts
☐ *www.asia* clause	______	2 pts
☐ banned words: go/went, say/said, good/bad, big/little (-1 for each use)	______	pts
¶1 Sentence Openers (number)		
☐ [2] prepositional	______	2 pts
☐ [3] -ly adverb	______	2 pts
☐ [6] vss	______	2 pts
MECHANICS		
☐ capitalization	______	1 pt
☐ end marks and punctuation	______	1 pt
☐ complete sentences (Does it make sense?)	______	1 pt
☐ spelling and usage	______	1 pt
VOCABULARY		
☐ vocabulary words - label *(voc)* in left margin or after sentence		
Total:	______	30 pts
Custom Total:	______	pts

Teachers are free to adjust a checklist by requiring only the stylistic techniques that have become easy, plus one new one. "EZ+1."

Lesson 20: Favorite Amusements, Part 1

Structure: IEW Unit 7: Inventive Writing (Body Paragraphs)

Style: #5 clausal opener (*www.asia.b*)

Writing Topic: Favorite Amusements, Entertainments, or Holidays

Optional Student Reading Assignment: Elementary students: With Lessons 20–22 read *Adam of the Road* by Elizabeth Janet Gray. Junior high and high school students: With Lessons 16–20 read *Winning His Spurs: A Tale of the Crusades* by G.A. Henty.

Teaching Writing: Structure and Style

Watch the sections for Unit 7: Inventive Writing. At IEW.com/twss-help reference the TWSS Viewing Guides.

UNIT 7: INVENTIVE WRITING

Lesson 20: Favorite Amusements, Part 1

Goals

- to be introduced to the Unit 7 Inventive Writing structural model
- to create a key word outline from a writing prompt
- to write two paragraphs about your favorite amusements, entertainments, or holidays
- to correctly add a new sentence opener: #5 clausal opener (*www.asia.b*)

Assignment Schedule

Note: Classes that meet weekly should complete Days 1 and 2 in class.

Day 1

1. In the following few lessons, you will learn how to structure a basic 4-paragraph composition. Please study the "My Dog" model of structure for such an essay in the SRP behind the Unit 7 tab.

   With a teacher read the Review and New Structure: Notes from the Brain sections on pages 172–173.
2. Since you need two body paragraphs, you need two topics to write about. As a class, list several possible topics.
3. You will practice in class as your teacher models the question process by choosing at least one topic to outline together. Do not copy the class KWO, but notice the process. Study the sample on page 173 for one topic.

Day 2

1. Use the blank outline on page 174 and note ideas for two topics. Begin with words that will help you write a topic sentence. Remember to ask yourself plenty of questions to get ideas about what to say. Also, try to include specific examples and descriptions. Page 175 should help.
2. With a teacher learn and practice the new #5 clausal opener (*www.asia.b*) on page 176.
3. Write the first paragraph from your key word outline, using the style practice ideas to guide you. Remember that each paragraph must follow the topic-clincher rule.
4. Follow the checklist on page 177. From now on you must include one clausal dress-up (underline) and one #5 clausal opener (number with [5]). Notice that the *because* clause dress-up has been combined with the *www.asia* clause. The acronym is now *www.asia.b* (when, while, where, as, since, if, although, because).

amusement parks
movies
books
biking
swimming
beach
Christmas
Thanksgiving
LEGO®S
robotics

Day 3

1. Write the second paragraph. Check off each item on the checklist when you are sure you have completed it. Let an editor proofread both paragraphs.
2. Although there are no new vocabulary words for Lesson 20, continue to review all words learned thus far.

Day 4

1. Write or type a final draft, making any corrections your editor asked you to make. Check off each item on the checklist that you have completed and indicated as instructed.
2. Let an editor proofread again. He or she should check that all elements of structure and style are included and labeled as instructed on the checklist. Paperclip the checklist to your final draft to be turned in.
3. If you are making a Magnum Opus Notebook, revise your Knights report from Lessons 17–18. (See Appendix II.) Do not lose this. We will be adding an introduction and conclusion paragraph to the report in Lesson 25.

Literature Suggestions

With Lessons 20–22 elementary students may read *Adam of the Road* by Elizabeth Janet Gray.

Junior high and high school students who are reading the suggested literature should obtain *The Kite Rider* by Geraldine McCaughrean for Lessons 21–23.

Review

Stretch the following sentence by adding each element of style as your teacher instructs. (Use the space around, above, and below the sentence to add elements to it.)

The roller coaster goes down the track.

Sentence Stretching

Put each of the elements of style on the whiteboard, one at a time. Each time, instruct the students to add the element to the sentence above using a ^.

strong verb (Replace *goes.*)

quality adjective

who/which clause (Place commas before and after the clause.)

#2 prepositional opener

Sample: [2] After a steep climb the exhilarating roller coaster, which appeared to defy gravity, flew down the track.

New Structure

Notes from the Brain

In Unit 7 lessons you will write without the help of source texts, but you will still need to make a key word outline of notes to organize your ideas. So, where are you going to get your notes? You are going to get them from your brain! To do so you must learn to ask yourself questions. Memorizing some question-starter words and phrases will help you.

What? Who? Where? When? Why? How? Best/Worst? Problems? Value? Meaning? Examples? Descriptions?

You will practice using these question words to give yourself ideas to write in response to the prompt below.

Prompt

The main entertainment and fun during medieval times was in the form of feasts, fairs, and festivals. Most villages had one each month, and they were often associated with religious holidays or events. They were fun days filled with food, music, and dancing. There were entertainers like jugglers, musicians, acrobats, and storytellers. There were competitions like archery, hammer throwing, jousting, and wrestling. Everyone looked forward to these fun-filled days.

Entertainment today is a bit different. We have access to many different kinds of amusements almost any day of the year.

Write two paragraphs about your favorite amusements, entertainments, or holidays.

You may write about two kinds of amusements, entertainments, or holidays you enjoy. In this case, each would be a topic. Another option is to write about one kind of amusement, entertainment, or holiday and discuss two reasons you enjoy it. The reasons would each be a topic. For example, if you choose amusement parks, each topic could be one of your favorite rides.

Sample Key Word Outline

Topic	I. Disneyland, Star Tours, ride
What?	1. Star Tours, r. coaster, simulator
Why like?	2. realistic, ex, line, = boarding
	3. 3D screen + sound + vib
See? Hear?	4. screen, w/space, buzzing, vib.
	5. = real, w/speed, dive
How feel?	6. grip, cover eyes
How show feel?	7. safe landing = ☺

Clincher

Sample

Key Word Outline

Who

What

When

Where

Why

How

How feel

Best thing

Worst thing

Problems

Value

Meaning

Examples

Describe
(Strong Image or Feeling)

II. Topic A: *Disneyland, Star Tours ride*

1. *r. coaster, simulator, movie*
2. *realistic, x, line, = boarding*
3. *3D screen + sound + vib*
4. *screen, w/space, buzzing, vib*
5. *= real, w/speed, dive*
6. *grip, cover, 👁👁*
7. *safe, landing, ☺*

Clincher

III. Topic B: *Disneyland, enchanting, atmosphere*

1. *spotless, beautiful, grounds*
2. *Disney, characters, wander*
3. *parades, P.M., fireworks, explode*
4. *ea, area, captivating, theme*
5. *pirates, Indiana Jones, T. Sawyer*
6. *future, w/robots, rockets*
7. *educational, shows, fun!*

Clincher

Lesson 20: Favorite Amusements, Part 1

Structure Practice

For some students, adding specific details, examples, and descriptions is the most difficult part of writing descriptive essays, but these help bring your writing to life. To help with this, do the following.

1. Add examples.

   Add *specific* details or examples to one or more of the ideas in your outline. For example, if you said something like *Movies are fun*, you could add something like the following:

   > *Movies tug at your emotions. They can make you despise a villain and cheer a hero like Captain America as he saves the world just in time. They can make you laugh, such as at the mishaps of Anne of Green Gables when her struggles to fit in only lead to minor disasters like an exploding cake. They can also make you cry, such as when ...*

   Movies are fun by itself is vague. It is boring. It says little. The additions are much more specific. They tell *why* and *how* movies are fun. Try to add such detail to an idea you have for one of your paragraphs. How or why is the entertainment you are writing about enjoyable? Be *specific*.

2. Add vivid descriptions by using strong verbs and quality adjectives.

   Look for things to describe. For example, which of the following is more descriptive and therefore more vivid?

   a. *My brother and I like to get up early on Christmas morning to wake up our parents so that we can open presents.*

   b. *When the sun is just starting to lighten our room, we know it is time. The house is cool, quiet, and still, but my brother and I run to my parents' room and shake them awake. "Time to open presents," we both chant. With tired eyes they smile.*

Now look at your outline. Find a place where you can either add a specific detail or example or where you can use a strong verb or quality adjective to create a strong image or feeling in your readers' minds. Write ideas below.

Ideas will vary with student topics.

Unit 7: Inventive Writing

New Style

#5 Clausal Opener

You have been using the *because* clause dress-up and the *www.asia* clause dress-up. We will now combine these into one dress-up and call it the *www.asia.b* clause dress-up. This clause begins with one of these words: *when, while, where, as, since, if, although, because.*

You must use this type of clause as a sentence opener as well as a dress-up. In other words, you must begin at least one sentence of each paragraph with a *www.asia.b* clause in addition to having such a clause in the middle or at the end of a sentence as a dress-up.

Remember, a clause that begins with one of the *www.asia.b* words cannot be a complete sentence by itself. Look at the sample sentences below. Each has a *www.asia.b* clause plus another complete thought.

[5] When the ship blasts into warp speed, I hang onto my seat.

[5] Although it is just a ride, I feel as if I am flying through the galaxy.

Remember the comma rules:

If the *www.asia.b* clause is at the beginning of the sentence, follow the entire clause with a comma. We do not usually put a comma before a *www.asia.b* clause.

When the *www.asia.b* clause is used as a sentence opener, it is simply numbered with a *5* in the left margin or with a [5] before the sentence. It is only underlined when it is used as a dress-up.

Practice

Write two ideas for a #5 clausal opener that you could use in your essay, each for a different paragraph. Don't forget the comma.

1. *[5] As I speed down the hills on my mountain bike, I feel as free as a bird.*

2. *[5] If it is a sunny day, the only place to be is the beach.*

Reminder

Each body paragraph must follow the topic-clincher rule: The topic sentence and the clincher sentence *must* repeat or reflect two or three key words. Make sure you highlight or bold the key words that repeat or reflect.

Unit 7 Composition Checklist

Lesson 20: Favorite Amusements, Part 1 body paragraphs

Inventive Writing

Institute for Excellence in Writing

Name: ______________________________

STRUCTURE

☐ MLA format (see Appendix I)	______	2	pts
☐ topic-clincher sentences repeat or reflect 2–3 key words (highlight or bold)	______	5	pts
☐ checklist on top, final draft, rough draft, key word outline	______	3	pts
STYLE (one of each in each paragraph)			
¶2 ¶3 Dress-Ups (underline)	(2 pts each)		
☐ ☐ -ly adverb	______	4	pts
☐ ☐ *who/which* clause	______	4	pts
☐ ☐ strong verb	______	4	pts
☐ ☐ quality adjective	______	4	pts
☐ ☐ *www.asia.b* clause	______	4	pts
☐ banned words: go/went, say/said, good/bad, big/little (-1 for each use)	______		pts
¶2 ¶3 Sentence Openers (number)			
☐ ☐ [2] prepositional	______	4	pts
☐ ☐ [3] -ly adverb	______	4	pts
☐ ☐ [5] clausal - *www.asia.b*	______	4	pts
☐ ☐ [6] vss	______	4	pts
MECHANICS			
☐ spelling, grammar, and punctuation	______	4	pts
VOCABULARY			
☐ vocabulary words - label *(voc)* in left margin or after sentence			
Total:	______	50	pts
Custom Total:	______		pts

Teachers are free to adjust a checklist by requiring only the stylistic techniques that have become easy, plus one new one. "EZ+1."

Unit 7: Inventive Writing

Lesson 21: Favorite Amusements, Part 2

Structure: IEW Unit 7: Inventive Writing (Introduction and Conclusion)

Style: no new stylistic techniques

Writing Topic: Favorite Amusements, Entertainments, or Holidays

Optional Student Reading Assignment: Elementary students: With Lessons 20–22 students may read *Adam of the Road* by Elizabeth Janet Gray. Junior high and high school students: With Lessons 21–23 students may read *The Kite Rider* by Geraldine McCaughrean.

UNIT 7: INVENTIVE WRITING

Lesson 21: Favorite Amusements, Part 2

Goals

- to practice the Unit 7 structural model
- to create key word outlines for an introduction and a conclusion paragraph
- to write an introduction and a conclusion paragraph
- to complete a 4-paragraph composition about your favorite amusements, entertainments, or holidays

Assignment Schedule

Note: Classes that meet weekly should complete Days 1 and 2 in class.

Day 1

1. In this lesson you will outline and add a paragraph of conclusion and a paragraph of introduction to the two body paragraphs you wrote in Lesson 20 about entertainments, amusements, or holidays.

   With a teacher read the Review section on page 180 and do the activities.

2. Learn about introductions and conclusions on pages 180–184. Follow the instructions to create a key word outline for a conclusion and for an introduction.

Day 2

1. Review your key word outlines. Tell back the ideas in complete sentences. If there is a note you do not understand, fix it.
2. Practice using sentence openers on page 185.
3. Write your conclusion paragraph. Remember to highlight or bold the topic words.

Day 3

1. Write your introduction paragraph. Remember to highlight or bold the topic words. Check off each item on the checklist when you are sure you have completed it. Let an editor proofread.
2. There are no new vocabulary words for Lesson 21, but continue to review all words learned thus far.

Day 4

1. Write or type a final draft of your entire composition by placing the introduction paragraph before your body paragraphs and the conclusion paragraph after them. As you do, make any corrections your editor asked you to make. Check off each item on the checklist that you have completed and indicated as instructed.

Review

Allow time for students to share. Help with topic sentences and clincher sentences as necessary.

Help with adding examples, details, or descriptions as necessary. To do so, scan a paragraph and look for a spot where an example or more description could be added. Ask the students questions that will help them make the addition. Be sure all students add something to one of their paragraphs.

2. Let an editor proofread again. He or she should check that all elements of structure and style are included and labeled as instructed on *both* checklists, pages 177 (body paragraphs) and 186 (introduction and conclusion). Paperclip both checklists (pages 177 and 186) to your final draft to be turned in.
3. If you are making a Magnum Opus Notebook, revise your King Richard report from Lesson 19. (See Appendix II.)

Literature Suggestions

Elementary students: With Lessons 20–22 read *Adam of the Road* by Elizabeth Janet Gray.

Junior high and high school students: With Lessons 21–23 read *The Kite Rider* by Geraldine McCaughrean.

Review

Read your topic and clincher sentences for Lesson 20 paragraphs. Did you remember to highlight or bold two or three key words that are repeated or reflected?

Share part of one of the paragraphs where you purposely added specific details, examples, or description.

Good writing requires writing, reading, editing, and re-writing. Take a few minutes to read the paragraphs you wrote for Lesson 20. Look for a place to add more vivid descriptions or a specific example or detail. If you are stuck, ask your teacher for help or work with a classmate. Oftentimes another person can ask questions to help you see where you could add more detail.

New Structure

Conclusion and Introduction

The job of the conclusion is to remind the reader of the topics and then to clarify what is the most important thing to remember about the subject and why. It ends with a general sentence about the subject that includes one to three words that can be used in a title.

The job of the introduction is to introduce the subject and topics of the essay. But the introduction has another important purpose. An introduction must grab the readers' attention; it must entice them to keep reading. If you begin with something boring, it is likely that your readers will put down the essay without finishing it.

It is often easier to outline and write the conclusion directly after writing the body paragraphs. This is because the conclusion must flow smoothly from the final body paragraph, and the details in all the body paragraphs will be fresh in your mind as you move to the conclusion. For this reason, we will outline the conclusion before we outline the introduction. Outlining and writing the introduction last makes it an easier task because you will know what you are introducing.

Study the sample conclusion and introduction on the following page. Note the elements labeled and the topic words in bold.

In these samples the required elements of the introduction and the conclusion have been labeled in brackets for clarity. When writing the introduction and conclusion, students must highlight or bold the topic words, but they should not label the elements.

Sample Conclusion

[Topic A] At Disneyland, **Star Tours** takes me into space and makes me feel as if I am flying with R2D2 and C3PO. **[Topic B]** Actually, every place in the park seems **magical**. **[Most significant]** Most significantly, Disneyland is not just about rides and atmosphere. **[Why]** It is much more. It is about having fun with friends and family. It is about escaping everyday chores, celebrating special days, and creating memories. **[Final sentence]** When I am caught up in the magic of Disneyland, it really does seem like "the happiest place on earth."

Sample Introduction

[Attention getter] Disneyland is magical. **[Background]** It is my favorite amusement park because it is much more than rides. It has Disney characters who roam around and who march in parades. Additionally, it has fireworks that light up the night sky with dazzling colors, fun fantastic food, charming shops, and so much more. **[Topic A]** Without a doubt my favorite ride is **Star Tours** because I love feeling like I am in a spaceship. **[Topic B]** Wherever I am in the park, I feel as if I am in a faraway, **enchanted** land.

Note: In these samples the required elements of the introduction and the conclusion have been labeled in brackets for clarity. When you write your introduction and conclusion, highlight or bold the topic words but do not label the elements.

Here is a sample conclusion outline for an essay about Thanksgiving; however, students should not copy this sample. Instead, they should write an outline that matches their subject and topics. Help them do so as you model each part.

Conclusion

Even though the introduction will come first in the composition, we will outline the conclusion first. Here are the components you must include:

Restate the topics: Write a sentence about each topic or list them in one sentence. Try to convey the main idea of each body paragraph; in other words, reword the topic sentences. Highlight or bold the topic words.

Most significant and why: What is the most important, most interesting, or most significant thing to remember about all that you wrote and *why*? What do you want your reader to realize and remember or apply?

You may choose one of your topics and tell why it is the most significant, or you may choose something that captures the importance of the entire subject. For example, study the "Most significant" and "Why?" in the sample conclusion on page 181.

Final sentence: End your paper with a final sentence from which you can create a title. Be sure your paper sounds complete.

Sample

IV. Key Word Outline for Conclusion

Topic A	*Th-, fun, w/, all, family*
Topic B	*eat, favorite, foods*
Most significant	*about, being, thankful*
	thinking, blessings
	family, loves, cares
Why?	*important, remember, appreciate*

Title repeats 1–3 key words from final sentence.

Discuss ideas for a final sentence that helps the paper sound complete. For example,

Thanksgiving is one of my favorite holidays.

Once you have written an outline, model how to use the notes to construct a paragraph with sentences that flow smoothly. Read your sample outline as a paragraph and then ask a few students to do the same with theirs. The above outline might turn into a paragraph like this:

Every Thanksgiving I have fun with my **grandparents**, **cousins**, **aunts**, and **uncles**. Everyone brings tasty **food**, and we have a feast, but Thanksgiving is not just about eating. Most importantly, it is about being thankful and thinking about all of the many blessings in my life. I am truly blessed to have a family that loves me and cares for me. Thanksgiving is a special day that helps me remember to appreciate them. It is one of my favorite holidays.

Introduction

Attention getter: Begin your report with something that will make your reader want to read more. Is there something especially intriguing about your subject? If you need help, consider trying one of the following:

1. Ask your reader a question.

   Example for Disneyland essay: *What is "the happiest place on earth"?*
   Example for Thanksgiving essay: *What is your favorite holiday?*

   Write a question that you might use to begin your introduction:

   Students' ideas will differ, depending upon the subject they chose.

2. Begin with a very short sentence (#6 vss).

   Notice that the sample introduction on page 181 begins this way with *Disneyland is magical.*
   Example for Thanksgiving essay: *I am blessed.*

   Write a very short sentence that you might use to begin your introduction:

   Students' ideas will differ, depending upon the subject they chose.

3. Begin with a famous quote.

   (If you do not know one, search on the Internet for a quote about fun, entertainment, amusement, or whatever your favorite activity or holiday is.) Be sure to connect it to what you say in your background information.

   Example for Disneyland essay: *Walt Disney once stated, "It is kind of fun to do the impossible." He built Disneyland to help visitors experience that kind of fun.*
   Example for Thanksgiving essay: *"Thanksgiving is a time of togetherness and gratitude" (Nigel Hamilton).*

   Find a quote that you might use to begin your introduction:

   Students' ideas will differ, depending upon the subject they chose.

For more ideas see the Attention Getters page in the SRP behind the Decorations tab.

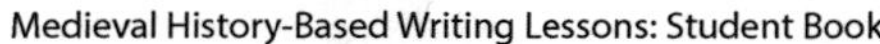

Here is a sample introduction outline for an essay about Thanksgiving; however, students should not copy this sample. Instead, they should write an outline that matches their subject and topics. Help them do so as you model each part.

Choose your favorite attention getter and write it in key words on the outline below; then, finish the introduction with these elements.

Background: Tell your reader what the essay is about but do not say anything similar to *"This essay is about ... ."* Simply make a general statement about the subject. In this composition the subject is your favorite amusement, entertainment, or holiday.

Then, give any background information you think would be interesting. (Notice how the sample introduction does this on page 181.) The background information should help you flow into mentioning your topics.

Topics: Try to write a complete sentence for each of your topics that tells the main idea of each body paragraph. In other words, re-word your topic sentences. You may need to add phrases or sentences to connect these ideas smoothly. List your topics in the same order that they appear in the body paragraphs. Bold the topic words.

Sample

I. Key Word Outline for Introduction

Attention getter *I, richly, blessed*

Background *busy, forget, thankful*

1x, yr, stop, reflect, blessings

____

Topic A *entire, fam, together, fun*

Topic B *lots, yummy, food*

Once you have written an outline, model how to use the notes to construct a paragraph with sentences that flow smoothly. Read your sample outline as a paragraph and then ask a few students to do the same. The above outline might turn into a paragraph like this:

I am richly blessed. However, my life is busy and gets crazy sometimes. In all of the busyness, I can forget to be thankful. At least once a year, I stop to remember and reflect upon how I am blessed. That day is Thanksgiving. It is one of my favorite holidays. On Thanksgiving my entire **family**, including grandparents, aunts, uncles, and cousins, gets together. We have tons of fun, and, of course, we have a fabulous feast of yummy **foods**.

Study the sample introduction and conclusion on page 181. Number the different sentence openers.

Sample Conclusion

[2] At Disneyland, **Star Tours** takes me into space and makes me feel as if I am flying with R2D2 and C3PO. [3] Actually, every place in the park seems **magical**. **[Most significant]** Most significantly, Disneyland is not just about rides and atmosphere. [6] It is much more. It is about having fun with friends and family. It is about escaping everyday chores, celebrating special days, and creating memories. [5] When I am caught up in the magic of Disneyland, it really does seem like "the happiest place on earth."

Sample Introduction

[6] Disneyland is magical. It is my favorite amusement park because it is much more than rides. It has Disney characters who roam around and who march in parades. [3] Additionally, it has fireworks that light up the night sky with dazzling colors, fun fantastic food, charming shops, and so much more. [2] Without a doubt my favorite ride is **Star Tours** because I love feeling like I am in a spaceship. [5] Wherever I am in the park, I feel as if I am in a faraway, **enchanted** land.

Style Practice

Your introduction and conclusion will each need to include the elements of style you have learned thus far. Each body paragraph should also have each element of style. You should check to see that you have underlined one of each dress-up and numbered one of each sentence opener in each of your body paragraphs. If you are missing some, you should add them.

Sentence Openers

Study the sample introduction and conclusion on page 181. Number the different sentence openers.

Look at your outlines for your introduction and conclusion. How could you express some of those ideas using sentence openers? Write one idea for each opener.

#2 (prepositional) *After the big meal the cousins like to go outside and play kickball.*

#3 (-ly adverb) *Suddenly the rollercoaster twists and dives.*

#5 (clausal - *www.asia.b*) *While the women are busy in the kitchen, the men are usually watching football.*

#6 (vss, 2–5 words) *I love Disneyland.*

Vocabulary Practice

Can you think of ways to add some vocabulary words anywhere in your essay?

Look at your outlines for your introduction and conclusion. How could you express some of those ideas using sentence openers? Write one idea for each opener.

Since students wrote about different topics, walk around the room and help students as necessary. Here are ideas for the Disneyland and Thanksgiving topics. It might be helpful to share them.

Teachers are free to adjust a checklist by requiring only the stylistic techniques that have become easy, plus one new one. "EZ+1."

Unit 7 Composition Checklist

Lesson 21: Favorite Amusements, Part 2 introduction and conclusion

Inventive Writing

Name: ____________________

Institute for Excellence in Writing

STRUCTURE

☐ MLA format (see Appendix I)	______	2 pts
☐ title centered	______	2 pts
Introduction		
☐ attention getter ☐ background ☐ topics stated (highlight or bold)	______	9 pts
☐ insert body paragraphs	______	2 pts
Conclusion		
☐ restate topics (highlight or bold) ☐ most significant/why ☐ final sentence repeats 1–3 key words for the title	______	9 pts
☐ checklist on top, final draft, rough draft, key word outline	______	4 pts
STYLE (one of each in **each** paragraph)		
¶1 ¶4 **Dress-Ups** (underline)	(1 pt each)	
☐ ☐ -ly adverb	______	2 pts
☐ ☐ *who/which* clause	______	2 pts
☐ ☐ strong verb	______	2 pts
☐ ☐ quality adjective	______	2 pts
☐ ☐ *www.asia.b* clause	______	2 pts
☐ banned words: go/went, say/said, good/bad, big/little (-1 for each use)	______	pts
¶1 ¶4 **Sentence Openers** (number)		
☐ ☐ [2] prepositional	______	2 pts
☐ ☐ [3] -ly adverb	______	2 pts
☐ ☐ [5] clausal - *www.asia.b*	______	2 pts
☐ ☐ [6] vss	______	2 pts
MECHANICS		
☐ spelling, grammar, and punctuation	______	4 pts
VOCABULARY		
☐ vocabulary words - label *(voc)* in left margin or after sentence		
Total:	______	50 pts
Custom Total:	______	pts

Lesson 22: Chivalry, Part 1

Structure: IEW Unit 7: Inventive Writing (Body Paragraphs)

Style: no new stylistic techniques

Writing Topic: Chivalry (Virtues)

Optional Student Reading Assignment: Elementary students: With Lessons 20–22 students may read *Adam of the Road* by Elizabeth Janet Gray. Junior high and high school students: With Lessons 21–23 students may read *The Kite Rider* by Geraldine McCaughrean.

UNIT 7: INVENTIVE WRITING

Lesson 22: Chivalry, Part 1

Goals

- to practice the Unit 7 structural model
- to create a key word outline from a writing prompt
- to write the body paragraphs of a 5-paragraph essay on chivalry
- to correctly use new vocabulary words: *credible, foremost, stymie, indolent*

Assignment Schedule

Note: Classes that meet weekly should complete Days 1 and 2 in class.

Day 1

1. With a teacher read the Review section and follow the instructions.
2. On page 188, read the prompt for the essay for this lesson. You will choose three topics (virtues) to write about.
3. Study pages 189–190 to understand the kinds of examples that could be used to support the topics of this essay.
4. Study page 191 to discuss topic sentences.
5. You will create a key word outline for one of the topics (virtues) with your teacher in class. You may choose to copy this key word outline if the virtue is one you will choose for your essay.

Day 2

1. Use the blank outline on page 192 to make a key word outline for Topic A. Begin with words that will help you write a topic sentence. Remember to ask yourself plenty of questions to get ideas about what to say. Also, try to include a specific example. Pages 189–190 should help.
2. Write the first body paragraph, Topic A. Remember that each paragraph must follow the topic-clincher rule. Follow the checklist.

Day 3

1. Complete your key word outlines for the remaining paragraphs, Topic B and Topic C.
2. Use the key word outlines to write the paragraphs for Topic B and Topic C. Check off each item on the checklist when you are sure you have completed it. Let an editor proofread.
3. Learn the new vocabulary words: *credible, foremost, stymie, indolent*. Can you include some in your paragraphs?

Day 4

1. Write or type a final draft, making any corrections your editor asked you to make. Check off each item on the checklist that you have completed and indicated as instructed.
2. Let an editor proofread again. He or she should check that all elements of structure and style are included and labeled as instructed on the checklist. Paperclip the checklist to your final draft to be turned in.

Review

Discuss the new vocabulary words for Lesson 22: *credible, foremost, stymie, indolent.*

Play a vocabulary game from the Teacher's Manual and include these words.

Share your attention getter from the composition you wrote for Lesson 21.

Structure

Prompt

The knights of Europe were expected to follow strict codes of chivalry. These codes promoted virtues such as courage, loyalty, respect for authority, honesty, perseverance, and compassion.

Write about three virtues that you believe are important.

Make each virtue the topic of a paragraph. Tell why the virtue is important and include examples of the virtue. Examples may be from people you know, personal experience, history, or literature (including children's stories). Many of the people you have read and written about thus far in this course would make good examples.

You will need three body paragraphs plus an introduction and a conclusion. In this lesson you will write the body paragraphs. In Lesson 23 you will add an introduction and conclusion.

Topics

Which three virtues will you write about?

____

Students may fill out the "Topics" line after you have read over examples and modeled a sample outline for one of the topic options.

Teachers of elementary students may opt to assign only two paragraphs. In this case, only two topics will be needed.

Structure Practice

Once you choose the virtues you will write about, you will need to think of examples for them. Below are several examples for a few virtues to help you understand the kinds of examples that will work. You may use some of these if you like them, or you may think of your own. Try to fill in some of the blanks with your own ideas. (You do not have to fill in every blank.)

For history and literature consider using some of the people you have read and written about thus far in this course. Many have shown virtues.

Courage (ability to do right despite danger or fear)

History

Augustine had courage to sail to England to tell the people about God. What was the result?

Can you think of another example of courage from history?

King Richard had courage to fight for the Holy Land. Even though he did not win, his efforts resulted in the Muslims allowing Christians to visit Jerusalem.

Literature/Children's Stories

In *One Thousand and One Arabian Nights*, Shahrazad has the courage to risk her life and marry the king. What was the result?

Can you think of another example of courage from literature?

Beowulf fights the dragon. He loses his life, but he saves his people from the dragon's terror.

Personal Experience

Have you ever done something despite your fear? Even things as simple as telling the truth, standing up for a friend, or performing in front of a large audience sometimes take courage.

Write an example below:

These will vary with students.

Perseverance (steadiness and persistence in purpose despite difficulties)

History

People of the Middle Ages devoted decades to building a cathedral. Those who began work on one knew they would not see it completed, yet they persevered. Why? What was the result?

Can you think of another example of perseverance from history?

Alfred the Great did not give in to the relentless Viking attacks. He continually stood strong against them. He eventually made peace with them and even won some over to Christianity.

Let students offer ideas. Especially encourage them to consider the people they have read about and written about this year from their Student Book and from the suggested literature.

Literature/Children's Stories

The tortoise in "The Tortoise and the Hare" did not let anything distract him from his purpose as the hare did. What was the result?

Can you think of another example of perseverance from literature?

The third pig in "The Three Little Pigs" persevered to build a house of bricks despite his brothers' jeering. He saved them all from the wolf.

Personal Experience

Have you ever wanted to quit or give up on something, but instead persevered and succeeded? Do you play a sport or a musical instrument that requires persistent practice? That is perseverance.

Write an example below:

These will vary with students.

Honesty (truthfulness, being without deceit)

Literature/Children's Stories

The boy who cried wolf was not honest. What happened?

The mayor in "The Pied Piper" did not keep his word. What happened?

Can you think of another example of honesty, or the lack thereof, from literature?

Pinocchio found himself in bad company and in misery because he did not tell the truth.

Personal Experience

Can you think of a time you had to tell the truth even though it might not have been pleasant? Has someone ever made you a promise that you are thankful they kept or were disappointed they did not keep? Who do you trust and why?

Write an example below:

These will vary with students.

Use your ideas to help you include examples in the key word outline on the page 192.

Lesson 22: Chivalry, Part 1

Topic Sentences and Clincher Sentences

Thinking about your examples will help you write clear topic sentences. Remember, each topic sentence must express the main idea you will communicate about the virtue. Your examples should help clarify this for you.

For example, if one of your topics is courage, what will your main idea about courage be? If you use the example of Shahrazad's courage to marry the king in *One Thousand and One Arabian Nights,* you know that by doing so she saved the lives of many women in her kingdom. You also know that she risked her own life to do so; therefore, a topic sentence might be something like this: *Courage gives us strength to see beyond ourselves in order to help others.*

If one of your topics is honesty, and you use the example of "The Boy Who Cried Wolf," you know that because the boy lied, he was not believed even when he told the truth. A topic sentence for your paragraph might be something like this: *Honesty builds trust.*

As you fill in the outline on the following page, try to write key words on the topic line for each virtue that will help you write a sentence that tells the main idea you want to communicate about that virtue.

Remember to end each paragraph with a clincher sentence that repeats or reflects two or three key words from your topic sentence.

Sample

Key Word Outline

Each Roman numeral indicates a topic sentence. What will the main idea about each virtue be? Write key words on each topic line. Then add details by answering any of the question words and including at least one example. When you write each paragraph, add a clincher.

Who?
What?
When?
Where?
Why?
How?
How feel?
Best thing?
Worst thing?
Problems
Value
Meaning
Examples
Describe (Strong Image or Feeling)

II. Topic A: *courage, strength, help*

1. *ex, Shahrazad, courage, 1001 Arabian Nights*
2. *👑, XX, wives, b/c, ⊘ trust*
3. *Sh-, married, stories, w/cliffhangers, ea ☾*
4. *courage, face, challenge, 👑*
5. *helped, 👑, trust, ♡*
6. *courage, saved, ♀, kingdom*

Clincher

III. Topic B: *perseverance → success, reward*

1. *quitters, ⊘, > accomplishments*
2. *ex. piano, practice, ⊘, fun*
3. *wanted, quit, many, Xs*
4. *persevered, now, able, ♫*
5. *perform, worship, others, ⊘*
6. *perseverance, paid*

Clincher

IV. Topic C: *honesty, = w/o deceit, → trust*

1. *ppl, ⊘, trust, liars*
2. *ex. boy, cried, wolf*
3. *deceived, → ppl, ⊘, trust*
4. *💬 help, ppl, ⊘, respond, b/c ⊘, blv*
5. *tragic, end, sheep XX*
6. *want, trust, honest*

Clincher

Unit 7 Composition Checklist

Lesson 22: Chivalry, Part 1 body paragraphs

Inventive Writing

Name: ______________________________

Institute for Excellence in Writing

Listen. Speak. Read. Write. Think!

STRUCTURE

☐ MLA format (see Appendix I)	______	2 pts
☐ topic-clincher sentences repeat or reflect 2–3 key **words** (highlight or bold)	______	4 pts
☐ checklist on top, final draft, rough draft, key word outline	______	2 pts

STYLE (one of each in each paragraph)

¶2 ¶3 ¶4 Dress-Ups (underline)	(2 pts each)	
☐ ☐ ☐ -ly adverb	______	6 pts
☐ ☐ ☐ *who/which* clause	______	6 pts
☐ ☐ ☐ strong verb	______	6 pts
☐ ☐ ☐ quality adjective	______	6 pts
☐ ☐ ☐ *www.asia.b* clause	______	6 pts
☐ banned words: go/went, say/said, good/bad, big/little (-1 for each use)	______	pts

¶2 ¶3 ¶4 Sentence Openers (number)		
☐ ☐ ☐ [2] prepositional	______	6 pts
☐ ☐ ☐ [3] -ly adverb	______	6 pts
☐ ☐ ☐ [5] clausal - *www.asia.b*	______	6 pts
☐ ☐ ☐ [6] vss	______	6 pts

MECHANICS

☐ spelling, grammar, and punctuation	______	8 pts

VOCABULARY

☐ vocabulary words - label *(voc)* in left margin or after sentence

Total:	______	70 pts
Custom Total:	______	pts

Teachers are free to adjust a checklist by requiring only the stylistic techniques that have become easy, plus one new one. "EZ+1."

Unit 7: Inventive Writing

Lesson 23: Chivalry, Part 2

Structure: IEW Unit 7: Inventive Writing (Introduction and Conclusion)

Style: no new stylistic techniques

Writing Topic: Chivalry (Virtues)

Optional Student Reading Assignment: Junior high and high school students: With Lessons 21–23 students may read *The Kite Rider* by Geraldine McCaughrean.

UNIT 7: INVENTIVE WRITING

Lesson 23: Chivalry, Part 2

Goals

- to practice the Unit 7 structural model
- to create key word outlines for an introduction and a conclusion paragraph
- to write an introduction and a conclusion paragraph
- to complete a 5-paragraph essay on chivalry

Assignment Schedule

Note: Classes that meet weekly should complete Days 1 and 2 in class.

Day 1

1. With a teacher read the Review section on page 196 and do the activities.
2. Use pages 196–197 to create key word outlines for a conclusion and an introduction.

Day 2

1. Review your key word outlines. Tell back the ideas in complete sentences. If there is a note that you do not understand, fix it.
2. Practice using sentence openers on page 198.
3. Write your conclusion paragraph. Remember to highlight or bold the topic words.

Day 3

1. Write your introduction paragraph. Remember to highlight or bold the topic words. Check off each item on the checklist when you are sure you have completed it. Let an editor proofread.
2. There are no new vocabulary words for Lesson 23, but continue to review all words learned thus far.

Day 4

1. Write or type a final draft of your entire virtues essay by placing the introduction paragraph before your body paragraphs and the conclusion paragraph after them. As you do, make any corrections your editor asked you to make. Check off each item on the checklist that you have completed and indicated as instructed.
2. Let an editor proofread again. He or she should check that all elements of structure and style are included and labeled as instructed on both checklists, pages 193 (body) and 199 (introduction and conclusion). Paperclip both checklists (pages 193 and 199) to your final draft to be turned in.
3. If you are making a Magnum Opus Notebook, revise your amusements composition from Lesson 21. (See Appendix II.)
4. If you are reading the suggested literature, obtain *Marco Polo* by Demi for Lesson 24.

Review

Play a review game such as Tic-Tac-Toe, 21 Questions, or Hang Man from the Teacher's Manual.

Share your topic sentences and clincher sentences from Lesson 22 paragraphs. What examples did you use to support each?

Structure

Conclusion

Follow the procedure taught in Lesson 21 to outline a conclusion for your chivalry essay. Here are some reminders and helps:

Restate the topics: Rewording each of your topic sentences usually works well for this; however, you may instead list the virtues in one sentence. Remember to highlight or bold the topic words.

Most significant and why: Why are virtues important? What do they help us accomplish or gain? Are they only for nobility? What application can the reader make to his life based on what you shared in your essay?

What happens when we practice virtues? What happens without virtues?

Final sentence: End your paper with a final sentence from which you can create a title.

Sample

V. Key Word Outline for Conclusion

Topic A	*courage, → right, regardless*
Topic B	*perseverance, → amazing, feats*
Topic C	*honesty, → trusted*
Most significant	*⊘, just, nobility, all*
	practicing, virtues, → character
Why?	*focus, others, + goals*
	helps, live, w/purpose

Title repeats 1–3 key words from final sentence.

Discuss ideas for a final sentence that helps the essay sound complete. Sample ideas:
Virtues are still important. Virtues are valuable.
When people live by virtues, the world is a better place.

Introduction

Follow the procedure taught in Lesson 21 to outline an introduction for your chivalry essay. Here are some reminders and helps:

Attention getter: Begin with a question, a very short sentence (2–5 words), or a quote (review page 183). For more ideas see the Attention Getters page in the SRP behind the Decorations tab.

Background: Since the prompt used the codes of chivalry of European knights as background, you could begin by talking about chivalry in the Middle Ages and the importance the nobility placed on it. This could help you then discuss the value of virtuous character for everyone of all time. You might even define what a virtue is and list several virtues.

Topics: After your discussion of virtues in general, you need to focus on the three topics about virtues that you will be discussing. Make one statement about each or list all three in one statement. List your topics in the same order that they appear in the body paragraphs. Remember to highlight or bold the topic words.

Sample

I. Key Word Outline for Introduction

Attention getter	*character, counts*
Background	*even, ppl, Mid-Ages, recognized*
	codes, promoted, virtues
	knights, > respected
	still, important, today
Topic A	*courage, = ability, stand*
Topic B	*perseverance, strength, endure → >*
Topic C	*honesty, heart, pure*

Unit 7: Inventive Writing

Style Practice

Your introduction and conclusion will each need to include the elements of style you have learned thus far. Let's practice the newest element of style, sentence openers.

Sentence Openers

Below are five sentences. *Choose three*. Add a different sentence opener to each: #2 (prepositional), #3 (-ly adverb), or #5 (clausal - *www.asia.b*).

1. *[2] Despite the brutality of the times,* knights and nobles recognized the importance of upholding virtues.
2. *[5] If we are honest,* people will trust us.
3. *[3] Clearly,* courage gives us strength.
4. *[2] Throughout history* perseverance has led to many amazing accomplishments.
5. *[3] Certainly,* virtues are the foundation of admirable character.

Can you think of a #6 (vss, 2–5 words) sentence that you could use in your introduction, possibly as your attention getter?

Character counts. *We must uphold virtues.*

Knights valued virtues. *Virtues are valuable.*

Vocabulary Practice

Can you think of ways to add some vocabulary words anywhere in your essay?

____

Unit 7 Composition Checklist

Lesson 23: Chivalry, Part 2 introduction and conclusion

Inventive Writing

Name: ______________________

Institute for Excellence in Writing

STRUCTURE

☐ MLA format (see Appendix I)	______	2 pts
☐ title centered	______	2 pts
Introduction		
☐ attention getter ☐ background ☐ topics stated (highlight or **bold**)	______	9 pts
☐ insert body paragraphs	______	2 pts
Conclusion		
☐ restate topics (highlight or **bold**) ☐ most significant/why ☐ final sentence repeats 1–3 **key words** for the title	______	9 pts
☐ checklist on top, final draft, rough draft, key word outline	______	4 pts
STYLE (one of each in each paragraph)		
¶1 ¶5 Dress-Ups (underline)	(2 pts each)	
☐ ☐ -ly adverb	______	4 pts
☐ ☐ *who/which* clause	______	4 pts
☐ ☐ strong verb	______	4 pts
☐ ☐ quality adjective	______	4 pts
☐ ☐ *www.asia.b* clause	______	4 pts
☐ banned words: go/went, say/said, good/bad, big/little (-1 for each use)	______	pts
¶1 ¶5 Sentence Openers (number)		
☐ ☐ [2] prepositional	______	4 pts
☐ ☐ [3] -ly adverb	______	4 pts
☐ ☐ [5] clausal - *www.asia.b*	______	4 pts
☐ ☐ [6] vss	______	4 pts
MECHANICS		
☐ spelling, grammar, and punctuation	______	6 pts
VOCABULARY		
☐ vocabulary words - label *(voc)* in left margin or after sentence		
Total:	______	70 pts
Custom Total:	______	pts

Teachers are free to adjust a checklist by requiring only the stylistic techniques that have become easy, plus one new one. "EZ+1."

Unit 7: Inventive Writing

Lesson 24: Descriptive Time Travel Diary

Structure: IEW Unit 7: Inventive Writing

Style: #1 subject opener and #4 -ing opener

Writing Topic: Marco Polo

Optional Student Reading Assignment: With Lesson 24 students may read *Marco Polo* by Demi.

UNIT 7: INVENTIVE WRITING

Lesson 24: Descriptive Time Travel Diary

Goals

- to practice a modified Unit 7 structural model
- to create a key word outline
- to write a fictional diary
- to indicate the #1 subject sentence opener
- to correctly add a new sentence opener: #4 -ing opener

Assignment Schedule

Note: Classes that meet weekly should complete Days 1 and 2 in class.

Day 1

1. In this lesson you will again write from a prompt, but you will focus on vivid descriptions in a modified structure: a fictional diary. With a teacher read the Review section and follow the instructions.
2. With a teacher read the prompt on page 202 and study the assigned structure on page 203.
3. Use your own paper to outline ideas for each entry of your diary. Use page 203 as a guide.
4. Write the first diary entry.

Day 2

1. Learn the #1 and #4 sentence openers on pages 204 and 205. Practice the #4 sentence opener.
2. Practice dress-ups on page 206.
3. Write the second and third diary entries. Remember to use dress-ups that create a strong image or feeling.

Day 3

1. Complete the last two entries in your diary. Check off each item on the checklist when you are sure you have completed it. Let an editor proofread.
2. There are no new vocabulary words for Lesson 24. Continue to review all and try to use some in your diary entries.

Day 4

1. Write or type a final draft, making any corrections your editor asked you to make. Check off each item on the checklist that you have completed and indicated as instructed.
2. Let an editor proofread again. He or she should check that all elements of structure and style are included and labeled as instructed on the checklist. Paperclip the checklist to your final draft to be turned in.
3. If you are reading the suggested literature, obtain *Crispin: The Cross of Lead* by Avi for Lessons 25–28.

Have students highlight or star the instructions on the next page to bring their knights report from Lessons 17–18 to class for Lesson 25.

Literature Suggestion

With Lesson 24 read *Marco Polo* by Demi.

Important: Bring your knights report from Lessons 17–18 to class next week.

Review

Share your introduction or conclusion of your chivalry essay from Lesson 23.

Play the sentence stretching game described in the Teacher's Manual.

Structure

Prompt

Marco Polo traveled far from his home in Italy to Asia. When he reached the empire of Kublai Khan (grandson of Genghis Khan), he could not believe what he was seeing and experiencing. He was in awe of the strange new land. Later, he wrote a book describing his experiences, but most of the people in Europe at that time did not believe his splendid descriptions.

Pretend you are a peasant of the Middle Ages who has time-traveled into the twenty-first century for five days. Write a diary entry for each day describing the things and people that you see and experience. Include your thoughts and feelings. Do not use terms that medieval people would not be familiar with.

The prompt instructs you to write one entry for each of the five days, so the "topic" of each "paragraph" will be each day, with the first day serving loosely as an introduction and the last day as a conclusion.

However, a diary is much more casual than a formal essay, so this assignment will not require topic sentences and clinchers. Additionally, the elements of style required on the checklist are required only once anywhere throughout the entire diary rather than in each entry. Do note, though, that each entry must have at least five sentences.

Use the next page as a guide.

Review

Use these basic sentences and requirements. Tell students to think of them in the context of someone being transported from the Middle Ages to the twenty-first century, describing what he sees and experiences.

1. I walked into the machine. (#5 opener, strong verb, quality adjective, *who/which* clause)

2. The man went across the street. (strong verb, quality adjective, *www.asia.b* clause)

3. The girl ate the ______________. (#2 opener, strong verb, -ly adverb, *who/which* clause)

Lesson 24: Descriptive Time Travel Diary

Key Word Outline

For this outline, use your own sheet of paper. Begin each entry with the day of the week written above it, Monday–Friday. Consider the following questions for each entry.

Who?
What?
When?
Where?
Why?
How?
How feel?
Best thing?
Worst thing?
Problems
Value
Meaning
Examples
Describe (Strong Image or Feeling)

Monday

I. Introduce yourself and explain how you stumbled upon a time travel machine and why or how you traveled to the twenty-first century.

1. Where and when did you arrive?
2. What did you see and hear?
3. Whom did you meet? How did the people react?
4. Where did you go? Did you go alone or with someone?
5. What did you think about everything you saw?
6. How did you feel?

For each Tuesday–Thursday

II.–III.–IV. Where did you go, and what did you do and see that day?

1. What happened? What did you learn?
2. What did you like or not like? Why?
3. What impressed you most? Why?
4. What confused you most? Why?

Friday

V. Explain how you got back to the Middle Ages.

1. What happened when you told your friends and family about your adventure?
2. What did you try to describe to them?
3. What was their reaction?

New Style

#1 Subject Opener

The #1 sentence opener is not really a new opener. You have used it many times. It is simply a sentence that begins with its subject. This is the kind of sentence you usually write if you do not purposely try to use one of the other sentence openers you have been taught. For this reason we have not yet discussed or labeled #1 sentence openers. Here are some examples:

[1] The time machine rattled and rumbled.

[1] I landed in the middle of a busy street.

[1] Several people rushed toward me, screaming at me.

In this example there is the adjective *several* in front of the subject, but that does not change the sentence structure. It is still a #1.

#4 -ing Opener

A #4 sentence opener follows this pattern: -ing word/phrase + comma + main clause.

This opener must follow these rules:

The sentence must begin with an action word that ends in -ing. This is called a participle. The -ing word/phrase and comma must be followed by a complete sentence. The thing after the comma must be the thing doing the -inging.

That is a lot to remember. Below are some sample sentences that should help you understand the #4 sentence opener. In each, notice that all of the rules above apply.

[4] Hoping to find help in this strange new world, I plodded on.

[4] Spotting a roaring metal bird overhead, I scrambled for cover.

In each of the above examples, an -ing phrase is followed by a comma, which is followed by a complete sentence. The subject of that sentence ("I" in both) is doing the -inging.

Imposter #4s

There are several imposters of the #4 sentence opener. These imposters begin with -ing words but do not follow the #4 sentence opener rules. Can you tell why each of the following would not be a #4 sentence opener?

1. During the fantastic trip I learned about a completely different way of life.
2. Explaining what I saw to people back home will be hard.

Lesson 24: Descriptive Time Travel Diary

Explanations

1. *During* is a preposition, not an action word. This sentence opener is a #2 (prepositional opener).
2. There is no -ing word/phrase followed by a comma, followed by a complete sentence. In this case *explaining* is actually the subject of the sentence: Explaining ... will be ... .

Imposters to Watch For

prepositions that end in -ing	*According to the timer, I had one day left.*
subject nouns that begin in -ing	*Cooking without fire is like magic.*

Practice

Write a sentence with a #4 -ing opener that you might be able to use in your diary.

Fearing that I would be struck or eaten by one of the metal boxes, I ran the other way.

Style Practice

Dress-Ups for Vivid Descriptions

This diary will require much description, so you will want to use a thesaurus when choosing your quality adjectives, strong verbs, and -ly adverbs.

Write descriptions of the following things using at least three descriptive words. Try to include at least one quality adjective, strong verb, and -ly adverb in each. You may write several sentences for each in order to accomplish this.

1. cars on the street *Shiny, colorful, metal boxes zoomed down the street, some making blaring noises. An enormous one occasionally spewed black fetid smoke that choked me.*

2. cheeseburger *The strange, circular meal was layered with warm, savory meat, gooey yellow cheese, and fresh vegetables between two soft, warm slices of bread. Greasy sauces oozed out slowly. The lettuce crunched in my mouth.*

3. common twenty-first century object of your choice *It looked like a tiny, empty room. When I walked in, two doors slid silently together and closed me in. I started to panic until I heard soft, soothing music. But, there were no musicians! The sound was coming from the walls. Suddenly there was a jolt, and I realized that the room was moving.*

Lesson 24: Descriptive Time Travel Diary

Unit 7 Composition Checklist
Lesson 24: Descriptive Time Travel Diary

Inventive Writing

Name: ______________________________

Institute for Excellence in Writing

STRUCTURE

☐ MLA format (see Appendix I)	______	2 pts
☐ title centered and repeats 1–3 key words from final sentence	______	2 pts
☐ each paragraph contains at least five sentences	______	5 pts
☐ checklist on top, final draft, rough draft, key word outline	______	2 pts
STYLE (one of each anywhere in the diary)		
Dress-Ups (underline)	(1 pt each)	
☐ -ly adverb	______	5 pts
☐ *who/which* clause	______	5 pts
☐ strong verb	______	5 pts
☐ quality adjective	______	5 pts
☐ *www.asia.b* clause	______	5 pts
☐ banned words: go/went, say/said, good/bad, big/little (-1 for each use)	______	pts
Sentence Openers (number; one of each as possible)		
☐ [1] subject	______	5 pts
☐ [2] prepositional	______	5 pts
☐ [3] -ly adverb	______	5 pts
☐ [4] -ing	______	5 pts
☐ [5] clausal - *www.asia.b*	______	5 pts
☐ [6] vss	______	5 pts
MECHANICS		
☐ spelling, grammar, and punctuation	______	4 pts
VOCABULARY		
☐ vocabulary words - label *(voc)* in left margin or after sentence		
Total:	______	70 pts
Custom Total:	______	pts

Teachers are free to adjust a checklist by requiring only the stylistic techniques that have become easy, plus one new one. "EZ+1."

Unit 7: Inventive Writing

Lesson 25: Knights, Part 3

Structure: IEW Unit 8: Formal Essay Models (Expanding Unit 6)

Style: no new stylistic techniques

Writing Topic: Knights

Optional Student Reading Assignment: With Lessons 25–28 students may read *Crispin: The Cross of Lead* by Avi.

Teaching Writing: Structure and Style

Watch the sections for Unit 8: Formal Essay Models. At IEW.com/twss-help reference the TWSS Viewing Guides.

UNIT 8: FORMAL ESSAY MODELS

Lesson 25: Knights, Part 3

Goals

- to be introduced to the Unit 8 Formal Essay structural model
- to review the components for an introduction and a conclusion paragraph
- to add an introduction and a conclusion paragraph to the body paragraphs written in Lessons 17–18

Assignment Schedule

Note: Classes that meet weekly should complete Days 1 and 2 in class.

Day 1

1. With a teacher read the Review section on page 210 and do the activities.
2. Use pages 211–213 to create key word outlines for a conclusion and an introduction for the knights paragraphs you wrote in Lessons 17–18.

Day 2

1. Review your key word outlines. Tell back the ideas in complete sentences. If there is a note you do not understand, fix it.
2. Practice using sentence openers on page 214.
3. Write your conclusion paragraph.

Day 3

1. Write your introduction paragraph. Check off each item on the checklist when you are sure you have completed it. Let an editor proofread.
2. There are no the new vocabulary words for Lesson 24, but continue to review all words learned thus far.

Day 4

1. Write or type a final draft of your entire composition by placing the introduction paragraph before your body paragraphs and the conclusion paragraph after them. As you do, make any corrections your editor asked you to make. Check off each item on the checklist that you have completed and indicated as instructed.
2. Place the bibliography that you wrote in Lesson 18 as the last page.
3. Let an editor proofread again. He or she should check that all elements of structure and style are included and labeled as instructed on the checklist. Paperclip the checklist to your final draft to be turned in.
4. If you are making a Magnum Opus Notebook, revise your chivalry essay from Lessons 22–23. (See Appendix II.)

Be sure to read the important note on the next page and page 221 to the students. Be sure they understand what to do in preparation for Lesson 26.

Important

Read page 219 of Lesson 26. Choose a prominent person of the Renaissance as the subject of your essay for Lesson 26. Find three fairly short sources of information about that person and bring them to class. There is list of possible subjects on page 219, but you may think of another.

Literature Suggestion

With Lessons 25–28 Read *Crispin: The Cross of Lead* by Avi.

Review

Play a game such as Hangman from the Teacher's Manual.

Share an entry from the diary you wrote in Lesson 24.

Review

For Hang Man, use these phrases:

TO BLOCK OR HINDER (Once solved, ask *"What is the vocabulary word?"* stymie)

INTRODUCTION, BODY, CONCLUSION (Once solved, ask, *"What should be included in an introduction?"* Attention getter, background, topics. *"In a conclusion?"* Topics, most significant and why, final sentence with one to three words for the title)

LOYALTY OR DEVOTION (Once solved ask, *"What is the vocabulary word?"* allegiance)

Lesson 25: Knights, Part 3

New Structure

Basic Essay Model

The basic essay model is outlined in the SRP behind the Unit 8 tab. This basic model suggests five paragraphs: three body paragraphs plus an introduction and conclusion. However, the model can be adapted by simply changing the number of body paragraphs.

You have already used this structure to write about chivalry in Unit 7. In this lesson you will use the same structure to complete the Unit 6 summary you wrote about knights in Lessons 17–18. You will simply add an introduction and a conclusion to the body paragraphs you already wrote.

Conclusion

Even though the conclusion will be placed last, we will outline and write it before the introduction. Here are some reminders about how to outline a conclusion.

Restate the topics: The best way to do this is to write a sentence about each topic. Remember to highlight or bold the topic words.

Most significant and why: What is the most important thing to remember about your subject and *why*? For the knights report, think about why knights are still remembered and studied today. What do you like about knights? What can we learn from their legacy?

Final sentence: End your paper with a final sentence from which you can create a title.

Sample

IV. Key Word Outline for Conclusion

Topic A	*many, duties, lord*
Topic B	*armor, symbolized, status*
Most significant	*upheld, virtues*
	served, others, → legends
Why?	*still, studied, admired*
	role models

Title repeats 1–3 key words from final sentence.

Discuss ideas for a final sentence that helps the essay sound complete.

Knights will never be forgotten. Their legend lives on.

Introduction

Attention getter: Begin with something intriguing that will make your reader want to read more. You could try one of the techniques below.

1. Ask your reader a question.

   Example: *Why are we still fascinated with knights of the Middle Ages?*

   Write a question that you might use to begin your introduction:

   Who has not heard of King Arthur and his noble Knights of the Round Table?

2. Begin with a very short sentence (#6 vss).

   Example: *Knights are legendary.*

   Write a short sentence that you might use to begin your introduction:

   Knights were fearless fighters.

3. Begin with a quote or fact you think is intriguing.

   (The Background Help on page 213 might be helpful.)

   Example: *Knights were like tanks of the Middle Ages.*

   Find a quote or write an intriguing fact about knights that you might use to begin your introduction. You may have to do a little research to find something you like for this.

   Boys of the Middle Ages dreamed of winning their spurs.

For more ideas see the Attention Getters page in the SRP behind the Decorations tab.

Background: Tell your reader the subject of the report but do not say anything similar to *"This report is about … ."* Simply make a general statement about the subject. Then, give any background information you think would be helpful. For example, when and where did knighthood begin? Where did knights live? For ideas, look at how each of the source texts on pages 145–149 begins. You may read other sources about knights or the Fun Facts on page 213 as well to find more ideas.

Topics: The simplest way to meet this requirement is to list the topics, but a list is not very interesting reading. Try to write one complete sentence for each of your topics—tell the main idea of each body paragraph. You may need to add phrases or sentences to connect these ideas smoothly. Ensure you list your topics in the order that they appear in the body paragraphs. Remember to highlight or bold the topic words.

Sample

I. Key Word Outline for Introduction

Attention getter	*who, ⊘, know, ♔ Arthur, + kn-?*
Background	*kn-, elite, "shining armor"*
	began, 9th century, → 12th w/ > crossbow
	revered, b/c, brave, chivalrous
Topic A	*loyal, lord, served*
Topic B	*recognized, armor, battle*

Background Help: *Below are a few fun facts about knights. If you find one of them interesting, you could use it in your introduction as an attention getter or as part of your background information. (Write in your own words, of course.)*

European knighthood began with Charlemagne, emperor of the Franks, in the ninth century. It declined quickly during the twelfth century because of the invention of the arbalest (a very powerful crossbow), which could pierce plate armor.

When a young man became a knight, he was given his own set of spurs. Thus, the term "winning his spurs" meant becoming a knight. When not in armor, these spurs showed everyone that the man was a knight.

A knight was identified by the coat of arms on his shield. The coat of arms was especially important in battle when faces were hidden inside helmets.

The Code of Chivalry held knights to high standards. When a knight was dishonored, his spurs were hacked, and his shield was turned upside down.

The most famous knights are probably King Arthur and his Knights of the Round Table. While loosely based on a real person in history, tales of their adventures are fancifully embellished with undaunted courage, magical swords, the majestic city of Camelot, and much more.

Unit 8: Formal Essay Models

Style Practice

Sentence Openers

Your introduction and conclusion will each need to include the elements of style you have learned thus far. For practice with sentence openers, *choose four of the sentences below*. Add a different sentence opener to each: #2 (prepositional), #3 (-ly adverb), #4 (-ing participle), or #5 (clausal - *www.asia.b*).

1. *[3] Loyally* knights served their lords.
2. *[5] Because they held themselves to a Code of Chivalry,* knights were revered.
3. *[2] On the battlefield* a young man could be dubbed a knight.
4. *[2] With the invention of a powerful crossbow,* knighthood began to fade away.
5. *[4] Inspiring many to noble deeds,* legends of knights will live on for centuries.
6. *[5] When we look back at the Middle Ages,* we can admire the knights who lived to serve others.

Can you think of a #6 (vss, 2–5 words) sentence that you could use in your introduction, possibly as your attention getter?

Knights served honorably.

Unit 8 Composition Checklist

Lesson 25: Knights, Part 3 introduction and conclusion

Formal Essay Models

Name: ______________________

Institute for Excellence in Writing

STRUCTURE		
☐ MLA format (see Appendix I)	______	1 pt
☐ title centered	______	1 pt
Introduction		
☐ attention getter ☐ background ☐ topics stated (highlight or bold)	______	9 pts
☐ insert body paragraphs	______	2 pts
Conclusion		
☐ restate topics (highlight or bold) ☐ most significant/why ☐ final sentence repeats 1–3 key words for the title	______	9 pts
☐ checklist on top, final draft, rough draft, key word outline	______	2 pts
STYLE (one of each in each paragraph)		
¶1 ¶4 Dress-Ups (underline)	(1 pt each)	
☐ ☐ -ly adverb	______	2 pts
☐ ☐ *who/which* clause	______	2 pts
☐ ☐ strong verb	______	2 pts
☐ ☐ quality adjective	______	2 pts
☐ ☐ *www.asia.b* clause	______	2 pts
☐ banned words: go/went, say/said, good/bad, big/little (-1 for each use)	______	pts
¶1 ¶4 Sentence Openers (number; one of each as possible)		
☐ ☐ [1] subject	______	2 pts
☐ ☐ [2] prepositional	______	2 pts
☐ ☐ [3] -ly adverb	______	2 pts
☐ ☐ [4] -ing	______	2 pts
☐ ☐ [5] clausal - *www.asia.b*	______	2 pts
☐ ☐ [6] vss	______	2 pts
MECHANICS		
☐ spelling, grammar, and punctuation	______	4 pts
VOCABULARY		
☐ vocabulary words - label *(voc)* in left margin or after sentence		
Total:	______	50 pts
Custom Total:	______	pts

Teachers are free to adjust a checklist by requiring only the stylistic techniques that have become easy, plus one new one. "EZ+1."

Unit 8: Formal Essay Models

Lesson 26: The Renaissance, Part 1

Structure: IEW Unit 8: Formal Essay Models (Body Paragraphs)

Style: no new stylistic techniques

Writing Topic: Prominent Person of the Renaissance

Optional Student Reading Assignment: With Lessons 25–28 students may read *Crispin: The Cross of Lead* by Avi.

UNIT 8: FORMAL ESSAY MODELS

Lesson 26: The Renaissance, Part 1

Goals

- to practice the Unit 8 structural model
- to practice scanning multiple sources to determine three topics for an essay
- to create source outlines from multiple sources
- to create fused outlines
- to write the first two body paragraphs of a 5-paragraph research essay

Assignment Schedule

Note: Classes that meet weekly should complete Days 1 and 2 in class.

Day 1

1. In the next two lessons, you will write a research essay about one of the great individuals of the Renaissance. With a teacher read the Review and Historical Information on page 218.
2. Read pages 219–221 to practice scanning for topics. Scan your own sources for possible topics. ***Note***: If you choose to write about Leonardo daVinci, you may use the source text on pages 220–221 as one of your sources.
3. Take out three sheets of paper. Format them like page 223. These papers are where you will write key word outlines from your sources. When you know the topic of each of your body paragraphs, write key words for each topic on the topic lines of each of the papers. You will use the first two of these papers this week.

Day 2

1. Make key word outlines for Topic A from all sources that contain information about that topic.
2. Once you have key word outlines from two or three sources for Topic A, organize them into one fused outline. Use page 224. Begin with the key words for a topic sentence. Then choose the facts from your outlines that you want in your paragraph and write them in an order that makes sense.
3. Using the fused outline, write your first body paragraph (Topic A). Follow the checklist requirements.

Day 3

1. Repeat steps 1 and 2 of Day 2 for Topic B. Fuse the notes onto page 225.
2. Write the second body paragraph (Topic B). Let an editor proofread both paragraphs.

Day 4

1. Write or type a draft of the two body paragraphs, making the corrections your editor asked you to make. Check off each item on the checklist that you have completed and indicated as instructed. Let an editor proofread again.
2. You will complete this essay in Lesson 27, so do not attach the checklist yet.
3. If you are making a Magnum Opus Notebook, revise your descriptive diary from Lesson 24. (See Appendix II.)

Bring your sources to class next week. If they are Internet sources, print them.

Review

Play a quick vocabulary game from the Teacher's Manual.

Historical Information

The end of the Middle Ages merged into a period of history known as the Renaissance. The term *Renaissance* comes from a Latin word meaning *rebirth*. During this time period, scholars and artists sought to return to the spirit of the Greek and Roman cultures that had valued the arts and learning. The Renaissance began in Italy in the 1300s and slowly spread throughout Europe. As a result, Europe experienced remarkable advances, especially in the arts and sciences. Most scholars agree that the modern era began with the Renaissance.

People living during the Renaissance did not just accept things as they were. They challenged old ideas and techniques. Renaissance artists set a new standard for art. They desired to portray humans and nature realistically. They experimented with perspective, color, light, and shading to achieve great masterpieces. Renaissance architects used Roman and Greek architecture as their inspiration; thus, many Renaissance buildings included columns and arches. Renaissance scientists, inventors, and explorers made great advances that had far-reaching effects. They began to challenge ancient teachings that had been commonly accepted for centuries. For example, Copernicus challenged the idea that the earth was the center of the universe. He proposed a sun-centered model. In addition, many devices were invented that helped great thinkers experiment and explore. For example, the telescope helped scientists study the heavens. Also, Gutenberg's printing press made it possible to share ideas and knowledge on a much grander scale. Many were inspired to explore the world and the universe. Some of the greatest explorers of the 1400s and 1500s, such as Christopher Columbus, were Italians exposed to the ideas of Renaissance thinkers. The world was forever changed by those who lived during the Renaissance.

New Structure

The Research Essay

For this research essay about one of the great individuals of the Renaissance, you will use the 5-paragraph essay model that includes an introduction, three body paragraphs, and a conclusion.

This lesson provides one source text for one possible subject: Leonardo da Vinci. It is on the next two pages. However, you will need to find other sources on your own, specific to the person you choose.

First, you need to choose your specific subject. Here are some options, but you may do your own research and choose any notable person of the Renaissance:

Artists		Scientists	
Leonardo da Vinci	Raphael	Nicolaus Copernicus	Francis Bacon
Michelangelo	Donatello	Paracelsus	Galileo
			Johannes Kepler

Once you determine the person you will research, find at least three sources of information about him or her. History textbooks, Internet articles (especially those labeled "for kids"), encyclopedia articles, and short children's books will make the best sources. Your parents or a librarian should help you choose short, easy sources. The difficulty of this essay will be determined largely upon the difficulty of the sources you use.

Choosing Topics

Once you decide on a subject, you will need to familiarize yourself with it by skimming your sources. Your goal will be to determine three topics. When writing about famous people, the following topics might work:

A. young life

B. what made them famous (their works and ideas)

C. later years/death

However, when writing about individuals who are famous for a variety of accomplishments, consider using each accomplishment as a topic. Look at the topics your sources cover and choose ones that will work best.

For practice, read the source text on the following pages. In the gray box in the margin by each paragraph, write its topic.

Once you have determined the topics covered in the sample source text, scan the sources you were asked to bring to class for the person you will be researching. Determine the topics you could use for your essay. Ask your teacher to approve your topics.

Note: If you choose to write about Leonardo da Vinci, you may use pages 220–221 as one of your sources. Here is how you would cite it in your bibliography:

Verstegen, Lori. "The Ultimate Renaissance Man." *Medieval History-Based Writing Lessons*, Institute for Excellence in Writing, 2018, pp. 220–221.

Unit 8: Formal Essay Models

Source Text

The Ultimate Renaissance Man

Introduction

He was ingenious. Leonardo da Vinci, who was born in Vinci, Italy, in 1452, has been called "the Ultimate Renaissance Man" because he excelled in so many fields of interest. In fact, he may have been the most multi-talented man to ever have lived. He studied many branches of science, engineering, and architecture, and he sketched plans for hundreds of inventions far ahead of his time. However, Leonardo was trained to be a painter, and that is what he is best remembered for.

education and training

As a child Leonardo had very little formal education, but at age fourteen he was apprenticed to a prominent artist in Florence named Verrocchio. While under Verrocchio's care, Leonardo learned many workshop skills. He was taught painting, drafting, metalworking, plaster casting, and carpentry. One day Verrocchio asked Leonardo to add an angel to the painting *The Baptism of Christ* that they were working on together. When Verrocchio saw how skillfully his student had painted the angel, it is said that he put down his brush and swore never to paint again. Leonardo soon branched out on his own and continued to learn and master new things.

Leonardo became a master painter. In every piece of work he painted, he strove to portray his subjects as realistically as possible. He became a master at using light and shadows to achieve perspective and depth, which other paintings of his day sorely lacked. His success is evident in the painting he is best known for, the *Mona Lisa*. This portrait of an unknown woman has intrigued the world

Lesson 26: The Renaissance, Part 1

for centuries. It is arguably the most famous painting in history. Interestingly, Leonardo never sold this work. He kept it and continually worked on it, striving for perfection. Today it is on display at the Louvre Museum in Paris, France. Its estimated value is well over $500 million (US dollars). His next most famous painting is *The Lord's Supper*. For this fresco he developed his own technique of painting onto the plaster of a wall. It took him three years to paint. This beautiful work of art is the most reproduced painting of all time. Truly, Leonardo da Vinci is one of the greatest painters who ever lived.

master painter

Leonardo was not just an artist; he was a scientist in the true sense of the word. He believed that close observation, repeated experimentation, and detailed recording were the keys to gaining knowledge. He kept a series of journals of over 13,000 pages in which he noted his observations, ideas, and discoveries. He meticulously studied and drew all parts of the human body in minute detail, which helped him paint more realistically. He drew pictures of ideas for inventions such as a helicopter, a hang glider, a parachute, war machines, motor cars, musical instruments, pumps, and other items. However, in his journal he wrote backwards, making it difficult for others to read. He also studied light, other aspects of physics, botany, and more. He developed many of his own theories from his observations. He was a scientific genius.

scientist

Despite having no formal education as a young child, Leonardo's inquisitive mind and diligence helped him develop into one of the world's most accomplished men. Today people still marvel not only at his masterful paintings, but at his brilliant mind. He typifies the Renaissance.

Conclusion

Unit 8: Formal Essay Models

Bibliography

Nelson, Ken. “Leonardo da Vinci Biography for Kids: Artist, Genius, Inventor.” *Ducksters*, Technological Solutions, June 2018, ducksters.com/biography/leonardo_da_vinci.php.

“Leonardo da Vinci Biography.” *Biography.com*, A&E Television Networks, 10 April 2018, biography.com/people/leonardo-da-vinci-40396.

“Leonardo da Vinci: Science.” *Leonardo-da-Vinci.ch*, leonardo-da-vinci.ch/science, Accessed 15 May 2018.

Note: See instructions on page 219 if you desire to cite “The Ultimate Renaissance Man.”

Sample

Lesson 26: The Renaissance, Part 1

Source Outlines

Prepare three sheets of paper for note taking in key word outlines by copying this format onto each. On each topic line, write key words to remind you of the topic you are working on.

Topic A: *little, education, training*

Source 1: *Verstegen*

II. Topic A: *little, education, training*

1. *< formal, education*
2. *@ 14, apprenticed, Verrocchio, training*
3. *learned, workshop skills*
4. *painting, drafting, carpentry*
5. *became, better, teacher*

Source 2: *Sources 2 and 3 will be sources obtained by students.*

II. Topic A: *little, education, training*

1. ___
2. ___
3. ___
4. ___
5. ___

Source 3: ___

II. Topic A: *little, education, training*

1. ___
2. ___
3. ___
4. ___
5. ___

Unit 8: Formal Essay Models

Fused Outline A

Choose facts from the key word outlines you made on your own paper from all sources for Topic A. Put them in an order that makes sense.

*II. Topic A: ____________________

1. ____________________
2. ____________________
3. ____________________
4. ____________________
5. ____________________
6. ____________________
7. ____________________

Clincher

*Topic A is paragraph II because a paragraph of introduction will be written in Lesson 27.

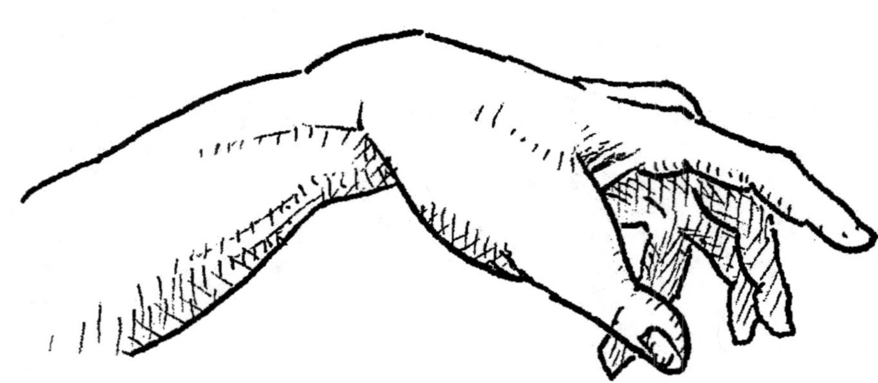

Lesson 26: The Renaissance, Part 1

Fused Outline B

Choose facts from the key word outlines you made on your own paper from all sources for Topic B. Put them in an order that makes sense.

*III. Topic B: ______________________________

1. ______________________________
2. ______________________________
3. ______________________________
4. ______________________________
5. ______________________________
6. ______________________________
7. ______________________________

Clincher

*Topic B is paragraph III because a paragraph of introduction will be written in Lesson 27. (You will work on Topic C in Lesson 27.)

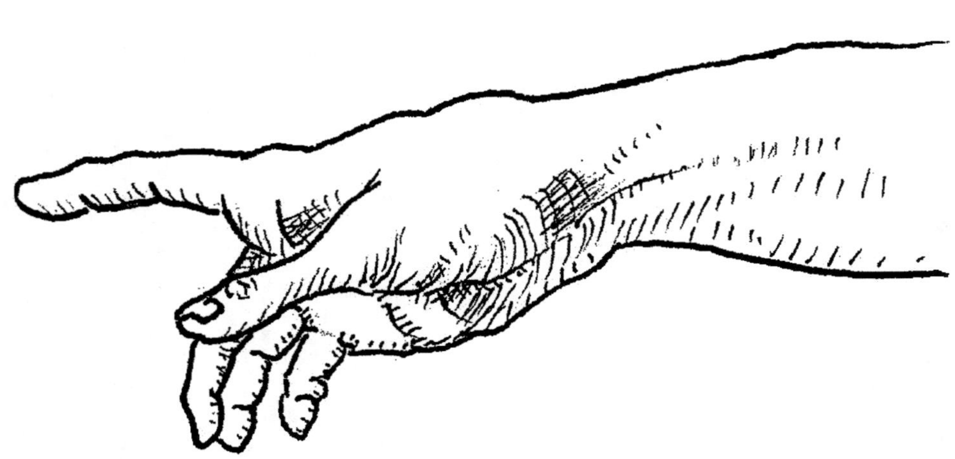

Unit 8: Formal Essay Models

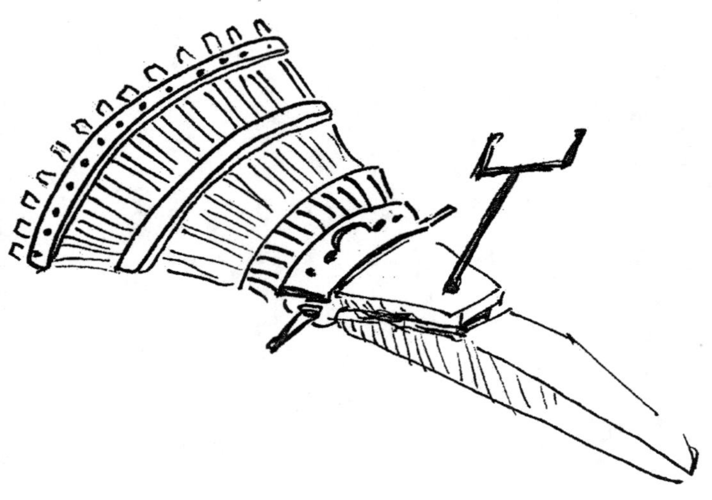

Lesson 27: The Renaissance, Part 2

Structure: IEW Unit 8: Formal Essay Models (Introduction and Conclusion)

Style: no new stylistic techniques

Writing Topic: Prominent Person of the Renaissance

Optional Student Reading Assignment: With Lessons 25–28 students may read *Crispin: The Cross of Lead* by Avi.

UNIT 8: FORMAL ESSAY MODELS

Lesson 27: The Renaissance, Part 2

Goals

- to practice the Unit 8 structural model
- to create key word outlines from multiple sources
- to create a fused outline
- to complete a 5-paragraph research essay with a bibliography

Do not collect the two body paragraphs from Lesson 26, but check to be sure the topic-clincher rule was followed.

Assignment Schedule

Note: Classes that meet weekly should complete Days 1 and 2 in class.

Day 1

1. With a teacher read and complete the Review section.
2. From two or three of your sources, create source outlines for Topic C for your Renaissance essay, as you did in Lesson 26 for Topics A and B. Read the Topic C Instructions on page 228 and use the paper you prepared in Lesson 26.
3. Fuse those notes into a fused outline on page 228.

   Note: Your teacher will decide how much of the above you must do in class and how much to complete at home. You should do enough to understand the main ideas of Topic C so that you can state Topic C in your introduction and conclusion.

Day 2

1. With the help of your teacher, create key word outlines and write a conclusion and an introduction for your research essay (page 229).
2. See Lesson 18, pages 157–158, to review how to create a bibliography page.

Day 3

1. Complete your 5-paragraph essay about a prominent person of the Renaissance, including a bibliography. Let an editor proofread.

Day 4

1. Write or type a final draft of your essay, making the corrections your editor asked you to make. Check off each item on the checklists (pp. 230–231) that you have completed and indicated as instructed.
2. Let an editor proofread again. He or she should check that all elements of structure and style are included and labeled as instructed on the checklists. Paperclip both checklists (pp. 230–231) to your final draft to be turned in.
3. If you are making a Magnum Opus Notebook, revise your knights research essay from Lesson 25. (See Appendix II.)

Unit 8: Formal Essay Models

Review

Read the topic and clincher sentences of each of the two body paragraphs you wrote for Lesson 26. Did you remember to highlight or bold two or three key words that are repeated or reflected?

Structure

Topic C Instructions

First, on the paper you prepared in Lesson 26, make source outlines from two or three of your sources for Topic C of your essay. Then, choose some of the notes in your outlines to put in the fused outline below. Put them in an order that makes sense. Remember to begin with key words that will help you write a topic sentence.

Fused Outline C

Choose facts from the key word outlines you made from all sources for Topic C.

IV. Topic C: ______________________________

1. ______________________________
2. ______________________________
3. ______________________________
4. ______________________________
5. ______________________________
6. ______________________________
7. ______________________________

Clincher

Here are sample outlines for an essay about Leonardo da Vinci:

Sample

Lesson 27: The Renaissance, Part 2

V. Key Word Outline for Conclusion

Topic A	*mostly, self-taught*
Topic B	*one, best, painters*
Topic C	*true, scientist*
Most significant	*⊘, ☺ w/old, strove, perfection*
Why?	*study, ➔ new, techniques*
	changed, art, forever

I. Key Word Outline for Introduction

Attention getter	*he, did, all*
Background	*Leo, multi-talented, Ren. Man*
	rebirth, arts, learning
	brilliant, led, way, 1400s
Topic A	*< formal, education, ? mind*
Topic B	*trained, artist. ➔ > painter*
Topic C	*+ studied, sciences ➔ > ideas*

Background Help: The paragraphs on page 218, which give background information about the Renaissance in general, might have facts that you could include in the background section of your introduction.

Unit 8 Composition Checklist

Lessons 26–27 : The Renaissance, Part 1 body paragraphs

Formal Essay Models

Institute for Excellence in Writing

Name: ______________________________

STRUCTURE		
☐ MLA format (see Appendix I)	______	1 pt
☐ topic-clincher sentences repeat or reflect 2–3 key words (highlight or bold)	______	3 pts
☐ checklist on top, final draft, rough draft, key word outline	______	2 pts
STYLE (one of each in each paragraph)		
¶2 ¶3 ¶4 Dress-Ups (underline)	(1 pt each)	
☐ ☐ ☐ -ly adverb	______	3 pts
☐ ☐ ☐ *who/which* clause	______	3 pts
☐ ☐ ☐ strong verb	______	3 pts
☐ ☐ ☐ quality adjective	______	3 pts
☐ ☐ ☐ *www.asia.b* clause	______	3 pts
☐ banned words: go/went, say/said, good/bad, big/little (-1 for each use)	______	pts
¶2 ¶3 ¶4 Sentence Openers (number; one of each as possible)	(1 pt each)	
☐ ☐ ☐ [1] subject	______	3 pts
☐ ☐ ☐ [2] prepositional	______	3 pts
☐ ☐ ☐ [3] -ly adverb	______	3 pts
☐ ☐ ☐ [4] -ing	______	3 pts
☐ ☐ ☐ [5] clausal - *www.asia.b*	______	3 pts
☐ ☐ ☐ [6] vss	______	3 pts
MECHANICS		
☐ spelling, grammar, and punctuation	______	6 pts
VOCABULARY		
☐ vocabulary words - label *(voc)* in left margin or after sentence		
Total:	______	45 pts
Custom Total:	______	pts

Teachers are free to adjust a checklist by requiring only the stylistic techniques that have become easy, plus one new one. "EZ+1."

Lesson 27: The Renaissance, Part 2

Unit 8 Composition Checklist

Lesson 27 : The Renaissance, Part 2 introduction and conclusion

Formal Essay Models

Name: ______________________

Institute for Excellence in Writing

STRUCTURE		
☐ MLA format (see Appendix I)	______	1 pt
☐ title centered	______	1 pt
Introduction		
☐ attention getter ☐ background ☐ topics stated (highlight or bold)	______	8 pts
☐ insert body paragraphs	______	3 pts
Conclusion		
☐ restate topics (highlight or bold) ☐ most significant/why ☐ final sentence repeats 1–3 key words for the title	______	8 pts
☐ checklist on top, final draft, rough draft, key word outline	______	3 pts
STYLE (one of each in each paragraph)		
¶1 ¶5 Dress-Ups (underline)	(1 pt each)	
☐ ☐ -ly adverb	______	2 pts
☐ ☐ *who/which* clause	______	2 pts
☐ ☐ strong verb	______	2 pts
☐ ☐ quality adjective	______	2 pts
☐ ☐ *www.asia.b* clause	______	2 pts
☐ banned words: go/went, say/said, good/bad, big/little (-1 for each use)	______	pts
¶1 ¶5 Sentence Openers (number; one of each as possible)		
☐ ☐ [1] subject	______	2 pts
☐ ☐ [2] prepositional	______	2 pts
☐ ☐ [3] -ly adverb	______	2 pts
☐ ☐ [4] -ing	______	2 pts
☐ ☐ [5] clausal - *www.asia.b*	______	2 pts
☐ ☐ [6] vss	______	2 pts
MECHANICS		
☐ spelling, grammar, and punctuation	______	4 pts
VOCABULARY		
☐ vocabulary words - label *(voc)* in left margin or after sentence		
Total:	______	50 pts
Custom Total:	______	pts

Teachers are free to adjust a checklist by requiring only the stylistic techniques that have become easy, plus one new one. "EZ+1."

Unit 8: Formal Essay Models

Lesson 28: "Genghis Khan and His Hawk," Part 1

Structure: IEW Unit 9: Formal Critique (Body Paragraphs)

Style: no new stylistic techniques

Writing Topic: "Genghis Khan and His Hawk"

Optional Student Reading Assignment: With Lessons 25–28 students may read *Crispin: The Cross of Lead* by Avi.

Teaching Writing: Structure and Style

Watch the sections for Unit 9: Formal Critique. At IEW.com/twss-help reference the TWSS Viewing Guides.

UNIT 9: FORMAL CRITIQUE

Lesson 28: "Genghis Khan and His Hawk," Part 1

Goals

- to be introduced to the Unit 9 Formal Critique structural model
- to create a key word outline
- to write the body paragraphs of a short story critique
- to correctly use some critique vocabulary
- to correctly use new vocabulary words: *analyze, aghast, tragic, rash*

Assignment Schedule

Note: Classes that meet weekly should complete Days 1 and 2 in class.

Day 1

1. With a teacher play a quick vocabulary game as suggested in the Review section.
2. With a teacher learn the basic structure of a critique by studying page 235.
3. With a teacher read "Genghis Khan and His Hawk" on page 236.
4. With a teacher key word outline paragraphs II–IV (the body paragraphs) that identify the main elements of the Story Sequence Chart on page 237. When you are done, tell back the meaning of each line of notes to be sure you understand them.

Day 2

1. Write the three body paragraphs of your critique. Remember, this is where you retell the basic elements of the Story Sequence Chart by identifying the setting, characters, conflict, climax, and resolution. *Use words from the Critique Thesaurus in Appendix III in your paragraphs*. For example, begin the first body paragraph with something such as *The setting of the story is* ____________________ or *The story is set in* ____________________.
2. Learn the new vocabulary words for Lesson 28: *analyze, aghast, tragic, rash*. How could you use these in your critique?

Day 3

1. Use your key word outline to finish writing the body paragraphs of the critique. Follow the checklist on page 244, Body and Style sections. Let an editor proofread.

Day 4

1. Write or type a final draft of your body paragraphs, making the corrections your editor asked you to make. Check off each item on the checklist on page 244 that you have completed and indicated as instructed.

2. Let an editor proofread again. He or she should check that all elements of structure and style are included and labeled as instructed on the checklist.
3. ***Important***: With a parent, discuss the questions on page 241. Be prepared to offer your responses in class next week.

Review

Play a quick vocabulary game from the Teacher's Manual. Include the new words for this lesson: *analyze, aghast, tragic, rash.*

Lesson 28: "Genghis Khan and His Hawk," Part 1

New Structure

The Critique Model

In this new unit you will be combining the skills of two previous units. You have learned the elements of a well-written story: the Story Sequence Chart. You have learned to write conclusion and introduction paragraphs for essays. In this unit you are going to use these skills to help you write critiques of literature.

When you critique a story, you do not retell it in its entirety. Instead, you explain the most important aspects of the story based on the Story Sequence Chart—just enough so your reader can follow your discussion of your opinion. This will create a brief summary of the story, with the setting, characters, conflict, climax, and resolution clearly identified. Then, you add a concluding paragraph in which you give your opinion about different aspects of the story. You tell what you like or do not like. Finally, you add an introduction paragraph to the beginning that gives some background information about the story and author.

The Unit 9 body paragraphs follow the Story Sequence Chart, and the elements required in the introduction and conclusion are specific to critiques.

Here is a model of the structure:

I. Introduction (attention getter, title, author, publisher, background)

II. Setting/Characters

III. Conflict/Problem

IV. Climax/Resolution

V. Conclusion (your opinion)

This model can be used to critique short stories, movies, novels, plays, TV shows, or anything that tells a story. An important part of a critique is the conclusion. Here you should tell what you like or dislike about the story without saying anything like "I think " or "in my opinion." For example, if you say, "It is a suspenseful story with plenty of thrilling action," your readers will know your opinion, but it will sound much more convincing than this: "I think it is a good story."

When you write a critique, the body paragraphs have clear opening sentences for *setting*, *conflict*, and *climax*, but they do not have clinchers. This is because the paragraphs move through the events of the story as each element of the Story Sequence Chart is discussed.

Source Text

Genghis Khan and His Hawk

Genghis Khan ruled the huge Mongolian empire in the early 1200s. He was a ruthless warrior and a respected king who commanded multitudes. When he was not at war, the khan enjoyed his favorite sport of hunting. And when he hunted, his loyal hawk always accompanied him. His hawk was his best friend. He loved his master, and he loved hunting. With his keen eyes and his master's great skill, their hunting expeditions were always a success.

One day while on a hunt, the khan wandered farther than he had intended. In an intense chase, a deer had led him out of the shade of the forest trees, and he found himself in a barren field with the sun beating down on his head. He was hot and thirsty. He had to find water soon, so he stopped pursuing the deer, which had disappeared anyway, and headed back to the forest to look for a stream.

As he approached the forest, he heard the soft, constant trickling of water. He followed the sound. It led him to a high cluster of massive rocks, over which a small flow of crystal clear water fell. It was a welcome sight! The khan quickly took his cup from his pack and placed it under the stream. When the cup was filled, he brought it to his lips, anticipating how cool and refreshing it would be. However, before he could take a drink, his hawk swooped down and knocked the cup from his hand. The khan was stunned and angered by this apparently cruel action and shouted, "You crazy bird! You've spilled my water all over the ground!"

The khan picked up his cup and again filled it with the water. But again when he lifted it to his lips, his hawk flew down and knocked the cup from his hand.

"Insolent bird!" he yelled as he waved his arms at his hawk. "You'll not deprive me of a drink a third time." With that, the khan readied his sword. When the bird dove for the cup a third time, the khan struck him with his sword. The bird plummeted to the ground, dead.

Now by the time the khan retrieved his cup, the flow of water had diminished so much that the cup was only filling one drop at a time. Impatiently, the khan decided to climb higher to find the source of the flow. As he neared the top ledge, he spotted a large pool. As he looked closer, he was aghast at what he saw. In the pool was a dead viper, cut at the throat so that all of its deadly venom had spilled into the water.

"What have I done?" he lamented, for at that moment he realized that his hawk had only been trying to save his life. "I have killed my best friend. What a rash fool I was not to have trusted him and to have let my temper consume me so."

With that, he climbed down the rocks, picked up the stricken bird, and headed home. He had lost a friend, but he had learned a valuable lesson he would never forget.

Sample

Lesson 28: "Genghis Khan and His Hawk," Part 1

Key Word Outline

In this lesson, key word outline and write only the body paragraphs that retell the story by identifying the Story Sequence Chart elements. Use words such as *setting*, *characters*, *conflict*, *climax*, *resolution* and their synonyms found on the Critique Thesaurus in Appendix III.

Characters and Setting

Describe the time and place the story occurs. This is the *setting*.

Name and describe each main character.

II. *set, forest, Mongolia, 1200s*

1. *characters, G. Khan, +, hawk*
2. *GK, ruthless, warrior, hunter*
3. *⊘, control, temper, rash*
4. *hawk, loyal, companion*
5. *begins, two, ☺ hunting*

Conflict or Problem

State the main problem of the story. In other words, what does the main character want or need? Identify this as the *conflict*.

Tell what the main characters do, say, and think in order to solve the problem.

Tell how the characters feel as they try to solve the problem.

III. *conflict, GK, needs, 💧*

1. *finds, dripping, rocks*
2. *fills, cup, hawk, ⬇, 2X*
3. *GK, irate, readies, sword*
4. *3rd X, kills, hawk*
5. *climbs, source, 💧*

Climax and Resolution

What event in the story reveals how the conflict will work out (whether the problem will be solved or not)? Identify this as the *climax*.

What is the outcome for the main characters at the end of the story? Identify this as the resolution.

IV. *climax, GK, 👁👁, viper, slit*

1. *water, poisoned*
2. *realizes, hawk, saved*
3. *hawk, XX, Khan, ⊘ 💧*
4. *khan, regrets, ⊘, trust*
5. *acting, anger, ➔ tragedy*

See the Body and Style sections of the checklist on page 244.

Use Precise Adjectives

(Examples: adventurous, sinister, impulsive, rash, reserved, kind, compassionate, loyal, honorable, untrustworthy ...)

Could you call one a hero or another a villain?

Unit 9: Formal Critique

Lesson 29: "Genghis Khan and His Hawk," Part 2

Structure: IEW Unit 9: Formal Critique (Introduction and Conclusion)

Style: no new stylistic techniques

Writing Topic: "Genghis Khan and His Hawk"

UNIT 9: FORMAL CRITIQUE

Lesson 29: "Genghis Khan and His Hawk," Part 2

Goals

- to practice the Unit 9 structural model
- to add an introduction and a conclusion paragraph to the short story critique
- to correctly use more critique vocabulary

Assignment Schedule

Note: Classes that meet weekly should complete Days 1 and 2 in class.

Day 1

1. In Lesson 28 you wrote the body paragraphs of a critique. In this lesson you will finish the critique by adding a conclusion and an introduction. With a teacher see page 235 to review the structure of a critique.
2. Discuss with your teacher what you like and do not like about the story. On your own paper, write down some ideas without using "I" or "my."
3. Using the blank outline on page 242 and the answers to the questions on page 241 to help you, write a key word outline for the conclusion.
4. Use page 243 to key word outline an introduction.

Day 2

1. Use your key word outline to write the conclusion paragraph of your critique. Follow the checklist on page 244 carefully. Let an editor proofread.

Day 3

1. Use your key word outline to write the introduction paragraph of your critique. Follow the checklist on page 244. Let an editor proofread.
2. There are no new vocabulary words. Review all.

Day 4

1. Write or type a final draft of your entire critique, making the corrections your editor asked you to make. This will be all five paragraphs from Lessons 28 and 29. In other words, add the introduction and the conclusion paragraph to the three body paragraphs you wrote in Lesson 28. Check off each item on the checklist (page 244) that you have completed and indicated as instructed.
2. Let an editor proofread again. He or she should check that all elements of structure and style are included and labeled as instructed on the checklists. Paperclip the checklist to your final draft to be turned in.
3. If you are making a Magnum Opus Notebook, revise your Renaissance essay from Lessons 26–27. (See Appendix II.)

Study for the Final Vocabulary Quiz. It will cover all of the vocabulary words.

Review

In the body paragraphs you wrote for Lesson 28, read the sentences in which you refer to the *setting, character, conflict, climax,* and *resolution*, using words found in the Critique Thesaurus in Appendix III.

Review the model of the structure for a critique:

I. Introduction (attention getter, title, author, publisher, background)

II. Setting/Characters

III. Conflict/Problem

IV. Climax/Resolution

V. Conclusion (your opinion)

New Structure

Conclusion and Introduction

The conclusion is where you must critique, or analyze. You must tell what you like or dislike about the story and why. Remember that you may not say anything like "I think " or "in my opinion." For example, if you say, "It is a suspenseful story with plenty of thrilling action," your readers will know your opinion, but it will sound much more convincing than this: "I think it is a good story."

Use the following pages to discuss and outline a conclusion and introduction for your critique of "Genghis Khan and His Hawk."

Lesson 29: "Genghis Khan and His Hawk," Part 2

The Conclusion

In the conclusion discuss what you like or dislike about the story and why. This will require you to consider each aspect of the story to determine what you like and what you do not like. The following questions should help.

Take time to discuss each of these questions with your students.

- What did you think of the story overall? What one word could you use to describe it? Begin your conclusion with a general statement that reveals your overall impression or opinion of the story. Do not use vague adjectives like *good, bad, interesting, wonderful,* and the like. Use specific adjectives. You may choose from the examples that follow or you may think of your own: *suspenseful, predictable, engrossing, boring, tragic, heart-wrenching, powerful, thought-provoking, inspiring, captivating.*
- Do not say *I* or *my*. Here is a template that may help:

  "*Genghis Khan and His Hawk*" is a ________________________________ story that

  ________________________________.

  Example: *"Genghis Khan and His Hawk" is a tragic story that teaches a powerful message.*

Then support your opinion by discussing *some* of the following.

- Is the style enjoyable? Does the author create vivid images? (Give examples.)
- What is the best part or aspect of the story? Why?
- What is the worst part or aspect? Why?
- Think about the characters. Were they appealing and realistic? Why or why not?
- Does the story have much action or adventure? Where?
- Was the conflict exciting? Why or why not?
- Does the story have suspense or mystery? Where? Did it intrigue you? Why?
- Why is the hawk's death so tragic? How will it affect readers?
- Was the climax (finding the serpent in the water) a surprise or predictable? What emotions will the reader feel at this point of the story?
- Are you happy with the resolution? Why or why not?
- Was it necessary that the hawk die? Would the message be as powerful if the hawk had only been injured?
- What are the messages? In other words, what does the story teach? What do you think about the messages? Do you agree with them?

The final sentence of the critique must repeat one to three words from the title.

Sample

Key Word Outline

Conclusion

Include some of your answers to the questions on page 241.

> Begin with your overall impression. (See page 241, top.)
>
> What do you like and dislike about the story? Why?
>
> Comments may be related to the characters, conflict, climax, resolution, or style. (See page 241.)
>
> What does the story teach? Did it do so effectively? How?
>
> Do you agree with the message? Why? Is it an important message that everyone could benefit from understanding? Why?

V. *"GK & H," ♥-wrenching, powerful, message*

1. *characters, intriguing, b/c GK, real*
2. *hawk, likeable, b/c loyal*
3. *mystery, hawk, knocking?*
4. *surprising, finds, viper*
5. *themes, powerful, b/c, hawk, XX*
6. *⊘ trust, anger ➔ regret*
7. *everyone, relate, b/c anger*

Title repeats 1–3 key words from final sentence.

Reminder: Never use *I*, *my*, *we*, *us*, *you*.

Sample

Lesson 29: "Genghis Khan and His Hawk," Part 2

The Introduction

The critique introduction differs from the introductions you have written in previous lessons. It begins similarly with an attention getter, but then it should contain basic information specific to the story: title, type of story, background of the story, author and his or her literary time, publisher, and date of publication.

Key Word Outline

Introduction

Attention getter	I.	*life, teaches, hard*
title, author	1.	*"GK & H," author ?, retold, L. Verstegen*
publisher, date	2.	*pub, IEW, 2018*
type of story	3.	*classic, moral tale*
background	4.	*GK, historical, Mongol [crown], 1200s*
	5.	*learns, tragic, lesson*

Background Help: For "Genghis Khan and His Hawk," there are several options for background information. You could give some facts about Genghis Khan since he is a real figure in history. The story tells that he was a ruthless warrior and king who ruled Mongolia in the 1200s. You could tell what happens in the story before the conflict develops. The conflict is that the khan needs water, so the background to this is that at the start of the story, the khan is on a hunting trip with his hawk and wanders out of the shade of the forest. You could also, instead, give a hint that the khan will learn a valuable lesson through a tragic mistake he makes on a hunting trip.

Unit 9 Composition Checklist

Lessons 28–29: "Genghis Khan and His Hawk," Parts 1 and 2

Formal Critique

Name: ______________________

Institute for Excellence in Writing

STRUCTURE			
☐ MLA format (see Appendix I)	______	2	pts
☐ title centered	______	4	pts
Introduction			
☐ attention getter	______	4	pts
☐ includes title, author, publisher and type of story, and background information	______	5	pts
Body			
☐ Unit 9: 3 paragraphs follow Story Sequence Chart (Unit 3) and include words from the Critique Thesaurus page in each paragraph	______	9	pts
Conclusion			
☐ your opinion of the story: well written or not, like/dislike and why, may also discuss character development, conflict, message, effect of story on reader	______	10	pts
☐ no "I," "my," "we," "us," "you" ☐ final sentence repeats 1–3 key words for the title	______	5	pts
☐ checklist on top, final draft, rough draft, key word outline	______	2	pts
STYLE (one of each in each paragraph)			
¶1 ¶2 ¶3 ¶4 ¶5 Dress-Ups (underline)	(1 pt each)		
☐ ☐ ☐ ☐ ☐ -ly adverb ☐ ☐ ☐ ☐ ☐ quality adjective	______	10	pts
☐ ☐ ☐ ☐ ☐ *who/which* clause ☐ ☐ ☐ ☐ ☐ *www.asia.b* clause	______	10	pts
☐ ☐ ☐ ☐ ☐ strong verb	______	5	pts
☐ banned words: go/went, say/said, good/bad, big/little (-1 for each use)	______		pts
¶1 ¶2 ¶3 ¶4 ¶5 Sentence Openers (number; one of each as possible)			
☐ ☐ ☐ ☐ ☐ [1] subject ☐ ☐ ☐ ☐ ☐ [4] -ing	______	10	pts
☐ ☐ ☐ ☐ ☐ [2] prepositional ☐ ☐ ☐ ☐ ☐ [5] clausal - *www.asia.b*	______	10	pts
☐ ☐ ☐ ☐ ☐ [3] -ly adverb ☐ ☐ ☐ ☐ ☐ [6] vss	______	10	pts
MECHANICS			
☐ spelling, grammar, and punctuation	______	4	pts
VOCABULARY			
☐ vocabulary words - label *(voc)* in left margin or after sentence			
Total:	______	100	pts
Custom Total:	______		pts

Teachers are free to adjust a checklist by requiring only the stylistic techniques that have become easy, plus one new one. "EZ+1."

Lesson 30: Character Analysis—"Seven in One Blow"

Structure: Response to Literature
Style: no new stylistic techniques
Writing Topic: "Seven in One Blow" ("The Brave Little Tailor")

RESPONSE TO LITERATURE

Lesson 30: Character Analysis—"Seven in One Blow"

Goals

- to be introduced to a Response to Literature model
- to correctly write a character analysis
- to be introduced to the TRIAC technique for developing a paragraph supporting an opinion

Assignment Schedule

Note: Classes that meet weekly should complete Days 1 and 2 in class.

Day 1

1. Begin class with the Final Vocabulary Quiz.
2. With a teacher play a vocabulary game as suggested in the Review section.
3. In Lessons 28–29 you learned to write a critique. In this lesson you will modify the model in order to focus on analyzing the character of a story.

   With a teacher read pages 246–247 to understand the structure of a character analysis paper. Also read the background information.
4. On pages 248–249 read the story "Seven in One Blow."
5. Using the blank outline on pages 250, write a key word outline of the introduction paragraph and Story Sequence Chart paragraph for your composition. Tell back the meaning of each line of notes to be sure you understand them.

Day 2

1. Use page 251 to discuss and key word outline a paragraph discussing whether the tailor is admirable. Words listed after the heading *Analysis* on the Critique Thesaurus (Appendix III) may help you express yourself.
2. Use your key word outlines to begin writing a 3-paragraph character analysis of the tailor. Follow the checklist carefully.

Day 3

1. Finish writing the 3-paragraph character analysis. Follow the checklist carefully. Let an editor proofread.

Day 4

1. Write or type a final draft, making the corrections your editor asked you to make. Check off each item on the checklist that you have completed and indicated as instructed.
2. Let an editor proofread again. He or she should check that all elements of structure and style are included and labeled as instructed on the checklist. Paperclip the checklist to your final draft to be turned in.

Review

Elements of the Story Sequence Chart:

I. Setting and Characters

II. Conflict or Problem

III. Climax and Resolution

Review

Play a vocabulary game from the Teacher's Manual to prepare for the final test.

What are the elements of the Story Sequence Chart?

Structure

Modifying the Critique Model: Character Analysis

In this lesson you will modify the critique model in order to focus on analyzing the character of a story. We call this type of composition a response to literature.

Here is the prompt:

Prompt

In the story on page 248, "Seven in One Blow," the tailor is a clever character who rids the town of a menacing boar and two evil giants, thus winning the princess and half of the kingdom. Read the story and decide whether the tailor is someone who should be admired. Defend your opinion with examples from the story.

Here is the model you will follow:

I. Introduction (attention getter, title, author, publisher, background)

II. Setting/Characters, Conflict/Problem, Climax/Resolution

III. Character Analysis

Notice that in the above model you will summarize the story in one paragraph rather than in three. This means that you will have to discuss only the most important elements and do so very briefly. You will have to leave much out. You will not retell all the details of the story.

Character Analysis: TRIAC

To help you structure the character analysis paragraph, you will learn a technique called TRIAC. TRIAC stands for five elements that should be part of your analysis paragraph. It is explained below, and there is a sample paragraph on the following page.

Topic	Begin with a topic sentence that answers the prompt.
Restrict	Restrict to a specific reason or point to support the topic.
Illustrate	Illustrate your reason or point with one or more passages from the story.
Analyze	Explain how or why the passage supports the topic.
Clincher	Repeat or reflect two or three key words from the topic sentence.

Lesson 30: Character Analysis—"Seven in One Blow"

Sample TRIAC Paragraph

Here is a sample paragraph using TRIAC to write a paragraph discussing whether the khan is admirable in "Genghis Khan and His Hawk."

[Topic] Genghis Khan is not admirable. **[Restrict]** He cannot control his anger, which makes him act rashly and foolishly. It also causes him to distrust his loyal friend. **[Illustrate]** When his hawk repeatedly knocks his cup of water from his hands, he does not take time to deduce the reason. In a fit of anger, he strikes his friend and kills him. **[Analyze]** He should have trusted his friend and not let his anger consume him so. He soon deeply regrets his hasty, evil deed. **[Clincher]** Because his anger causes him to kill his friend, the khan should be scorned, not admired.

Background Help: "Seven in One Blow" is a classic medieval fairy tale that appeared in a collection of stories by the Grimm brothers. They called it "The Brave Little Tailor." It has been retold many times by many people. Some versions have other titles, such as "The Valiant Tailor" and "A Dozen at One Blow." You can find longer versions in libraries or on the Internet. Walt Disney even made a cartoon of it in which Mickey Mouse plays the tailor. In each, the tailor bravely faces one or two giants.

Note: Jacob and Wilhelm Grimm lived in Germany in the late 1700s and early 1800s. They collected and wrote down over two hundred stories that had previously only been told orally, passed down for generations by the common people. Their book, *Grimms' Fairy Tales*, went through many revisions and is one of the best-selling books of all time. It includes stories such as "Cinderella," "Snow White," "Rapunzel," "Sleeping Beauty," "Little Red Riding Hood," "The Elves and the Shoemaker," "Hansel and Gretel," along with "The Brave Little Tailor" and many other familiar stories. The Grimm brothers are sometimes cited as the authors of these stories, but actually they were the editors.

Source Text

Seven in One Blow

It was a hot, humid summer day. A tailor sat in his shop with flies buzzing all around. Finally he became so perturbed that he grabbed a broom and—whack—he killed seven in one blow! He was so proud of himself that he decided everyone should know what a great thing he had done. So, he made a belt for himself. On the belt he stitched in large, fancy letters SEVEN IN ONE BLOW. Then he sauntered out into the village so everyone could see his belt and ask about his great feat. Sure enough, his belt caused quite a stir.

"Did you really kill seven with just one blow?" a woman asked.

"I sure did," bragged the tailor. Then he began to embellish the story a bit, conveniently forgetting to mention that his enemies were mere flies. "They had me surrounded, way overhead, high in the air and all around, but that did not scare me. I pulled out my weapon and struck."

Some of the people who heard the tailor tell his story thought he was talking about killing giants, for there had been several giants terrorizing the land. They ran to tell the king. The king sent for the tailor.

"Good tailor, I have heard that you killed seven giants in one blow. I need such a man as you to help rid the forest of a boar that continues to kill my men. If you will do this for me, I will give you half of my kingdom and my daughter to be your wife."

The tailor could not believe his good fortune. He wanted to be rich and to marry the princess, so he gladly accepted the challenge and headed for the forest. He did not confess that he had not killed giants. Eventually he spotted the boar. He also spotted an

Lesson 30: Character Analysis—"Seven in One Blow"

empty hut, and that gave him an idea. He opened the door and window of the hut. Then he summoned the boar. The boar angrily chased the tailor right into the hut, so the tailor jumped out the window and locked the door. He had trapped the beast.

When the tailor returned to the king, he asked for the princess.

The king replied, "That challenge was just a test. Your real challenge is to kill two more giants. They are brothers, and they live by the river. Can you do it?"

"Of course I can," boasted the tailor, "I killed seven in one blow!"

Soon the tailor found the two giants sleeping under a tree. He knew what to do. He filled his pockets with rocks and climbed the tree. He dropped rocks on one of the giants. The giant woke up and yelled at his brother, "Why are you hitting me?"

"I didn't hit you. You must be dreaming. Go back to sleep!"

The giants drifted back to sleep, and the tailor again dropped rocks, but this time on the other giant. He woke up angry.

"I told you I didn't hit you! Why are you hitting me now?" he yelled.

"I didn't hit you! Now *you* are dreaming."

When the giants fell back asleep, the tailor dropped rocks again, this time on both of them. They both woke up so angry that they fought and fought until they killed each other.

The tailor whistled a happy tune as he returned to tell the king of his success. The king gave him his daughter and half of his kingdom, just as he had promised. They all lived happily ever after.

Sample

Key Word Outline "Seven in One Blow"

Introduction

Attention getter Title, Author Publisher, Date Type of Story Background (See page 247 for help.)

I. *What makes 1 admirable?*

1. *"7 in 1 Blow," 1st, author?*
2. *retold, LV, pub, IEW, 2018*
3. *1, Bros. Grimm, fairy tales*
4. *many, versions, titles*
5. *tailor, defeats, giant(s)*
6. *tailor, worthy, praise?*

Hint: In response to literature papers in which you are answering a question from a prompt, you may repeat the basic question at the end of the introduction: *Is the tailor admirable?*

Story Sequence Chart

Briefly identify and describe the **setting** and main **characters**. What is the main **conflict**? (What is the main problem or want of the main character?) What happens? (What do the characters do, say, think, and feel?) What is the **climax**? (At what point in the story do you know if the main character will get what he wants?) What is the **resolution**? (What is the outcome for the main characters at the end of the story?) What does the story teach?

II. *set, medieval, town*

1. *tailor, clever, brave*
2. *conflict, desires, praise, + $$*
3. *XX, 7 flies, belt, "7 in 1"*
4. *ppl, think, XX, giants,*
5. *[speech bubble], [crown], calls, tailor*
6. *➔, praise, princess, ½ kingdom*
7. *teaches, cleverness, valor, rewarded*

(Use the next page for paragraph III.)

Lesson 30: Character Analysis—"Seven in One Blow"

Sample

Character Analysis

Note: You may use more than three words for each section. Illustrate and Analyze will likely require notes for more than one sentence.

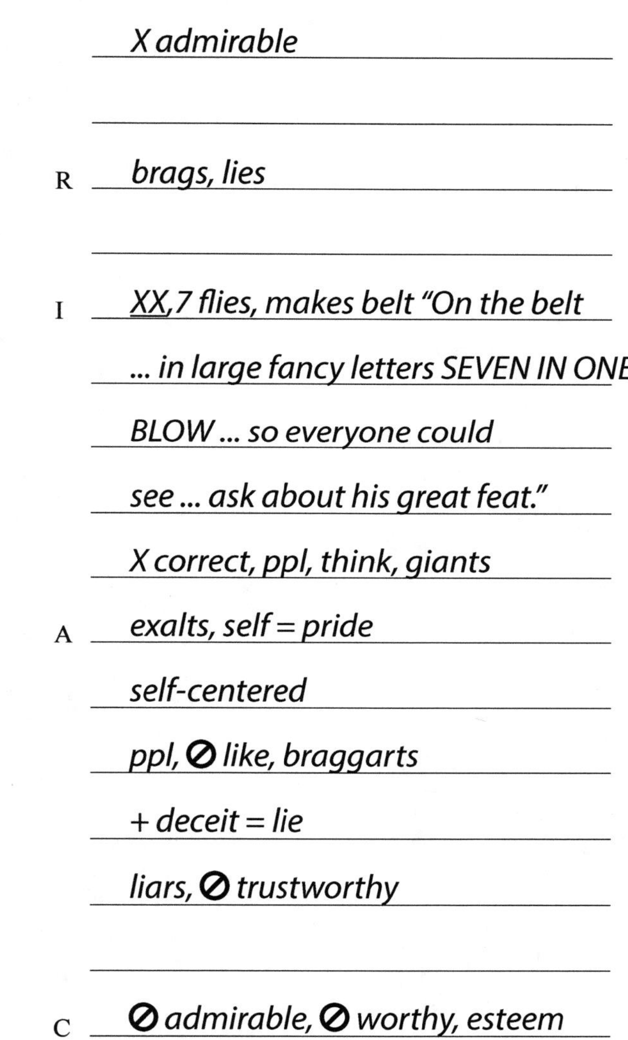

What makes 1 admirable?
III. T despite, success, tailor,
X admirable
R brags, lies
I XX,7 flies, makes belt "On the belt
... in large fancy letters SEVEN IN ONE
BLOW ... so everyone could
see ... ask about his great feat."
X correct, ppl, think, giants
A exalts, self = pride
self-centered
ppl, ⊘ like, braggarts
+ deceit = lie
liars, ⊘ trustworthy
C ⊘ admirable, ⊘ worthy, esteem

Topic sentence *(Is the tailor admirable?)*

Restrict to a specific reason *(Why or why not?)*

Illustrate with a specific passage or passages from the story

For example

Analyze *(How do passages support the topic? In other words, how do passages show the tailor is admirable or not admirable?)*

Clincher *(Repeat or reflect 2–3 key words from the topic sentence.)*

Title repeats 1–3 key words from final sentence.

To Illustrate

Students may give one passage as an example from the story, or they may give more than one passage.

To Analyze

Students may use words listed after the heading *Analysis* on the Critique Thesaurus (Appendix III) to express themselves.

Response to Literature

Composition Checklist

Lesson 30: Character Analysis—"Seven in One Blow"

Response to Literature

Institute for Excellence in Writing

Name: ______________________

STRUCTURE

☐ MLA format (see Appendix I)	______	2 pts
☐ title centered and repeats 1–3 key words from final sentence	______	4 pts
Introduction		
☐ attention getter	______	5 pts
☐ includes title, author, publisher and type of story, and background information	______	5 pts
Body		
☐ paragraph follows Story Sequence Chart (Unit 3) and includes words from the Critique Thesaurus page	______	9 pts
Character Analysis		
☐ TRIAC model	______	10 pts
☐ topic-clincher sentences repeat or reflect 2–3 key words (highlight or bold)	______	5 pts
☐ checklist on top, final draft, rough draft, key word outline	______	2 pts

STYLE (one of each in each paragraph)

¶1 ¶2 ¶3 Dress-Ups (underline)		(1 pt each)	
☐ ☐ ☐ -ly adverb	☐ ☐ ☐ quality adjective	______	6 pts
☐ ☐ ☐ *who/which* clause	☐ ☐ ☐ *www.asia.b* clause	______	6 pts
☐ ☐ ☐ strong verb		______	3 pts
☐ banned words: go/went, say/said, good/bad, big/little (-1 for each use)		______	pts
¶1 ¶2 ¶3 Sentence Openers (number; one of each as possible)			
☐ ☐ ☐ [1] subject	☐ ☐ ☐ [4] -ing	______	6 pts
☐ ☐ ☐ [2] prepositional	☐ ☐ ☐ [5] clausal - *www.asia.b*	______	6 pts
☐ ☐ ☐ [3] -ly adverb	☐ ☐ ☐ [6] vss	______	6 pts

MECHANICS

☐ spelling, grammar, and punctuation	______	5 pts

VOCABULARY

☐ vocabulary words - label *(voc)* in left margin or after sentence

Total:	______	80 pts
Custom Total:	______	pts

Teachers are free to adjust a checklist by requiring only the stylistic techniques that have become easy, plus one new one. "EZ+1."

Bonus Lesson: Vocabulary Story

Writing Topic: Familiar Story of Choice

If you have not been teaching the vocabulary portion of these lessons, please see the *Medieval History-Based Writing Advanced Additions e-book* for instructions for writing a rhyming story.

JUST FOR FUN

Bonus Lesson: Vocabulary Story

Goals

- to master the use of the vocabulary words
- to write an original version of a familiar story or to borrow a conflict to write an original story

Assignment Schedule

Note: Classes that meet weekly should complete Days 1 and 2 in class.

Day 1

1. With a teacher read the Review section.
2. Read pages 254–255 and follow the instructions.

Day 2

1. Key word outline your story idea using page 256.
2. Begin to write your story. Have the vocabulary chart in front of you to help you include as many vocabulary words as possible.

Day 3

1. Complete your story. (There is no checklist for this story. Just label your vocabulary words.) Let an editor proofread.

Day 4

1. Write or type a final draft, making the corrections your editor asked you to make.
2. Let an editor proofread again.
3. If you are making a Magnum Opus Notebook, revise your "Genghis Khan and His Hawk" critique from Lessons 28–29. (See Appendix II.)

Review

Introduction, three Story Sequence paragraphs (Setting/Characters; Conflict/Problem; Climax/Resolution), conclusion

Introduction, one Story Sequence paragraph; character analysis paragraph

T= Topic
R= Restrict to a specific reason
I= Illustrate with a passage from the story
A= Analyze how the passage supports the topic
C= Clincher

Review

What is the structure of a formal critique?

What is the structure of a 3-paragraph character analysis?

What does each letter of TRIAC stand for?

Structure

Vocabulary Story

This last lesson is a "just for fun" assignment. Writing a vocabulary story is not only a fun way to end the year, but it serves as a great review of the vocabulary words that you have learned.

The instructions are simple: Write a story using as many vocabulary words as you can. You may write a familiar story (such as an Aesop fable, a children's story, or a fairy tale), or you may make up your own story by borrowing a conflict from a familiar story. Borrowing a conflict is explained below.

Here are the rules:

1. Words must be used correctly and fit naturally.
2. You may not put more than three adjectives in front of one noun. (For example, you may not say something like this: *the fetid, massive, smug, tenacious monster*)

There is no checklist for this assignment, but tickets will be given as follows:

- One ticket is given for each vocabulary word used well and either underlined or bolded.
- If you use at least fifty vocabulary words, you earn 100 tickets. (Repeated words do not count.)

Read the sample at the end of this lesson to get the idea.

Borrowing a Conflict

It is difficult to come up with a completely original story; however, it is not as difficult to borrow a conflict in order to create your own story. Borrowing a conflict means that you take the basic "problem" of a story and change the characters and setting.

For example, the conflict of "The Tortoise and the Hare" is that one character (the hare) is proud and makes fun of another character (the tortoise) because he believes he is not as good at something (running). But the second character challenges the first to a contest and wins. How could we borrow this basic conflict and set the story in the Middle Ages with different characters?

How about an arrogant knight who constantly makes fun of a squire until the squire challenges him to a jousting contest. The arrogant knight could be distracted by showing off to a beautiful lady, which causes him to be off guard long enough for the squire to knock him from his horse.

Structure Practice

1. Below, list at least five children's stories. If you would like to try to change the setting and characters of your story, write an idea for doing so below each. Since this is a medieval history-based course, try to set your story in the Middle Ages. Remember, it is not required that you change the characters and setting. You may write any story and simply add many vocabulary words to it.

Here are a few examples:

"The Ugly Duckling"
"The Gingerbread Man"
"Little Red Riding Hood"
"Cinderella"
"Jack and the Beanstalk"
"Rumpelstiltskin"
"Goldilocks and the Three Bears"
"The Three Little Pigs"
"The Three Billy Goats Gruff"
"The Lion and the Mouse"

2. Now open to your chart of vocabulary words on pages 274–275. For each story you listed, see if you can quickly think of ways to use several of the vocabulary words in your story. If you cannot do so for one story idea, you should probably choose another to write.

Do not skip this step. Ask a few students to share their ideas.

You may want to host a class party. Encourage students to read the vocabulary story or a favorite story from Unit 5 or Unit 7. Consider having an auction in which students can use their tickets to buy prizes. (See Appendix VI for details about the auction.) If you prefer not to do an auction, consider a final review game such as simplified *Jeopardy*, also explained in Appendix VI.

Just for Fun

Key Word Outline—Story Sequence Chart

Characters and Setting

I. ______________________________

1. ______________________________
2. ______________________________
3. ______________________________
4. ______________________________
5. ______________________________

When does the story happen?

Who is in the story?

What are they like?

Where do they live or go?

Conflict or Problem

II. ______________________________

1. ______________________________
2. ______________________________
3. ______________________________
4. ______________________________
5. ______________________________

What does the main character need or want?

What do the characters do, say, think, and feel?

What happens before the climax?

Climax and Resolution

III. ______________________________

1. ______________________________
2. ______________________________
3. ______________________________
4. ______________________________
5. ______________________________

What leads to the problem being solved (the climax)?

What happens as a result?

What is learned? (message, moral)

Title repeats 1–3 key words from final sentence.

Bonus Lesson: Vocabulary Story

VOCABULARY STORY SAMPLE

Bonus Lesson

Daniel O.

Sir Braveone

In Ataland, by the **serene** Lake of Desire, there lived a **renowned** king with his three beautiful, **devout** daughters. Beyond the **massive** castle walls were four knights, who were raised to defend the land. However, Sir Lazyone sat **indolently** on the couch all day and dreamed about **ravishing** damsels. Sir Busyone spent all day **embellishing** and shining his armor until it sparkled like the stars. Sir Vainone enjoyed staring at himself **incessantly** in the mirror, fixing his **impeccable** hair this way and that. But Sir Braveone, because he was **intrepid**, **benevolently toiled** to rescue all the fair maidens in the kingdom. He never **fled** when there was a plea for help.

There were many damsels in distress in Ataland, especially the king's three beautiful daughters because they were so highly desired. The king's first daughter, Lady Beautifulone, was held **interminably** captive in the top of a **vacant** tower, **stymied** by a **devious** king. Sir Braveone asked, "Who will help me save Lady Beautifulone?"

"Not I," **rashly** replied Sir Lazyone.

"Not I," **smugly scowled** Sir Busyone.

"Not I," **hastily** hummed Sir Vainone.

"Then I will," **proficiently proclaimed** Sir Braveone. And he did.

The next day the king's second daughter, Lady Faithfulone, was cornered by a **fetid**, ferocious, fire-**spewing** dragon. Sir Braveone **bellowed**, "Who will help me **pursue** this beast and save Lady Faithfulone?"

"Not I," **rashly** replied Sir Lazyone.

"Not I," **smugly scowled** Sir Busyone.

"Not I," **hastily** hummed Sir Vainone.

"Then I will," **proficiently proclaimed** Sir Braveone. And he did.

The next day, the king's third daughter, Lady Fairone, was **wantonly apprehended** by an evil, **tenacious** knight. Sir Braveone yelled, "Who will help me save Lady Fairone?"

"Not I," **rashly** replied Sir Lazyone.

"Not I," **smugly scowled** Sir Busyone.

"Not I," **hastily** hummed Sir Vainone.

"Then I will," **proficiently proclaimed** Sir Braveone. And he did.

Imminently the king held a grand banquet to procure a suitor for his eldest daughter. Sir Lazyone jumped off the couch and rushed to the banquet. Sir Busyone dropped his armor and stormed to the castle. Sit Vainone turned from the mirror and paraded to the banquet. Sir Braveone was already there, making certain the king's young beautiful daughters were safe. When the king entered the banquet hall, he asked, "Who will marry Lady Beautifulone?"

"I will," volunteered Sir Lazyone.

"I will," **pleaded** Sir Busyone.

"I will," announced Sir Vainone.

But the king **earnestly** and **resolutely rebuked**, "Because, all by himself, Sir Braveone **nobly** and **astutely** rescued Lady Beautifulone from the devious king, Lady Faithful from the fire-breathing dragon, and Lady Fairone from the evil knight, he shall marry Lady Beautifulone. And he did. After that, whenever there were damsels in distress in need of being rescued, Sir Braveone had three knights who were eager to **brandish** their swords.

Contents

Appendices

Appendix I: Modified MLA Format

Format your paper in the following manner:

1. Double-space the entire composition, including the heading and title. Set 1-inch margins all the way around.
2. Only the first page should have the heading in the upper left corner with your name, lesson number, and the date.
3. If your paper is more than one page, every page (including the first) must have a header in the top right corner with your last name and page number. Look at the example below.
4. The text should be left justified. Use 12 pt Times New Roman or similar serif font. Paragraphs should be indented half an inch. There should only be one space after end punctuation to separate sentences.

Your essay should use the format shown below at 3/4 scale.

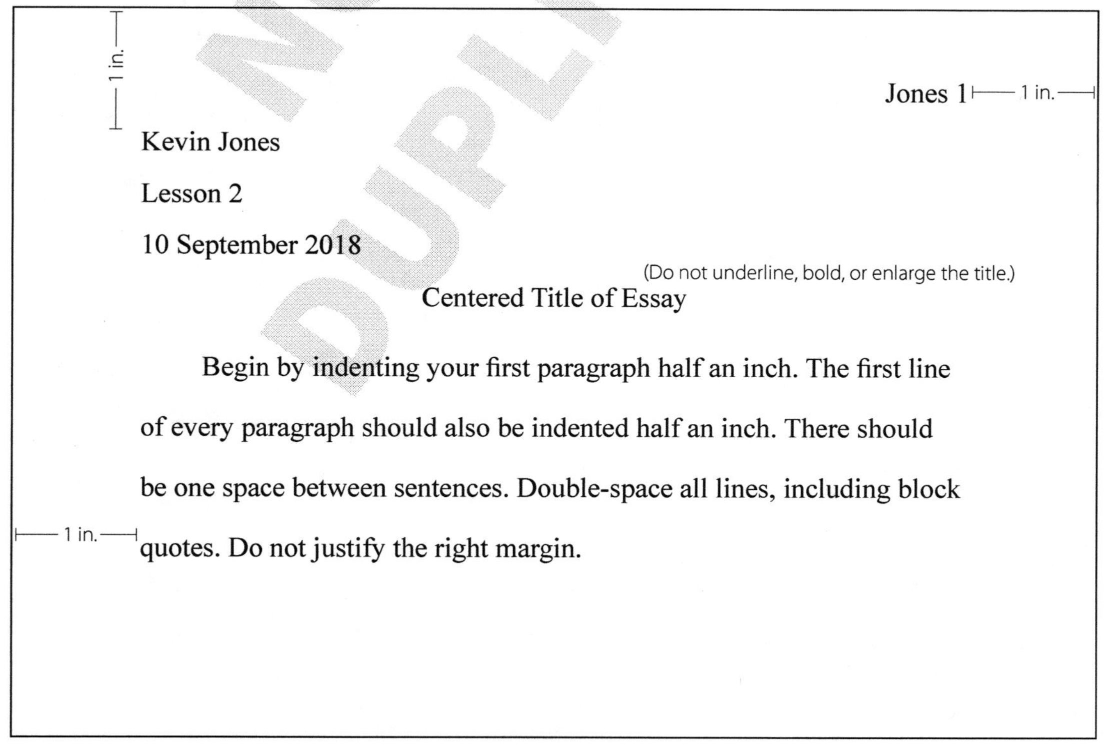

Kevin Jones

Lesson 2

10 September 2018

Centered Title of Essay

Begin by indenting your first paragraph half an inch. The first line of every paragraph should also be indented half an inch. There should be one space between sentences. Double-space all lines, including block quotes. Do not justify the right margin.

Appendices

Appendix II: Magnum Opus Notebook and Keepsake

If you choose to make a Magnum Opus Notebook, students should make the corrections noted by the teacher. Parents should help their students understand the reason for each correction. This last draft should have the stylistic technique markings removed.

The following page is the checklist that should be attached to each Magnum Opus draft if teachers require them to be turned in. To check, teachers simply make sure that each correction marked on the final draft has been made and that a picture has been added if desired.

Once returned, the Magnum Opus drafts should be kept in a half-inch binder in clear sheet protectors *with the original, labeled final drafts hidden behind the first page of each Magnum Opus draft.* At the end of the year, students will have a fine collection of a variety of types of compositions that move through major themes in medieval history.

Each student also may do an "About the Author" page as his title page. This can either be a paragraph about himself or an acrostic poem. For the poem option, each student writes his name in large, bold letters in a column down the page. He then uses each of the letters of his name as the first letter of each line of the poem describing himself. With either option, students may include a picture of themselves.

Another fun idea is to make a picture collage of the class for each of the students to put in the front of their notebooks. The students also sign one another's books on blank paper placed at the end of the notebook (like a yearbook) in a clear sheet protector. All these things make the Magnum Opus Notebook a wonderful keepsake of the year.

In a class setting, the teacher may display the Magnum Opus Notebooks at the end of the year at a Parent Day party.

Make copies of this page. You will need one checklist for each lesson.

Magnum Opus Draft Checklist

Each item is worth 5 points.

- ☐ Magnum Opus draft is in clear sheet protector(s) with the original final draft and checklist hidden behind the first page.
- ☐ Composition is neat and double-spaced.
- ☐ Elements of style missing on final draft have been added.
- ☐ Grammar and spelling corrections have been made.

Picture is added. (Optional)
(You may draw, or you may cut and paste from the Internet.)

***Note*:** Magnum Opus drafts do not have to be relabeled.

Total ___________/20

Magnum Opus Draft Checklist

Each item is worth 5 points.

- ☐ Magnum Opus draft is in clear sheet protector(s) with the original final draft and checklist hidden behind the first page.
- ☐ Composition is neat and double-spaced.
- ☐ Elements of style missing on final draft have been added.
- ☐ Grammar and spelling corrections have been made.

Picture is added. (Optional)
(You may draw, or you may cut and paste from the Internet.)

***Note*:** Magnum Opus drafts do not have to be relabeled.

Total ___________/20

Appendix III: Critique Thesaurus

Introduction	
Story	tale, saga, narrative, epic, legend, mystery, tragedy, comedy, romance, novel, yarn, anecdote, myth
Type	sad, nature, science fiction, love, adventure, historical, horror, folk, fairy, animal, moral, space, descriptive
Characters	players, actors, heroes, personae, participants, figures, villain, victim, protagonist, antagonist, foil
Role	main, central, leading, major, minor, subordinate, lesser, supporting, shadowy, background, secondary, foil
Types	adventurous, tragic, comic, bumbling, retiring, extroverted, pliant, scheming, sordid, acquisitive, inquisitive, impulsive, sinister
Analysis	well- or poorly-drawn, convincing, fully or underdeveloped, consistent, lifeless, too perfect, overly evil, idyllic, static, dynamic, flat, round
Setting	
Time	long ago, ancient or biblical times, Middle Ages or medieval, modern, contemporary, futuristic, mythical
Place	rural, urban, small town, frontier, pioneer, war, space, slums, ghetto, exotic
Mood	mysterious, foreboding, tragic, bland, comic, violent, suspenseful, compelling, sad, supernatural, emotional
Conflict	
Stages	initiated, promoted, continued, expanded, resolved
Intensity	exacerbated, heightened, lessened
Analysis	over- or under-played, realistic or unrealistic, convincing, contrived, stretched, sketchy
Plot	plan, conspiracy, scheme, intrigue, subplot, sequence of events, action, narrative, episode, unfolds
Climax	turning point, most exciting moment, dramatic event, high point, crisis, anticlimactic, inevitable conclusion
Theme	message, moral, lesson, topic, sub-theme, matter, subject
Literary Techniques	foreshadowing, symbolism, quality of language, short sentences, repetition, revelation of subplot to the narrative, suspense

Appendix IV: Adding Literature

Great literature will be a valuable addition to these lessons. There are many great books set in medieval times. The books below are suggested because their stories provide background to the compositions students will write in these lessons. Many of them make good read-aloud stories, and the G.A. Henty books are available as wonderful audiobooks.

Note: The Middle Ages was a dark and violent time in Europe. Some stories depict this more graphically than others. Notes of cautions are included for some of these to help you determine what would be appropriate for your children.

Lessons	Book
2–5	For elementary students: ***The Story of King Arthur and His Knights*, retold by Tania Zamorsky.** (This is a Classic Starts book published by Sterling Children's Books.) For junior high and high school students: ***King Arthur: Tales from the Round Table* by Andrew Lang** (Dover Evergreen Classics) Both of the above versions retell some of the most famous stories of the legendary King Arthur and his Knights of the Round Table, Merlin, Camelot, Excalibur, and more.
6–8	***One Thousand and One Arabian Nights* by Geraldine McCaughrean** or a younger children's version: ***Arabian Nights*** from the Classic Starts series (Sterling Publishing) ISBN 978-1-4027-4573-7 Set in Arabia, these stories tell of a king who has decided that to be sure a wife will never have time to betray him he must take a new bride each day and kill the former each night. So brave Shahrazad marries him and devises a clever plan to stop him. Each night she tells him a story that keeps the king wanting to hear more. He eventually grows to truly love her. In these books children will meet famous characters such as Sinbad the Sailor, Aladdin, and Ali Baba. Read all the stories or choose a few. ***Cautions***: The version by Geraldine McCaughrean is elegantly written and filled with wonderful similes; however, there are a couple of cautions. First, the story of Ali Baba includes content that may be disturbing. Parents should read it first and decide if those two chapters are appropriate for their children. Second, because it is an Arabian story, there are many references to Allah.

Lessons	Book
9–12	***The King's Shadow* by Elizabeth Alder or *Wulf the Saxon* by G.A. Henty** Both of these books are action-packed stories filled with history surrounding the Battle of Hastings. G.A. Henty was a Christian writer, and virtuous character is prominent in his stories, but his book is a more difficult read. A downloadable audio version of *Wulf the Saxon* is available at *LibriVox*. ***Caution***: In the first chapter of *The King's Shadow*, the main character is left dumb when villains cut out his tongue. It is tastefully depicted, but parents may want to read over this part and simply explain it to younger children.
13–15	***Robin Hood* by J. Walker McSpadden or a children's version** The legend begins with the transformation of young, noble Robert Fitzooth into Robin Hood, a gentleman robber and friend to the peasants. He leads a band of "merry men" in robbing the rich to give to the poor when England is suffering under the rule of greedy Prince John while King Richard is off fighting the Third Crusade.
16–18	**For elementary students: *The Door in the Wall* by Marguerite de Angeli** Set in England during the time of the Black Death, a ten-year-old boy, who is sent away from home to train to become a knight, loses the use of his legs. Robin finds himself alone as his parents are away, but he is befriended by a monk, Brother Luke. Through their adventures together, Brother Luke helps Robin find strength in his weakness. Brother Luke tells him, "Thou hast only to follow the wall long enough and there will be a door in it."
16–20	**For junior high and high school students: *Winning His Spurs: A Tale of the Crusades* by G.A. Henty** This is a wonderful book filled with exciting history about the struggle between Saxons and Normans in England, King Richard, the Crusades, and much more. Almost every page is filled with action and adventure. Being a G.A. Henty book, it extols virtuous character. It is available at *LibriVox*.

Appendix IV

Lessons	Book
20–22	**For elementary students:** ***Adam of the Road*** **by Elizabeth Janet Gray** Set in medieval England, this is the story of Adam, the son of Roger the jester. When the two are accidentally separated, Adam never gives up hope of finding his father as he travels the countryside.
21–23	**For junior high and high school students:** ***The Kite Rider*** **by Geraldine McCaughrean** This story is set in thirteenth-century China when Kublai Khan is ruling. It is the story of a poor peasant boy who is given the chance to escape poverty by becoming a kite rider in a circus. The story is a window into China's medieval culture and superstitions. ***Caution***: This story includes gambling, drinking, and murder. All are clearly portrayed as evil, but parents' discretion is advised for younger students.
24	***Marco Polo*** **by Demi** This is a 64-page picture book that can be read in a day or two. It is filled with beautiful pictures and fascinating information about medieval Europe, the Middle East, and China.
25–28	***Crispin: The Cross of Lead*** **by Avi** This is a Newbery Award winning story set in fourteenth-century England. *Book Report* says, it "is a superb combination of mystery, historical fiction, and a coming-of-age tale ... Breathlessly paced, beautifully written, and filled with details of life in the Middle Ages."

Appendices

Weekly Literature Response Sheet

Each week, **as you read**, do the following:

1. Circle unfamiliar words or words that you particularly like and might want to use in your own writing.
2. Highlight or underline a few elements of style that you particularly like, such as dress-ups and decorations that you have learned and vivid descriptions. *(If you are not allowed to mark in your book, use sticky notes.)*

After you are finished reading each section, do the following:

At the top of a paper, under your name and date, write the book title and the chapter numbers you read. Then format your paper like this:

Vocabulary

Under this heading, write two of the words you circled. Follow each with its definition and the sentence and page number in which it was used in the book.

Dress-Ups

Under this heading, write one of the dress-ups you highlighted or underlined. Write the entire sentence in which it occurs and underline the dress-up.

Summary

Write the most significant events of each chapter you read. Write three to five sentences per chapter.

When you finish the entire book, fill out the Final Literature Response Sheet (page 271) instead of doing the above.

Final Literature Response Sheet

After you finish a book, use your own paper to answer the following questions. Then discuss your answers with the class.

1. What is the title and author of the book?
2. What is the setting of the book? Describe it.
3. Describe each main character (no more than four).
4. What is the main conflict of the story? (What is the main problem, want, or need of the main character?) Write in complete sentences, but be brief.
5. Are there other important conflicts?
6. What is the climax of the main conflict? (What event leads to the conflict being solved?)
7. What is the resolution? (How do things work out in the end?)
8. Is there a message in the story? If so, what did the main character learn, or what should you, as the reader, have learned?
9. What is your favorite part of the story? Why?
10. What other things do you like or not like about the story?

Appendices

Appendix V

Appendix V: Vocabulary

Most of the lessons have a sheet of four vocabulary cards. In lessons that have cards, you will be instructed to cut them out and place them in a plastic bag or pencil pouch for easy reference. Each week you should study the words for the current lesson and continue to review words from previous lessons. You should try to use the vocabulary words in your compositions. For this purpose, you may use any of the words, even from lessons you have not yet had if you would like to look ahead.

For convenience, the following chart shows the words that go with each lesson and where quizzes fall. Quizzes are cumulative and cover all the words listed above them.

Quizzes can be found after the chart. Teachers who do not want students to see the quizzes ahead of time may ask you to tear them from your books and turn them in at the beginning of the school year. This is at the discretion of your teacher.

Vocabulary at a Glance

Lesson 1	fetid	stinky
	massive	huge
	dilapidated	partly ruined; broken down
	intrepid	fearless
Lesson 2	capably	having ability
	tenaciously	without giving up or letting go
	brazenly	without shame; boldly disrespectful
	benevolently	kindly; with a desire to help others
Lesson 3	reverently	with feelings of deep respect
	astutely	wisely; with understanding and skill to make the right choice
	earnestly	sincerely; seriously
	pursue	to chase
Quiz 1		
Lesson 4	resolutely	with determination; firm in purpose
	uniformly	without changing; of the same form or manner
	nobly	in a way that shows high moral character
	opulently	richly
Lesson 5	fatally	in a way that causes death or disaster
	hastily	quickly and with little thought
	spew	to force out in a large amount, especially in anger or disgust
	brandish	to wave threateningly
Lesson 6	extol	to praise highly
	flee	to run away, as from danger
	rebuke	to blame or find fault with
	intrigue	to captivate; to cause to be curious or fascinated
Quiz 2		
Lesson 7	proclaim	to announce or declare
	retreat	to withdraw
	embellish	to decorate; to add fanciful details
	deduce	to figure something out based on what you know
Lesson 8	disclose	to uncover or reveal
	contritely	sorrowfully; being sincerely sorry
	scowl	to look angry
	dislodge	to remove or force out
Lesson 9	reform	v: to improve; n: an improvement
	restrain	to hold back from doing something
	apprehend	to seize; to capture
	renowned	famous; of good reputation
Lesson 10	wanton	merciless; uncalled for and cruel
	merciless	having no compassion
	imminent	happening soon
	unrivaled	supreme; having no equal
Quiz 3		

Appendix V

Lesson 11	prominent	standing out; leading, important, or well-known
	myriad	a great number
	virtuous	having moral or admirable qualities
	bestow	to give or grant
Lesson 12	endure	to hold out against; to last
	smug	highly pleased with oneself
	proficient	skilled or expert
	treacherous	dangerous; untrustworthy
Lesson 13	relish	to like very much
	scramble	to move quickly in a panicked manner
	bewildered	puzzled
	anguish	great suffering in mind or body
Lesson 14	din	a loud, confused, or clanging noise
	cower	to crouch in fear or shame
	brim	the upper edge of anything
	frantically	emotionally out of control
Quiz 4		
Lesson 15	gravely	seriously; solemnly
	fatigued	tired or worn out
	insolent	disrespectful; boldly rude or insulting
	scorn	to reject with disgust
Lesson 16	grandiose	grand in an impressive way
	serene	calm and peaceful
	toil	to work hard; to labor
	contrive	to scheme
Lesson 17	primarily	mostly; chiefly
	elite	a socially superior group
	allegiance	loyalty or devotion
	impeccable	perfect
Lesson 18	agile	able to move quickly and easily
	devoted	zealous or fervent in attachment and loyalty
	feeble	weak (may be in body or mind)
	clad	clothed
Quiz 5 No new words for Lessons 19–21		
Lesson 22	credible	believable
	foremost	first in place, order, or rank
	stymie	to block or hinder
	indolent	lazy
No new words for Lessons 23–27		
Lesson 28	analyze	to examine the parts of something
	aghast	struck with horror, fright, or overwhelming amazement
	tragic	extremely unfortunate
	rash	too hasty in action; reckless
Final Quiz No new words for Lessons 29–30		

Appendices

Vocabulary Quiz 1 Answer Key

astutely	capably	fetid	pursue
benevolently	dilapidated	intrepid	reverently
brazenly	earnestly	massive	tenaciously

Fill in the blanks with the appropriate word. Be sure to spell correctly.
Two words in the box are not used.

1. stinky	1. *fetid*
2. huge	2. *massive*
3. fearless	3. *intrepid*
4. without giving up or letting go	4. *tenaciously*
5. kindly; with a desire to help others	5. *benevolently*
6. to chase	6. *pursue*
7. sincerely; seriously	7. *earnestly*
8. having ability	8. *capably*
9. partly ruined; broken down	9. *dilapidated*
10. wisely; with understanding and skill	10. *astutely*

Appendices

Vocabulary Quiz 2 Answer Key

brandish	fatally	intrepid	opulently	reverently
brazenly	flee	intrigue	rebuke	spew
extol	hastily	nobly	resolutely	uniformly

Fill in the blanks with the appropriate word. Be sure to spell correctly.

1.	without shame; boldly disrespectful	1.	*brazenly*
2.	to run away, as from danger	2.	*flee*
3.	with feelings of deep respect	3.	*reverently*
4.	fearless	4.	*intrepid*
5.	with determination; firm in purpose	5.	*resolutely*
6.	without changing; of the same form	6.	*uniformly*
7.	to blame or find fault with	7.	*rebuke*
8.	quickly and with little thought	8.	*hastily*
9.	in a way that shows high moral character	9.	*nobly*
10.	to force out in a large amount	10.	*spew*
11.	richly	11.	*opulently*
12.	in a way that causes death or disaster	12.	*fatally*
13.	to wave threateningly	13.	*brandish*
14.	to praise highly	14.	*extol*
15.	to captivate	15.	*intrigue*

Vocabulary Quiz 3 Answer Key

apprehend	disclose	extol	rebuke	restrain
contritely	dislodge	imminent	reform	retreat
deduce	embellish	proclaim	renowned	wanton

Fill in the blanks with the appropriate word. Be sure to spell correctly.

1.	to praise highly	1. *extol*
2.	to blame or find fault with	2. *rebuke*
3.	to uncover or reveal	3. *disclose*
4.	to announce or declare	4. *proclaim*
5.	to remove; to force out	5. *dislodge*
6.	to decorate; to add fanciful details	6. *embellish*
7.	to figure something out based on what you know	7. *deduce*
8.	sorrowfully; being sincerely sorry	8. *contritely*
9.	to improve	9. *reform*
10.	to hold back from doing something	10. *restrain*
11.	to withdraw	11. *retreat*
12.	happening soon	12. *imminent*
13.	to seize; to capture	13. *apprehend*
14.	famous; of good reputation	14. *renowned*
15.	merciless; uncalled for and cruel	15. *wanton*

Vocabulary Quiz 4 Answer Key

anguish	contritely	merciless	proficient	treacherous
bewildered	cower	myriad	scramble	unrivaled
brim	din	opulently	smug	virtuous

Fill in the blanks with the appropriate word. Be sure to spell correctly.

1.	richly	1.	*opulently*
2.	sorrowfully; being sincerely sorry	2.	*contritely*
3.	having no compassion	3.	*merciless*
4.	supreme; having no equal	4.	*unrivaled*
5.	skilled or expert	5.	*proficient*
6.	a great number	6.	*myriad*
7.	having moral or admirable qualities	7.	*virtuous*
8.	highly pleased with oneself	8.	*smug*
9.	dangerous; untrustworthy	9.	*treacherous*
10.	to move quickly in a panicked manner	10.	*scramble*
11.	puzzled	11.	*bewildered*
12.	great suffering in mind or body	12.	*anguish*
13.	a loud, confused, or clanging noise	13.	*din*
14.	to crouch in fear or shame	14.	*cower*
15.	the upper edge of anything	15.	*brim*

Appendices

Vocabulary Quiz 5 Answer Key

astutely	devoted	fatigued	intrigue	serene
bestow	elite	grandiose	relish	toil
contrive	endure	impeccable	scorn	wanton

Fill in the blanks with the appropriate word. Be sure to spell correctly.

1.	wisely; with understanding and skill	1.	*astutely*
2.	to captivate	2.	*intrigue*
3.	merciless; uncalled for and cruel	3.	*wanton*
4.	to give or grant	4.	*bestow*
5.	to hold out against; to last	5.	*endure*
6.	to like very much	6.	*relish*
7.	tired or worn out	7.	*fatigued*
8.	to reject with disgust	8.	*scorn*
9.	grand in an impressive way	9.	*grandiose*
10.	to work hard; to labor	10.	*toil*
11.	calm and peaceful	11.	*serene*
12.	to scheme	12.	*contrive*
13.	a socially superior group	13.	*elite*
14.	perfect	14.	*impeccable*
15.	zealous or fervent in attachment and loyalty	15.	*devoted*

Final Vocabulary Quiz   Answer Key

aghast	credible	frantically	primarily	retreat
agile	embellish	imminent	prominent	smug
analyze	fatally	indolent	pursue	stymie
anguish	feeble	insolent	rash	tragic

1.	to chase	1. *pursue*
2.	in a way that causes death or disaster	2. *fatally*
3.	to withdraw	3. *retreat*
4.	to decorate; to add fanciful details	4. *embellish*
5.	to block or hinder	5. *stymie*
6.	happening soon	6. *imminent*
7.	standing out; leading	7. *prominent*
8.	great suffering in body or mind	8. *anguish*
9.	emotionally out of control	9. *frantically*
10.	disrespectful; boldly rude or insulting	10. *insolent*
11.	weak	11. *feeble*
12.	mostly; chiefly	12. *primarily*
13.	able to move quickly or easily	13. *agile*
14.	highly pleased with oneself	14. *smug*
15.	believable	15. *credible*
16.	to examine the parts of something	16. *analyze*
17.	struck with horror, fright, or amazement	17. *aghast*
18.	extremely unfortunate	18. *tragic*
19.	too hasty in action; reckless	19. *rash*
20.	lazy	20. *indolent*

Appendix VI: Motivating Students: Tickets and Games

Students should be rewarded for jobs well done. Positive reinforcement is a wonderful motivator. In my classes I have found a ticket system extremely effective. To use such a system, purchase a roll of raffle tickets from an office supply store. In addition, make 5-, 10-, and 25-point tickets printed on colored paper. (A table with two columns and five rows works well.)

Give tickets for any of the advanced additions done and for anything done particularly well. I always give a ticket for each vocabulary word used.

Periodically I have contests for tickets, such as "Best Title" or the best of each type of dress-up or decoration. I also give tickets for winning review games such as those described below. Tickets may be used in an auction twice a year: once just before Christmas and once at the end of the year.

The Auction

There are many ways to do an auction. Here is how I do mine. You will want a calculator.

1. Students bring one to three items to auction to class. These can be new, or they can be items they have at home and think someone else would like. I sometimes fill in with items from the dollar store and with candy. Two items per student works well.
2. Students put their tickets in an envelope with their name and number of tickets written on the outside and turn them in to you.
3. You write the students' names and number of tickets on a whiteboard in order from greatest to least. Instead of having students physically hand you tickets when they buy and sell, you can add and subtract from their totals.
4. To begin, ask the student with the most tickets which item he would like to be auctioned first. When he chooses, he is bidding, so he should choose something he would like. Bids must begin at 25 or higher.
5. Students who would like the item continue to bid. The highest bidder receives the item. His bid is subtracted from his ticket total and added to the total of the person who brought the item. (***Note***: I set a maximum of 100 tickets to be added, regardless of how many tickets were paid.)
6. Repeat this process, letting the second student listed on the board choose the next item. Then the third student, and so forth.
7. ***Important***: Once a student has purchased an item, he may not bid on another item until everyone has bought one item. (This means that the last person will get his pick of what is left for 25 tickets.)
8. Once everyone has one item, it is open bidding for what is left.

Games

The best motivator I have found in all my years of teaching is playing games that teach and review concepts. Below are a few that are suggested in the lessons.

No-Noose Hangman

This is a great game to play at the beginning of class as you wait for last minute stragglers to arrive. It allows you to review any concept from previous lessons while engaging the students right from the start.

1. Think of anything you would like to review. Put it into a simple list or phrase. For example, if you want to remind your students to highlight the key words in their topic sentence and clincher, you might use “highlight key words” as your phrase.
2. On a whiteboard, write a blank for each letter in your phrase:

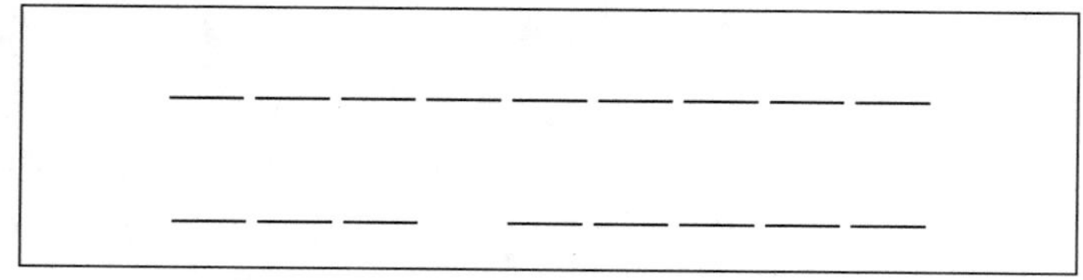

3. Students take turns guessing letters, one letter per turn. If the letter is in the puzzle, place it on the correct blank(s) and give the student a ticket for each time it is used. (Exception: Do not give tickets for vowels.) If the letter is not in the puzzle, write it on the bottom of the whiteboard so no one else will guess it.
4. Anytime a student knows the phrase, he may raise his hand to solve the puzzle. *It does not have to be his turn.*
5. If he solves the puzzle correctly, he receives 3 tickets. If he can then answer a bonus question about the phrase, he receives 2 more. (A bonus question for the above puzzle could be, “In which sentences do you highlight the key words?”)
6. Repeat with several puzzles.

Vocabulary Hangman

To play with vocabulary words, use the definition as the puzzle. When solved, the student who solved it must give you the matching word to receive the points or tickets.

Vocabulary around the World

This is my other "start of class" game.

1. Start with two students. Read a definition. The first to shout the correct vocabulary word receives a ticket and moves on to challenge the next student.
2. Continue in the same way. The winner always moves on to the next student. If one student makes it all the way "around the world" (beats everyone in the class), he receives five extra tickets.

Vocabulary Elimination

1. Divide the class into groups of three or four students. Try to have an even number of groups. Go to one group. Read a definition of a vocabulary word. The first student in that group to shout out the matching word gets a ticket. Continue with the first group until one student has three tickets. He has eliminated the rest of his group. Repeat with the other groups.
2. Repeat with half of the winners as one group, then with the other half. Finally, repeat with the two remaining students. The winner of that round receives five extra tickets.

Vocabulary Lightning

Supplies needed: a stack of vocabulary cards (borrow from a student)
a timer

Divide the class into two or three teams. Then, for each round, do the following:

1. Choose one or two players from one of the teams to come up in front of their team. Show them the stack of vocabulary cards with the word sides up. (They may not look at the definition side.)
2. Their job will be to try to get their team to say as many of the vocabulary words as they can in one minute. To do so, once the timer is set, they look at the first word and give their team clues, such as saying the definition if they know it, acting out the word, or describing the picture on the card. They may not say things such as what letter the word begins with or what it rhymes with. (***Optional***: Do not allow talking—only acting.)
3. As soon as someone from their team shouts the correct word, you (the teacher) should place the card on a table and move to the next word. If they get stuck on a word, they may "pass" it, but they will be penalized one point. Be sure to place passed word cards in a separate stack from the word cards they guess correctly.
4. When the time is up, count the number of words their team guessed. Subtract the number of words they passed. That difference is their score for that round. Then, let the other team(s) have a turn in the same way. The team with the highest score wins that round. Play several rounds if you have time.

Vocabulary Pictionary (A favorite!)

Supplies needed: two whiteboards (or one large one with a line sectioning it) or substitute paper and pencils
two whiteboard markers
a die (optional)

1. Divide the class into two teams. Assign each a whiteboard. Call one person from each team to the front of the class. Have them each roll the die to determine the number of points their team will receive if they win the round. Instruct them to write that number on the top of the whiteboard, so it is not forgotten. (The die is optional. You can just make each round won worth a point.)
2. Show the two students who came up which vocabulary word you want them to draw. They will both draw the same word.
3. When you say, "Go," they must draw a picture to try to get their team to say the chosen word. They may not include any letters or numbers in their drawings. The first team to guess the word receives the number of points rolled on their die. The other team erases the points they rolled. Play again with two new drawers.

Find the Card

Write each of the vocabulary words you wish to review on a separate 3x5 inch note card. Spread them out face up on a table and let the students study them for thirty seconds. Then turn them all face down. (In a large class, use larger cards and a pocket chart.)

Players (or teams), in turn, do the following:

1. The teacher reads the definition of one of the words. The first team must turn over one of the word cards, trying to find the word that matches the definition.
2. If the word matches the definition, that team receives two points, and the word card is returned to its spot on the table face down so that all word cards remain on the table the entire game. Play would then continue with the next team and the next definition.
3. If the word card does not match the definition, the word card is returned, and the next team attempts to find the correct word for the same definition. Now the correct word is worth three points. If missed again, the next team tries for four points. Continue in this way until the correct word is found. Limit the point value to 6.

   Note: When an incorrect word is turned over, award one point if the team that picked it can give its correct definition.
4. Continue as above until all definitions have been used. The player or team with the most points wins.

Tic-Tac-Toe (or Connect Four)

Supplies needed: about twenty questions

(Make your own, use vocabulary definitions, or choose from pages 296–297.)

a whiteboard or paper and pencil

two dice

1. Draw a Tic-Tac-Toe board on a whiteboard or paper. Number the squares 1–9.
2. Players are divided into an X team and an O team. They take turns trying to answer one of the questions. (You read one to them.)
3. If they answer correctly, place their X or O in the square of their choice. They then roll two dice. The dice will determine whether they make special moves:

(Write this on the whiteboard for all to see.)
A total of 7 = Take an extra turn.
Double 1, 2, or 3 = Erase an opponent's mark.
Double 4, 5 = Erase an opponent's mark and replace it with yours.
Double 6 = WILD. Go anywhere. You may erase your opponent's mark if need be.

4. Play until one team has three in a row or all squares are filled.
5. Repeat until one team has won two out of three or three out of five games.

Twenty Questions (or whatever number you desire)

Supplies needed: a whiteboard

a die

Choose questions from the list on pages 296–297. (I usually choose twenty). Number each differently each time you play.

Write the numbers 1 through 20 (or however many questions you want to ask) on a whiteboard.

1. Divide the class into three teams.
2. On each team's turn, they choose a number, and you read the corresponding question from your list. If a team answers correctly, they roll the die for points, and you erase the number from the board, so that question will not be chosen again.
3. If they answer incorrectly, you circle the number. That team gets no points. Now another team may choose that number for double points on their turn.
4. To add some fun, write "Lose a turn" or "Free roll" by two of your numbers.
5. Play until most questions have been chosen and teams have had an equal number of turns. Each player on the team with the most points receives five tickets.

Simplified Jeopardy!®

This makes a good end-of-the-year game. To prepare, you must write questions on 3 x 5 inch note cards. The questions should be categorized as pertaining to *Structure*, *Style*, or *Vocabulary*. They should also be ranked with respect to their level of difficulty (1 = easy; 2 = medium; 3 = difficult). Write a question on one side of each card and the category and level of difficulty on the other side. You may write as many questions as you like for each category.

Supplies needed: all of the cards
three dice
a whiteboard

1. Lay the cards, question side down, across a table in three rows by three columns. Stack cards of matching category and level of difficulty.

Structure	Style	Vocabulary
1 (easy)	1 (easy)	1 (easy)
2 (medium)	2 (medium)	2 (medium)
3 (difficult)	3 (difficult)	3 (difficult)

2. Divide the class into three teams. Teams take turns choosing a question by category and level of difficulty. If the team chooses a Level 1 (easy) question, they may roll one die to determine its point value. If they choose a Level 2, they roll two dice. For a Level 3, three dice.
3. If the team answers the question correctly, they receive the points indicated on the dice. Keep track of points on the whiteboard.

   If they do not answer correctly, they do not get any points. Do not give away the correct answer yet. The missed card should be placed face up as a jeopardy question. This means another team may choose it when it is their turn. Any team that can answer a previously missed question receives double the point value that they roll with two dice. However, if they miss it, they must subtract the points rolled (not doubled).
4. Jeopardy!: If a team rolls a total of 5, the question becomes a jeopardy question. This means that if they miss it, 5 points will be subtracted from their point total. However, if they answer correctly, they receive double points, which will be 10 points.
5. Play until time runs out, but be sure each team has had the same number of questions.

Sentence Stretching

This is fun to play at the beginning of class as a "warm up."

1. Write a basic subject-verb sentence on the whiteboard.

   Example: The boy fell.

2. Under this write at least three elements of style you would like to review. I usually do one or two dress-ups, a sentence opener, and a decoration. Of course, you can only include elements you have taught thus far. The decorations (*alliteration, similes, metaphors, and 3sss*) are taught in the *Advanced Additions e-book* of this course. If you have not taught them, leave them out.

   Example: quality adjective, *who/which* clause, #5 opener, alliteration

3. Divide students into teams and give them two minutes to stretch the basic sentence by including all the elements of style you listed. They may add ideas to the basic sentence, but it should still be one sentence. Encourage them to also include at least one vocabulary word. These are worth bonus points. (***Note***: If you desire to practice a 3sss (an Advanced Addition), they may add this after the basic sentence.)

4. When time is up, each team reads their sentence(s). They receive two points for each of the listed elements of style they used *and labeled* correctly. If they used an element but did not label it, I give them one point. Then, in addition to that score, add one point for each vocabulary word used.

5. Play several rounds. It is fun to hear the different sentences that are made from the same basic sentence.

Sample scoring of sentences created from *The boy fell*:

[5] As he was running home, the ecstatic boy, who thought he would be the winning run, ***fatally*** *fell flat* on his *face*. allit

8 pts for all four requirements + 1 pt for a vocab word (fatally) = 9 points

[5] When he leaned his chair too far back, the surprised boy, who had not listened to the teacher's *wise words of warning*, toppled over. *He hit the floor. He was embarrassed. Everyone laughed.*

8 pts for all four requirements met = 8 points Optional: 2 pts. for extra decoration (3sss) = 10 pts

Questions (for any of the question games)

Style (Dress-Ups)

1. What dress-ups have we learned thus far? How should you label them? *(underline)*
2. If you take a *who/which* clause out of a sentence, what should be left? *(a complete sentence)*
3. What are the banned words? *(go, went, say, said, big, little, good, bad)*
4. Where does a comma go with a *because* clause (and *www.asia* clause)? *(after the entire www.asia.b clause)*
5. Improve this sentence by changing the banned word: *Knights were good soldiers. (answers will vary)*
6. Improve this sentence by changing the banned word and adding a *because* clause:

   The dragon went into the town. (answers will vary)

Structure (Units 2–4)

7. What do we call the time and place of a story? *(setting)*
8. What do we call the problem, want, or need of the main character of a story? *(conflict)*
9. What do we call the event that leads to the conflict being solved? *(climax)*
10. When summarizing a reference, what should each paragraph of a summary report begin with? *(topic sentence)*
11. What is the topic-clincher rule? *(The topic sentence and the clincher sentence must repeat or reflect two or three key words.)*
12. Do narrative story paragraphs have topic sentences? *(no)*

Style: Sentence Openers

13. What sentence openers have you learned? How do you label them? *(number)*
14. How many -ly adverbs do you need at minimum in each paragraph? *(2: one as a dress-up and one as a #3 opener)*
15. Give six prepositions that can begin a #2 sentence. *(see page 112)*
16. What is a #5 sentence opener? *(www.asia.b clause)* What do these letters stand for? *(when, while, where, as, since, if, although, because)*
17. With which is a comma always required, and where do you place the comma: #5 opener or *www.asia.b* dress-up? *(opener; comma goes after the entire clause)*
18. How many words may be in a #6 sentence? *(2–5)*
19. Give an example of a sentence with a #4 sentence opener. *(answers will vary)*

Structure (Units 5–9)

20. When writing a three-paragraph story from three pictures, how should you begin each paragraph? *(with the central fact of one of the pictures)*

21. When writing a research report (using more than one source text), after you have your sources, what must you do BEFORE you begin making key word outlines? *(choose topics)*

22. Should each note page for a research report have all the notes from the *same source* or all the notes for the *same topic*? *(same topic)*

23. What is a fused outline? *(the outline you make by picking notes from key word outlines you made from more than one source; it is the outline you use to write your paragraph)*

24. When you must write without a source text (your own thoughts), how can you get ideas for what to say? *(ask yourself questions)*

25. What are the question starter words that can help you ask questions to think of more details to add to your writing? *(who, what, when, where, why, how, how feel, best thing, worst thing, examples, details, descriptions) (see page 174)*

26. What is the structure of a basic five-paragraph essay? *(introduction, three body paragraphs, conclusion)*

27. What must an introduction paragraph include? *(attention getter, background, and the topics of the body paragraphs)*

28. What are some techniques for creating attention getters? *(ask a question, use a vss, use a quote, begin with an intriguing fact)*

29. What must a concluding paragraph include? *(restate the topics, tell what is most something (significant, interesting, ...) and why, end with a final sentence that repeats one to three words in the title)*

30. What is the purpose of a critique? *(to give and support an opinion about a story)*

31. What should you *not* say in a critique? *("I" or "my," as in "I think" or "in my opinion")*

32. What is the structure of a basic five-paragraph critique? *(introduction paragraph, paragraph for setting and characters, paragraph for conflict, paragraph for climax and resolution, conclusion paragraph that analyzes the story)*

555
× 21
555
+ 11100

1,345
+ 601
1,946

26
22
9

4,532
− 2,055
2,477

4,582
− 4,055
0737

2891
× 12
5782
28910
3,41 02

2891
× 12
5682
10